Blogging
and RSS
A Librarian's
GUIDE
Second Edition

Blogging
and RSS
A Librarian's
GUIDE
Second Edition

Michael P. Sauers

Information Today, Inc.
Medford, New Jersey

First Printing, 2010

Blogging and RSS: A Librarian's Guide, Second Edition

Copyright © 2010 by Michael P. Sauers

Library of Congress Cataloging-in-Publication Data

Sauers, Michael P.
   Blogging and RSS : a librarian's guide / Michael P. Sauers. --2nd ed.
      p. cm.
  Includes bibliographical references and index.
     ISBN: 978-1-57387-399-4
1. Libraries--Blogs. 2. Library science--Blogs. 3. Librarians--Blogs.
4. Library Web sites--Design. 5. RSS feeds. 6. Communication in library
science--Technological innovations. I. Title
    Z674.75.S63S38 2010
    025.04--dc22

                                           2010028824

Printed and bound in the United States of America.

President and CEO: Thomas H. Hogan, Sr.
Editor-in-Chief and Publisher: John B. Bryans
Managing Editor: Amy M. Reeve
VP Graphics and Production: M. Heide Dengler
Book Designer: Kara Mia Jalkowski
Cover Designer: Shelley Szajner

www.infotoday.com

For my wife

Contents

Acknowledgments ix

Introduction xi

Chapter 1 An Introduction to Blogs 1

What Is a Blog? 1

Types of Blogs 2

The Blog Effect 3

Why Blog? 7

**Chapter 2 The Library Blogosphere,
Part 1: The Blogs** 9

Librarian Blogs 9

Library Blogs 43

Miscellaneous Blogs 52

Just One More 65

**Chapter 3 The Library Blogosphere,
Part 2: The Bloggers** 67

Chapter 4 Creating a Blog 81

Why Blog? 81

Methods for Creating Your Blog 82

Creating Your First Blog 83

Blog Options 99

Chapter 5 An Introduction to RSS 137

What Is RSS? 137

History of Feed Development 138

What's in a Feed File? 139

Feed Types 142

Identifying Feeds 144

Finding Feeds 148

Using Feeds 149

Chapter 6 Using an Aggregator 155

What Is an Aggregator? 155

Types of Aggregators 156

Google Reader 162

Podcasting and RSS 202

Chapter 7 Noteworthy Feeds 209

Library and Library-Related Feeds 209

News Feeds 213

RSS Services 220

Miscellaneous Feeds and Services 223

Chapter 8 Creating Feeds 231

Hand Rolling 231

Semi-Automated 232

Fully Automated 246

Placing Outside RSS Content on Your Site 247

Chapter 9 Microblogging With Twitter 259

Why Use Twitter? 259

Twitter Basics 261

Tweeting 101 267

Next Steps 282

Afterword 287

Recommended Reading 289

Appendix: Feed Code Examples 297

Glossary 307

About the Author 311

Index 313

Acknowledgments

I'd like to thank the following individuals and institutions for their contributions to the writing of this book: David Bigwood, Walt Crawford, Jason Griffey, Holly Hibner, Mary Kelly, Mary Sauers, Diana Norman, Sara Norman, Jessamyn West, and all of my coworkers at the Nebraska Library Commission. Oddly enough, this is my first book in which no part was written while in an airport.

Introduction

To those of you who are picking up this book for the first time, welcome. To those of you who read the first edition and are now reading this second edition, welcome back. Chances are you're a librarian, but even if you're not, you're someone who wants to know more about blogging and RSS. Even if you're not ready to dive in head first, I'm assuming you are interested enough to take a closer look. Blogs and RSS have received a lot of press in recent years: 2004 was widely hailed in the press as "The Year of the Blog," and blogging has proliferated at a remarkable pace since then. I realized blogs had gone mainstream while watching an episode of *The Daily Show with Jon Stewart* in 2004. Stewart was listening to a report from one of his "correspondents" about what was going to happen in Iraq the next day, as though it had already occurred. When Stewart questioned the fact that the correspondent had written his report in advance and asked what he'd do if something different and significant happened, the correspondent responded, "Jon, that's what the bloggers are for."

Now that it's 2010, some have declared that both blogging and RSS are dead, while others claim that they're at least on life support. These doubters claim that with newer services such as Facebook and Twitter (on which I've written an entire chapter), no one wants to read long-form blog-based content any more. I strongly disagree.

I think what has happened is that both blogging and RSS are now so mainstream that it's not just the cool kids who are doing it, so it must no longer be interesting. Cool or not, blogging is still an amazing platform you can use to get information out to your patrons and get them to participate in a discussion about your library and the services you offer.

Blogs and RSS continue to receive a significant amount of attention in the library world. Today, librarians use blogs to share their experiences with their peers, and libraries as institutions use blogs to get information out to patrons. In some cases, blogs are the core of a library's website. Go to any major library conference, especially Computers in Libraries or Internet Librarian, and you'll find entire tracks devoted to these topics. The movers and shakers among next generation librarians are blogging, and if you're not reading what they're saying, you're falling behind.

This book is designed to give you a baseline from which to start taking advantage of blogging and RSS technologies. As readers of my previous books will know, my style is practical and straightforward. Yes, the book will discuss history and theory, but its central purpose is to give you practical advice on how to get started at little or no cost. There may be other more advanced ways to accomplish some of the tasks I'll be discussing, but typically, such options involve significant financial investment or technological know-how, or both. There are plenty of other places you can go for that information. This book is for those of you who want to be able to read blogs and RSS feeds tomorrow, and to have your own blog up and running the next day. With these two goals accomplished, you can always move on (if you like) to mastering some of the more advanced and complex options that are available.

So, what exactly will I be covering in this book?

In Chapter 1, we'll be taking a look at just what blogs are, where they came from, and the significance of the blogging phenomenon. In Chapter 2, we'll learn about some of the most significant blogs in the library world today and about dozens of other blogs of potential interest to library professionals. In Chapter 3, we'll meet the people behind some of these blogs.

Chapter 4 discusses creating your first blog and various blog-creation services and software packages, but in the interest of cost and ease of use, the focus will be on Blogger.com. This free web service will allow you to have your own blog up and running in less than five minutes. Once your blog is live, I'll walk you through the options available for customizing it.

In Chapter 5, we'll move on to RSS. Here, we'll start with an introduction to RSS, explaining what it is, where it came from, and what it's good for. This chapter will also demonstrate XML code, but don't let that scare you. I'm a firm believer in showing the "back-end" once—in this case, if you feel like forgetting it after that, that's okay. In Chapter 6, we'll take our knowledge of what RSS is and apply it to life as a librarian. Here we'll explore the world of RSS aggregators—specifically Google Reader. Aggregators are websites or software solutions that let you take advantage of RSS feeds in order to get all your information in one location.

Chapter 7 is a directory of RSS feeds you might consider subscribing to, although not all of them are directly LIS-related. Some might be useful in reference situations while others simply illustrate the possibilities of the technology. Chapter 8 will show you how to create your own RSS feeds. There are several options and, depending on the source of your original material, setting up your first RSS feed can take as little as two minutes and typically no more than 20.

Lastly, and new to this edition, Chapter 9 is an introduction to microblogging, using a service you've probably heard of by now: Twitter. If you haven't used Twitter already, this chapter will get you up and running quickly and give you a great overview of how to use it to both gather and distribute information.

Although I wrote *Blogging and RSS* to be read from cover to cover, you may prefer to browse only the topics that are of greatest interest to you. If you are just looking for a basic background in these technologies, you can read Chapters 1 and 5 for now. If you already have some background and are interested in starting places and resources as an information consumer, look to Chapters 2, 3, 6, and 7. If you're already using blogs and RSS and are planning to become an information supplier, Chapters 4 and 8 are for you. Those interested in both sending and receiving information with a minimum of fuss and muss, head over to Chapter 9.

Regardless of how you approach the book initially, I recommend that you eventually read it in its entirety. As a trainer for the past 15 years, I've discovered that there's always something new you can learn about a topic, even if you already know "everything." You never know where and when a gem might turn up.

Welcome to the blogosphere!

Author's Note: Late in the editing process of this book, Blogger decided to make a significant change to one of its publishing features that would affect only ".05% of their users." Of course, my personal blog, travelinlibrarian.info, was one of those affected. Because of this, I was forced to move my blog from Blogger and onto the WordPress platform; therefore, some of the examples shown in this book will no longer match my live website. I still continue to recommend Blogger as a great starting point for anyone looking to blog, and my move away from it personally does not imply that I no longer recommend it to others.

Chapter 1

An Introduction to Blogs

Welcome to the wonderful world of blogs, bloggers, and blogging! In this chapter, I'll essentially be answering the following questions:

- What are blogs?

- Why are blogs important in today's online world?

- What can blogs do for you and your library?

By the end of this chapter, you'll be ready to start using blogs, not only as an information consumer but also as an information provider.

What Is a Blog?

According to Wikipedia, a blog is "a type of website, usually maintained by an individual with regular entries of commentary, descriptions of events, or other material such as graphics or video. Entries are commonly displayed in reverse-chronological order."[1] Blogging is the act of creating posts for a blog, and the person who creates those posts is known as a blogger. The collective environment of all blogs and bloggers is commonly referred to as the blogosphere.

Blog is a shorthand form of the word *weblog*, which in this context is pronounced "we blog."[2] The term weblog (pronounced "web log") is older than the concept of blogs and refers to the computer files generated by web servers to log their activity. When blogging became popular, some technologists decided that, to prevent confusion between the two concepts, weblog would be pronounced as "we blog." This, in turn, was shortened to *blog*, from which other blog-based terms arose.[3]

The first important part of the Wikipedia definition of blog is *website*. A blog is, most simply, just another website. However, a website comprised of your thoughts and interesting links isn't necessarily a blog. One of the key components of a blog is the automatic generation of a page comprised of individually created entries known as posts. Bloggers can use either a web-based service, such as Blogger.com (covered in detail in Chapter 4) or a server-based program, such as Movable Type. Posts are created using one of these methods, after which the software takes over and generates the code needed to display the posts to readers.

The other crucial part of the definition of blog is *reverse chronological order*. This means that the newest posts are presented at the top of the page, followed by older posts. When a new post is added to a blog, it appears as the first item to be read and shifts other posts down. As the definition notes, posts are "not necessarily" presented in reverse chronological order, but this is the prevailing practice by far.

Common practice has established some additional features of blogs not mentioned in the Wikipedia definition:

- Blog posts are marked with the date and time of publication. This is important both for conveying timeliness and for the functioning of aggregators. (Aggregators are covered in Chapter 6.)

- A blog is more than just a list of sites that someone thinks are cool. The original intent of blogging was to create online journals. In many cases, bloggers link to other sites of interest, but they usually add commentary as to *why* these sites are of interest.

- Unlike items on a standard webpage, which may be modified regularly, a blog entry typically remains unchanged once posted. A topic discussed in one post may be revisited in a new post or in updates appended to an existing post. Revising and deleting old posts often warrants, at a minimum, a harsh and public verbal flogging.

- Most blogs by individuals allow readers to post comments. These comments are automatically attached to the end of a post for all readers to view. Blogs from large organizations tend not to have this feature, as allowing public comment may be determined as more hassle than it's worth. An organization that needs to retain control of its public image may not want to host uncensored reader commentary on its blog.

Types of Blogs

From the user's perspective, there are three types of blogs: individual, subject, and organizational.

Individual blogs are created and maintained by individuals for their own reasons. This model is the original blog style. Typically resembling an online journal, these blogs are commonly personal in nature, relating to the blogger's life experiences or professional life. Examples of individual blogs in the LIS (Library and Information Science) circle include my own blog The Travelin' Librarian (travelinlibrarian.info), Karen Coombs's Library Web Chic (www.librarywebchic.net/wordpress), and Michael Stephens's Tame the Web (tametheweb.com).

Subject blogs can be produced by one or more people and are focused on a particular topic: hobbies, politics, pets, or any other topic of interest to an online community. War blogs have become popular due to the recent wars in Afghanistan and Iraq. One notable LIS subject blog is LISNews (www.lis news.org). Other subject blogs include The Huffington Post (www.huffington post.com), which comments on the news and politics of the day, and Gizmodo (www.gizmodo.com), which reviews the latest gadgets, gizmos, and technology.

Organizational blogs represent the views, opinions, and events of an organization. For example, the home page of the Ann Arbor District Library (www.aadl.org) is in essence a blog designed to inform patrons about events at the library. (In fact, the home page comprises the most recent posts from several different blogs that the library has created.) Sun Microsystems encourages all its employees to blog and has developed a platform for them to do so at blogs.sun.com. (Many of these blogs reflect what employees are doing at Sun, although this is not a requirement.) The Microsoft Developer Network has a blog called Channel 9 (named for the channel on which passengers can listen to tower communications while on an airplane), where Microsoft developers post details about current projects.

It is important to keep in mind that these three categories are generalizations to help you learn about blogging and are not meant as hard and fast rules. Many blogs may fall into more than one category or may not easily fit into any of them.

The Blog Effect

Merriam-Webster's 2004 word of the year was *blog* (www.m-w.com/ info/04words.htm). *TIME* magazine's 2004 Person of the Year issue included an article titled, "Person of the Year 2004: 10 Things We Learned About Blogs" (www.time.com/time/personoftheyear/2004/poymoments.html). Why was 2004 a watershed year for blogs? Several events that year made it clear that blogs were a force to be reckoned with. Two such events impacted "traditional" media, while the influence of other events was felt in the world of search engines, specifically Google.

The Impact of Blogs on Traditional Media

By the end of 2004, the traditional print, radio, and television media could no longer ignore the impact that bloggers were having on how people received their news. In that year alone, there were two significant cases in which blogs and bloggers either scooped major media or directly influenced how or if a story was reported:

- John Kerry's Choice of Vice Presidential Running Mate: On the morning of July 6, 2004, John Kerry announced that his choice for a vice presidential running mate was Senator John Edwards. Unfortunately for the Kerry campaign, the announcement was not the big surprise it was meant to be. On the previous evening, an airport technician in the hangar where new decals were being applied to Kerry's campaign plane saw the decals and posted the news to the USAviation.com message board. The information was quickly picked up by bloggers and posted on hundreds of sites within hours. The word was out, and the bloggers spread the word ahead of the traditional media.

- 60 Minutes and "Memogate": In September 2004, Dan Rather anchored a report on CBS's *60 Minutes II* about a memo allegedly written by Lt. Col. Jerry Killian in 1973, which stated that President George W. Bush had not fulfilled his National Guard duties. The memo turned out to be a fake, a fact first reported by a blogger on the Free Republic blog (www.freerepublic.com). The post pointed out that the typeface used in the memo was generated by a computer rather than a typewriter—something not likely in 1973. In response to this post, many other bloggers took up the charge and continued the investigation. Traditional media picked up the story and eventually confirmed the suspicions. CBS offered an official retraction in October.

Bloggers have continued to gain greater attention in the mainstream media throughout the past six years, as shown by the media interest in blogs such as Fat Man Walking (www.thefatmanwalking.com), documenting Steve Vaught's walk across America to lose weight; Blogging Fifth Nail (fifthnail. blogspot.com), written by Joseph Duncan who was later convicted of kidnapping and murder; MLBlogs (www.mlb.com/blogs), the official blogging service of Major League Baseball; and the Mars Rover Blog (www.marsroverblog. com) documenting the travels of the Mars Rover in the first person. A further demonstration of the power of blogs came during the presidential candidacy of Barack Obama, which used many different types of social networking tools, including blogs, to help him get elected as President of the United States. On the down side, blogs have also been the cause of both military demotions[4] and high-profile firings.[5]

The Effect of Blogs on Search Engines

Search engines started to feel the effects of blogging in 2003, but those effects grew in 2004 during the presidential election cycle and carried on through the 2008 election. Google became a victim of what is known as *Google bombing*. To understand how this works, here is a quick introduction to how Google ranks its search results.

Google's relevancy ranking algorithm (PageRank) is complex, but one of its main criteria is the number of other pages that link to a page. The more links found, the higher the ranking of the page in search results. Additionally, Google looks at how that linking occurs. If the linked text also contains the keywords searched, that page receives an even higher ranking. To influence Google's ranking system, all someone needs to do is pick a word or phrase and then convince a lot of people to link to the exact same page using the exact same text as the link. This might take tens of thousands of pages, all creating the same link to the same page, but that isn't as difficult as it may sound.

Two cases of Google bombing involving blogs received significant press in 2004. The first involved the phrase *miserable failure*. When this phrase was searched in Google, the first result was the official biography page of President George W. Bush on the White House website. Through January 2007, this remained the first result returned by Google for this search. Now, performing this same search retrieves mostly links to webpages about the story itself (Figure 1.1). For the most part, the effect of the prank on Google was considered minimal since most users viewed this as a humorous and essentially harmless manipulation of the system.[6]

In another case, a Google search on the word *Jew* resulted in the site for Jew Watch—which bills itself as "Keeping a Close Watch on Jewish Communities & Organizations Worldwide"—rising to first position. In this case, there was considerable public outcry, given the anti-Semitic nature of the site.[7] In retaliation, bloggers banded together, creating thousands of links to the Wikipedia article on Judaism and bumping the Jew Watch site to the fifth or later position. Today, the first result for this search isn't an actual result—it's a link to a Google page explaining "offensive results" (Figure 1.2).

Both cases of Google bombing were the direct result of bloggers banding together to create the exact same link on their sites with the express purpose of influencing Google results (blogsearch.google.com). Google continues to adjust its ranking system constantly to combat the effect of these kinds of pranks. In fact, in 2009 Google launched Google Blogs, which allows you to search specifically for results from blogs. This doesn't necessarily mean that blogs will come up any more or less in a traditional Google search, but it does acknowledge that blogs are a significant resource and a large portion of on online content being generated today.

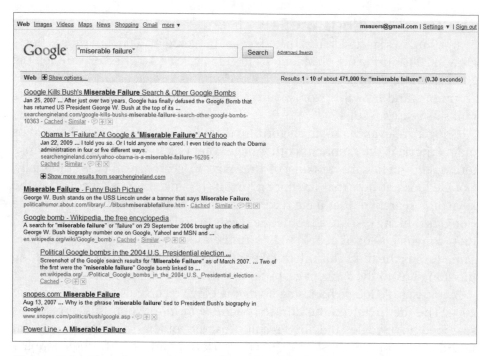

Figure 1.1   Google search results for *miserable failure*

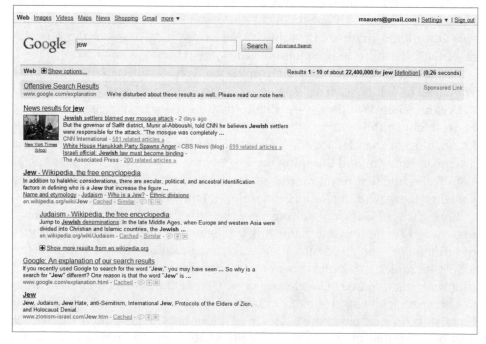

Figure 1.2   Google search results for *Jew*

Why Blog?

What makes blogs an important information resource and tool for you and your library? There are two perspectives from which this question can be answered: from the perspective of an information user and from the perspective of an information provider.

All librarians are information users. We constantly retrieve, access, sort, and store information for our patrons. Blogs are just one more source of information. Blogs, however, are unique in several ways:

- *Blogs are timely*. They are typically updated more frequently than most websites—many times a day in some cases. Unlike newspapers and other traditional publications where reporting is fact-checked and edited as part of the publishing process, the information provided in blogs is likely to be raw and unfiltered (and in some cases, the lack of editorial review may be viewed as a downside). News and information can be posted with minimal delay, and if it is sufficiently interesting or important, it will be quickly picked up and spread by other bloggers.

- *Blogs are opinionated*. More often than not, a blogger has a personal point of view and expresses it in no uncertain terms in his or her postings. Of course, whether a particular blogger's opinions are valid is subjective.

- *Blogs are accessible*. While many websites are difficult to navigate or make users jump through hoops to read (or just to find) what they're looking for, blogs are designed for open access. A blog that *isn't* accessible won't be widely read or referenced and will eventually disappear.

- *Blogs are omnipresent*. In February 2002, *Wired* magazine reported that there were "more than 500,000 [blogs]."[8] In April 2006, Technorati reported that it was monitoring more than 35.3 million blogs—doubling its numbers from the previous six months[9]—and in December 2007, it announced that it was indexing 112 million blogs.[10] Finally, in 2008, Technorati—the one site considered to have a vaguely accurate count of blogs—decided to no longer report the number of blogs it monitored or indexed because accuracy just wasn't possible any more. Any information resource of this magnitude clearly has the potential to affect the results presented in search engines (as with the *miserable failure* and *Jew* episodes).

Blogs are an excellent means by which a library can fulfill its role as an information provider. Calendars of events along with news of recent acquisitions, upgrades, and staff changes can be efficiently disseminated through a library blog. As we'll see in Chapter 4, the level of technical know-how needed to begin a blog is minimal, and the cost is even less. Because blogs are so widely accessible, they can help to increase your library's website traffic. Once a blogger starts supplying his or her posts via RSS feeds (covered in Chapters 5–8), accessibility further increases.

Now that you have a basic understanding of how blogs have developed and what they can be used for, let's look at a number of excellent blogs that you can use both as resources and models.

Endnotes

1. "Blog," Wikipedia, The Free Encyclopedia, en.wikipedia.org/wiki/Blog (accessed March 16, 2010).

2. Rebecca Blood, *We've Got Blog*, Perseus Publishing, 2002, p. 7.

3. Then again maybe not. According to Scott Rosenberg in *Say Everything: How Blogging Began, What It's Becoming, and Why it Matters,* "In May 1999, Peter Merholz … posted a little note in the side margin of Peterme.com … 'I've decided to pronounce the word weblog as wee'blog. Or blog for short.' … It was a lark, a riff making fun of the term *weblog* which at that point was only just gaining currency among web insiders. The coinage didn't exactly spread like wildfire."

4. Joseph R. Chenelly, "Guardsman punished after criticizing Iraq war," *Army Times* (AZCentral.com), July 30, 2005, www.azcentral.com/arizonarepublic/local/articles/0730blogger.html (accessed July 7, 2010).

5. Ellen Simonetti, "Perspective: I was fired for Blogging," CNET News, January 6, 2004, news.cnet.com/I-was-fired-for-blogging/2010-1030_3-5490836.html (accessed April 27, 2010), and Sewell Chan, "CNN Producer Says He Was Fired for Blogging," *New York Times*, February 14, 2008, cityroom.blogs.nytimes.com/2008/02/14/cnn-producer-says-he-was-fired-for-blogging (accessed April 27, 2010).

6. More information on *miserable failure* and Google can be found in "Google's (and Inktomi's) Miserable Failure" by Danny Sullivan (searchenginewatch.com/se report/article.php/3296101).

7. More information on *Jew* and Google can be found in a discussion from the Association of Jewish Libraries' electronic mailing list (www.mail-archive.com/hasafran@lists.acs.ohio-state.edu/msg02143.html) and "Jew Watch, Google, and Search Engine Optimization" by Seth Finkelstein (www.sethf.com/anticensor ware/google/jew-watch.php).

8. Farhad Manjoo, "Blah, Blah, Blah and Blog," Wired News, February 18, 2002, www.wired.com/news/culture/0,1284,50443,00.html (accessed April 27, 2010).

9. "State of the Blogosphere, April 2006, Part 1: On Blogosphere Growth," Technorati, April 17, 2006, www.sifry.com/alerts/archives/000432.html (accessed April 27, 2010).

10. "About Technorati," Technorati, technorati.com/about-technorati (accessed April 27, 2010).

Chapter 2

The Library Blogosphere, Part 1: The Blogs

This chapter will introduce you to a number of noteworthy blogs by librarians and from libraries, along with some additional blogs that may be of interest. The related chapter that follows, "The Library Blogosphere, Part 2: The Bloggers," will take a closer look at some of the most notable librarian bloggers in the field today. Much of the information presented in these two chapters was gleaned from the bloggers themselves through interviews, email exchanges, and blog posts. I found it fascinating and I hope you will, too.

For each blog listed, you'll find the title, author name, URL, and a brief description of the blog—in the blogger's own words when available—followed by an excerpt (or excerpts) intended to give you a feel for the tone and content of its posts. In many cases, the excerpted posts originally included links to other posts, blogs, and online resources; those links do not appear in this text.

Note that my coverage of these blogs is based on the content that was available at the time I viewed them. As with all web resources, blogs will come and go and metamorphose over time.

Librarian Blogs

There are hundreds of blogs written by librarians, library staff, library school students, and other bloggers in the LIS field. This chapter contains a sample of what I believe to be some of the best written, most informative, and in a few instances, the funniest blogs by librarians. In many cases, there are RSS feeds associated with these blogs that will make them easier for you to track. I'll show you how to take advantage of feeds in Chapters 5–8.

025.431: The Dewey Blog
Joan Mitchell with contributions from the Dewey editorial team
ddc.typepad.com

"Everything you always wanted to know about the Dewey Decimal Classification system but were afraid to ask ..." (Figure 2.1).

Sleep, Memory, and Learning

"Don't Knock Naps, They Make You Smarter" (*USA Today Science Fair*) and "Naps Clear Brain's Inbox, Improve Learning" (*National Geographic Daily News*) are news reports on research by Matthew Walker, University of California, Berkeley. The research was described in a press release entitled "An Afternoon Nap Markedly Boosts the Brain's Learning Capacity" but presented at the 2010 Annual Meeting of the American Association for the Advancement of Science under the title "Current Models of Mechanisms of Sleep-Dependent Memory." Here is an excerpt from USA Today Science Fair:

> In the study, a group of 39 healthy young adults were divided into a nap and no-nap group. Each were given a difficult to-learn task at noon, designed to push hard on the hippocampus, the region of the brain that helps store fact-based memories. Research has shown that fact-based memories are first stored in the hippocampus, then moved to the prefrontal cortex for long-term storage.
>
> Both groups did about the same.
>
> At 2:00 PM in the afternoon the nap group got a 90-minute siesta. Then at 6:00 PM both groups got a new set of learning tasks. The ones who hadn't gotten any shut-eye did markedly worse. Those who had caught 40 winks did much better and improved their capacity to learn.
>
> Walker says this helps confirm his group's hypothesis, that sleep clears the brain's short-term memory storage to make room for new learning.

The interdisciplinary numbers for sleep, memory, and learning are in psychology. The interdisciplinary number for sleep is **154.6 Sleep phenomena**, e.g., *The Mind in Sleep: Psychology and Psychophysiology*. The number for memory is **153.12 Memory**, e.g., *Memory*. The number for learning is **153.15 Learning**, e.g., *Human Learning*. Many works treat memory and learning together; they are classed in **153.1 Memory and learning**, e.g., *Learning and Memory: Basic Principles, Processes, and Procedures*. According to the rule of application, works about the effect of sleep on memory and learning are classed with memory and learning (see also Introduction section 5.7 [A]).

Works on the physiology of human sleep, memory, and learning are classed in subdivisions of **612.82 Brain**. Works that focus on sleep are classed in **612.821 Sleep phenomena**, e.g., *The Neuroscience of Sleep and The Physiologic Nature of Sleep*. Works that focus on memory are classed in **612.823312 Memory—human physiology** (built with **612.8233 Conscious mental processes and intelligence** plus **12** from **153.12 Memory**, following instruction at **612.8233**), e.g., *Neural Plasticity and Memory: From Genes to Brain Imaging and Neuroimaging of Human Memory: Linking Cognitive Processes to Neural Systems*. Works that focus on learning are classed in **612.823315 Learning—human physiology** (built with **612.8233** plus **15** from **153.15 Learning**, following instruction at **612.8233**), e.g., *The Autonomous Brain: A Neural Theory of Attention and Learning*.

Awful Library Books

Holly Hibner and Mary Kelly

awfullibrarybooks.wordpress.com

"This site is a collection of public library holdings that we find amusing and maybe questionable for public libraries trying to maintain a current and relevant collection. Contained in this site are actual library holdings. No libraries are specifically mentioned to protect our submitters who might disagree with a particular collection policy. (A good librarian would probably be able to track down the holding libraries without too much trouble anyway …)" (Figure 2.2).

Bring on the Oblivion!

The Encyclopedia of Psychoactive Drugs

Quaaludes: The Quest for Oblivion

Snyder

1985

I snagged this from a teen section. Don't you just love the creepy cover? I am not even sure what to say. I wonder if today's teens are still seduced by this quest for oblivion. The content of this book is heavy on charts, graphs and icky black and white photos of people doing a variety of drugs. Interestingly, none of the pictures feature quaalude abuse. I get the feeling that they slapped quaaludes on the front of a generic "drugs are bad" book. Of course drug information is probably suspect after 5 years, so I am going to go out on limb and suggest that perhaps this book's time has come and gone. Weed it, please!

Beyond the Job

Sarah Johnson and Rachel Singer Gordon

www.beyondthejob.org

"Articles, job-hunting advice, professional development opportunities, and other news and ideas on how to further your library career" (Figure 2.3).

ALA-NMRT Conference Mentoring Program
seeks experienced libraries

Dear Colleagues,

The New Members Round Table (NMRT) Mentoring Committee is pleased to announce that they are accepting applications for their Conference Mentoring Program for the ALA Annual Conference in June!

Do you have experience attending ALA conferences?

Do you find yourself wishing that someone would have been there to teach you all that you now know about attending conferences?

Do you find yourself wondering to whom you can impart all this hard-fought knowledge?

In that case, we have just the person!

The Conference Mentoring Program is open to all ALA members and is designed to connect a first time conference attendee with a 'seasoned professional' who can help them navigate the ALA Annual Conference.

Volunteer to be a Conference Mentor today!

Interested in volunteering as a Conference Mentor? For the guidelines and an online application form please visit http://www.ala.org/ala/mgrps/rts/nmrt/oversightgroups/comm/mentor/conferenceMentorApp.cfm

The application deadline is May 15, 2010 for first consideration.

Applicants will be matched with a Conference Mentee in June and communicate via email or telephone prior to the conference and then meet during the conference.

If you have questions, please contact the NMRT Mentoring Committee at nmrt_mentoring@yahoo.com. Please feel free to share this invitation with your colleagues.

Please note that this mentoring program is not structured to provide career guidance, it is focused on issues related to the ALA Annual Conference. NMRT also offers a Career Mentoring program that will begin taking applications at the end of the summer. Please watch your email for an announcement regarding Career Mentoring later this year.

Catalogablog

David Bigwood

catalogablog.blogspot.com

"Library cataloging, classification, metadata, subject access and related topics" (Figure 2.4).

SkyRiver

There is plenty of coverage of the new bibliographic utility, SkyRiver, so I'll not rehash all that's been said. The article by Marshall Breeding in *Library Journal* is a good place to start. However, one aspect that has not been covered is the authority file they offer. MARC authority records are available from LC, but the process of downloading them is painful. It is not easy, maybe not possible, to create a file and import them once. Each record has to be downloaded and then imported into the local system. Then the next record is downloaded, etc., etc., etc. An improvement in this process, if it was inexpensive would be greatly welcomed here.

Another bibliographic utility with an authority file that can be edited means it may be possible for smaller libraries to participate in NACO. We have no money in our budget to become full members of OCLC. Yet, in planetary science, our community, we have very good access to most of the authors. We're the folks who host the Lunar and Planetary Science Conference that brings all the community together for a week each year. Nice access. We could be an excellent source of authority records and corrections to existing records if we could become part of NACO. I'd guess there are plenty of other special libraries that have similar expertise that could benefit other libraries.

This is not to say it will ever be offered. There are rules about how often the database has to be updated and how changes in the local one be uploaded to LC. Nothing on their website mentions NACO, but still I dream.

Copyfight

Donna Wentworth, Ernest Miller, Elizabeth Rader, Jason Schultz, Wendy
   Seltzer, Aaron Swartz, and Alan Wexelblat

copyfight.corante.com

"Here we'll explore the nexus of legal rulings, Capitol Hill policy-making, technical standards development, and technological innovation that creates—and will recreate—the networked world as we know it. Among the topics we'll touch on: intellectual property conflicts, technical architecture and innovation, the evolution of copyright, private vs. public interests in Net policy-making, lobbying and the law, and more" (Figure 2.5).

Dear Ralph Lauren—Choose Your Targets Carefully

Actually that probably should be addressed to Ralph Lauren's lawyers, but in theory they're acting on behalf of the company, so we get to mock R.L., Inc.

The whole thing started with a photoshop disaster, reproduced here so you can see what we're talking about. The wholescale massacre of peoples' images for advertising purposes is well documented. You can go to YouTube and find a hundred videos showing Photoshop "makeovers"—one of the best is the "Dove evolution." But the gist is that anytime you see a model (almost always female) in a magazine, on a billboard, or any other advertising medium, she's been styled, made up, and then digitally altered so as to bear very little resemblance to how she actually looks. There are interesting Copyfight issues here about what is an original and what is a derivative work in this chain of illusion, but that's not what we're here to talk about.

No, instead I want to talk about how stupid a corporate lawyer can be. You see, that image there on the right? That's a Photoshop disaster. The retouching techniques have been taken so far that the person has ended up looking like a cartoon. If you search the blogosphere for *lollipop head* and *ralph lauren* you'll get a wad of scathing commentary on just how badly the image has been distorted. In fact the image was up on the "Photoshop disasters" blog for a while until they got a DMCA takedown notice and they or their ISP caved to it. (Interestingly, the top photoshop disaster currently shown is almost exactly the same disaster done to Brad Pitt, whose head and shoulders are grotesquely out of proportion to his hips and legs in the Edwin Jeans ad.)

Then a DMCA notice landed on boingboing's ISP. Dear lawyers, don't do that. Because not only will you not get your stuff taken down by doing that, you'll get mercilessly mocked. Which you roundly deserve. Copyfight salutes Boingboing's ISP for ignoring this threat and proffers a hat-tip to Cory for reminding us that sometimes humor is the best defense.

Digitization 101

Jill Hurst-Wahl

hurstassociates.blogspot.com

"The place for staying up-to-date on issues, topics, lessons learned and events surrounding the creation, management, marketing and preservation of digital assets" (Figure 2.6).

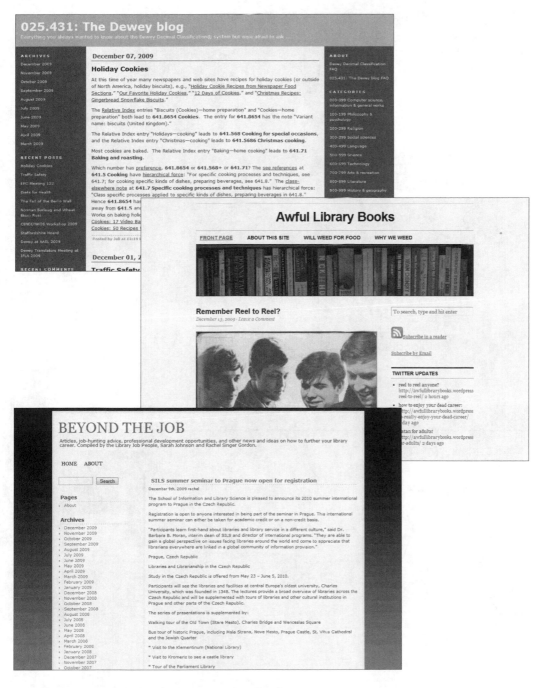

Figure 2.1   025.431: The Dewey Blog (top)

Figure 2.2   Awful Library Books (middle)

Figure 2.3   Beyond the Job (bottom)

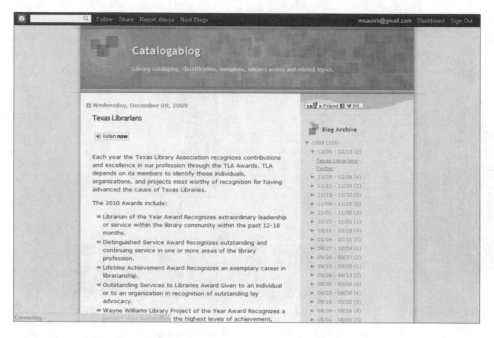

Figure 2.4 Catalogablog

Figure 2.5 Copyfight

Article: Google's Book Search: A Disaster for Scholars

This topic has been in the news recently and this article does an excellent job discussion the metadata problem. The comments below the article are also informative. The article's author, Geoffrey Nunberg, wrote:

Google's five-year head start and its relationships with libraries and publishers give it an effective monopoly: No competitor will be able to come after it on the same scale. Nor is technology going to lower the cost of entry.

And later goes onto say:

it's so disappointing that the book search's metadata are a train wreck: a mishmash wrapped in a muddle wrapped in a mess.

He then goes on to provide examples of the flawed metadata. Later he writes:

And while Google's machine classification system will certainly improve, extracting metadata mechanically isn't sufficient for scholarly purposes. After first seeming indifferent, Google decided it did want to acquire the library records for scanned books along with the scans themselves, but as of now the company hasn't licensed them for display or use ...

Digital content needs to findable. We don't have the luxury of looking at a shelf of hardcopy books and manually looking at the indexes and table of contents in order to find what we want. Online we rely on metadata and computer generated information. If those are flawed or non-existent, then the content may be unfindable. And if we can't find it, then having it online is meaningless.

Free Range Librarian

Karen G. Schneider

freerangelibrarian.com

"K. G. Schneider's blog on librarianship, writing, and everything else" (Figure 2.7).

One more notch up Maslow's hierarchy

Today is the go-live day of MPOW's OCLC authorization for interlibrary loan. Prior to this, our ILL procedure involved paper forms, which partly explains why we did 4 ILLs last year, the other half of that being that we charged patrons, and the third half being that we hadn't conditioned patrons that we provide this service.

So let me digress from the momentous occasion to ponder charging for ILLs. If we buy a book we think patrons might use, we don't charge them. If we buy a book a patron requests, we don't charge them. So why do some libraries—most of them, perhaps?—charge patrons for interlibrary loans, in some cases passing on the entire cost, in other cases charging a flat fee?

The answer can't be that libraries are poor, because the syllogism then fails, due to the other conditions. My guess is it's a mix of habit plus a view of the library budget that is focused on thingies rather than services (the ownership/access seesaw). Charging for ILLs is also oriented toward the idea that the library makes most of the collection decisions. An ILL is, after all, a patron-driven selection.

Meanwhile, I need to get up and out, but—call me Nerdbrarian—my heart flutters that My Place of Work now has the capability to request and provide items worldwide. We're still in need of procedures, policies, training, and marketing, but we have a chassis with four wheels and an engine in it!

Oh, and on conditioning patrons: at the EPA library I managed in the late 1990s, my boss, an engineer and a huge library supporter, said "People need to be conditioned to use libraries." It's absolutely true. A library is a truly amazing service, so amazing that no one could possibly divine all the things it can do for people. We can have wonderful services, but if patrons don't know about them, the job isn't complete.

Information Wants to Be Free

Meredith Farkas

meredith.wolfwater.com/wordpress

"A librarian, writer, educator and tech geek reflecting on the profession and the tools we use to serve our patrons" (Figure 2.8).

Roles and responsibilities for 2.0 technologies

I get asked a lot of things via email from librarians, but very few actually make it to this blog. This question was so interesting and probably better answered by the "hive" than just by little old me. I am also curious how others would respond.

I was wondering if you had any advice or links to websites or professional literature that deal with this issue. That issue is: how do libraries deal with the roles and responsibilities of 2.0 technology? Some of it crosses borders and/or job descriptions. Who is in charge or responsible for tweets on twitter, the library marketing director, the reference librarian, the library director, etc. I suspect this is something that we will just have to work out as an organization. I'm just wondering if anyone else has any wisdom they might share in this regard.

My take on this is that there probably isn't much professional literature on this topic because how the roles and responsibilities are assigned depend very much on organizational size, organizational structure, and who is really interested in doing it. At a library with a very small staff (like the Luria Library at Santa Barbara City College) it may be an interested director who takes responsibility for these 2.0 initiatives. At libraries where the lines between tech and public service are very clearly delineated, it may be the tech folks who are in charge of the Twitter account, whereas, at a library (like mine) where tech librarians do reference shifts and public service librarians are well-trained in library technologies (and every line is extremely blurred), it may be a joint responsibility or the responsibility of the public services librarians. In some libraries (perhaps most?), people have taken this on because they're simply the ones most into marketing and/or web 2.0 tools. In bigger libraries where there is a marketing direc-tor or an outreach librarian or a digital branch manager, that person may be in charge of these initiatives.

But I'm curious, what are your thoughts on this? Especially with regards to 2.0 tools that are created in an effort to reach out to patrons, who should be responsible? What makes the most sense? Should it be the person who has the most contact with the public? The most tech-savvy person? The per-son with the most authority (the Director)? This is one of those questions that has myriad answers, so I wanted to open it up to see how other libraries handle it (or how you think libraries should handle it).

ITART

ITART members
www.nebraskalibraries.org/ITART

"The Information Technology and Access Round Table of the Nebraska Library Association" (Figure 2.9). (*Author's Note:* This is a blog with which I'm involved.)

Edit Google Docs in Office

Officially, Google Docs files are compatible with Microsoft Word. Yeah, there are some limitations but if you want online access to a document or want to collaborate on a document with others, Google Docs is a great tool.

Because of this compatibility you've always been able to edit a Google Doc in Office. The problem was, you had to log in to Google Docs, down-load the file, open it in Word (or Excel), edit it, save it, and upload it back to Google Docs. That's hardly an efficient use of your time.

But what if you could access your Google Docs transparently via Office? Now you can when you download and install OffiSync! Once installed in either Office 2007 or 2010 (I've not tested it in Office 2003 yet) you'll get an additional ribbon which allows you to directly access your Google Docs files.

Ok, technically it does the downloading and uploading for you, so you're technically not live editing as you can with others when logged into Google Docs directly, but if you just need to edit a doc, and you're more comfortable in Office, this is the tool for you.

librarian.net

Jessamyn West

www.librarian.net

"Putting the rarin back in librarian since 1999" (Figure 2.10).

what's in my librarian toolbox?

Keeping with what Roy Tennant mentioned a few weeks back, here's what i told Blake about my librarian toolbox.

1. **Hardware/Software** – I can use computers with basically any operating system with nearly equal fluency. Mac, Windows, Linux, command line. Firefox, Opera, IE, Chrome. I don't expect other people to have this flexibility, but it's good to know if a problem you're looking at is due to a misfit in terms of this sort of thing.
2. **Access** – It's sort of a dirty secret, but I have library cards (mine or loaners) at maybe ten different libraries which gives me access to pretty much any database that I might need access to. Looking up stuff that is a little esoteric is just a few clicks away. Knowing which database has what then becomes the big trick.
3. **Discerning Eyes** – I can usually tell if an answer is in my Google results list without even clicking on the link. This helps me be fast and accurate.
4. **Wetware** – I'm pretty patient and pretty tolerant but at the same time, I know when to say "no" and know when to say "that is a suboptimal solution." It's important that as professionals we need to be able to "play it as it lays" but also be open to newer and better solutions.
5. **Tenacity** – I don't like to let go of a problem, particularly a technological problem, until I've solved it.
6. **The hot potato thing** – If I find out something that is awesome, I want to pass it around. This goes equally well for my ideas as well as the ideas of others. Pass it along so that others can benefit too!

What's in yours?

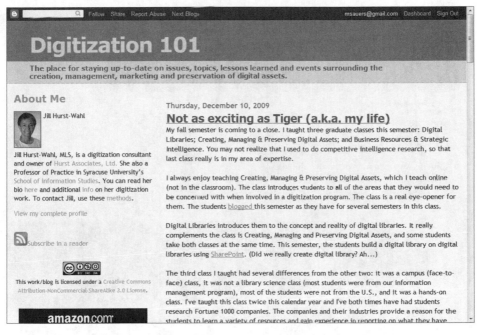

Figure 2.6   Digitization 101

Figure 2.7   Free Range Librarian

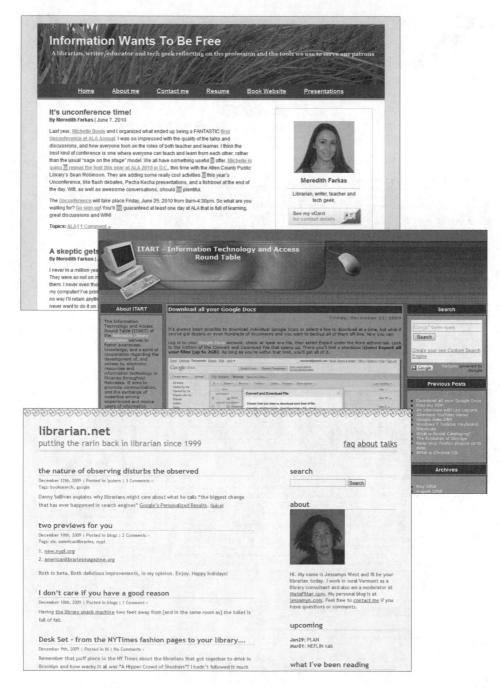

Figure 2.8   Information Wants to Be Free (top)
Figure 2.9   ITART (middle)
Figure 2.10 librarian.net (bottom)

Librarian in Black

Sarah Houghton-Jan

librarianinblack.net

"Amazingly informed & therefore properly opinionated" (Figure 2.11).

Social Network, Blog, and Comment Policies

Social Media Governance offers a database of Social Media Policies, a selection of corporate and government agency policies regulating their staff use of social networks, the internet in general, email, and more. There are also policies meant for their website's users, such as commenting policies. These literally run the entire spectrum from the overly-restrictive and horribly unrealistically impractical to the open and modern policies we're used to seeing in libraries.

And on that note, if you really want a look at a policy for staff that might be a good starting place for your own staff policy, take a look at the Electronic Frontier Foundation's "How to Blog Safely (About Work or Anything Else)."

Then again, there are hundreds of libraries out there too, with similar policies that are specifically written for a library environment. So look at those too :-) There are hundreds of examples of blog/comment/Facebook policies meant for the public's use, and even more governing staff's use … sadly, most of those are hidden behind intranet walls. A few have been posted as part of presentations or PowerPoints, so you can look for those with simple web searches too. The important thing is to keep it brief & direct—be general instead of trying to figure out every possible eventuality and problem. Take my own blog policy as an example:

No spam, personal attacks, or rude or intolerant comments.

Comments need to actually relate to the blog post topic.

Easy right?

Library Garden

Peter Bromberg with additional contributors

librarygarden.net

"Library Garden has been conceived as an ongoing conversation among librarians with differing perspectives (public, academic, consortial, state, youth, LIS) but one shared goal: ensuring the health and relevance of libraries" (Figure 2.12).

A Ph.D. in Library Science?

Posted by Emily Knox

Not long ago a participant on a listserv that I am on asked if she should consider getting a Ph.D. in library science. The answers were swift and almost all were negative—the poster should get a Ph.D. in anything but library science. Although it's hard to believe now, this was something I considered before starting my Ph.D. program. Would I be boxing myself in if I studied library science? Should I get a doctorate in an area that is primarily identified by a professional master's degree?

I told that poster that she should get a Ph.D. in an area that interests her. Ph.D.s take so much time and commitment that it is difficult to finish if you start one in an area that doesn't interest you. According to the Council for Graduate Schools, the average completion rate for *all* Ph.D.s hovers at around 50%.

My area of interest, intellectual freedom and censorship, is a classic field within the library and information science. If this area were part of another discipline, I would be in another department. However, what has been most surprising to me throughout my coursework at Rutgers is how much I love studying libraries. I enjoy thinking about them, researching them, and having arguments with my fellow students about their status in society. Even the information science classes weren't as bad as I had anticipated since they broadened my understanding of how people interact with data/information/knowledge in the world.

I find it disheartening that other librarians think research in our field is only necessary for teaching other librarians and has nothing to say to the wider academic community. We must encourage research in LIS in order to have a stronger voice in academia and to boost the status of libraries throughout the world. If we don't believe that a doctorate in LIS is as worthwhile as one in another area, who will?

LibraryLaw Blog

Mary Minnow and Peter Hirtle
blog.librarylaw.com/librarylaw

"Issues concerning libraries and the law—with latitude to discuss any other interesting issues. Note: Not legal advice—just a dangerous mix of thoughts and information" (Figure 2.13).

How much will the Google subscription database cost?

Two efforts to get the following blurb into the latest issue of Current Cites have failed for technical reasons, so I am going to go ahead and post it here:

Cairns, Michael. A Database of Riches: Measuring the Options for Google's Book Settlement Roll Out s.l.:Information Media Partners, 22 April 2010. (http://www.scribd.com/full/30334705?access_key=key-23rh5w2lwcdmcmzph2k4).

Everyone is eagerly anticipating a decision on whether the court will accept the proposed amended settlement of the suit brought by some authors and publishers against Google's library program. The recent confirmation of Judge Chin to the Court of Appeals may indicate that we will have to wait longer (though there is at least some speculation that he might seek permission to address this one last case).

In the absence of a decision, we can only guess what the final GBS database might look like. In this new report, Michael Cairns, a former president of R.R. Bowker, a publishing consultant, and the author of an earlier study on how many orphan works there might be in the database, has turned his attention to the business models Google might adopt. It is the first public analysis of which I am aware that attempts to determine how much an institutional subscription might cost.

One can quibble with some of Cairn's assumptions about the price of an average subscription or whether the level of market penetration he predicts would satisfy the settlement's requirement of "the realization of broad access to the Books by the public, including institutions of higher education."

What surprised me the most was the substantial amount of money that could be generated for the rights holders from these out-of-print titles. Even at a relatively low subscription price and with modest market penetration, Cairns estimates that the database could generate $260 million a year, 70% of which, or $182 million, would go to the rights holders. It is not enough to come close to justifying Google's investment in the project, but for authors and publishers, it represents an enormous pot of "found money." The analysis also demonstrates that low subscription prices and broad market penetration may be more profitable than the normal library model of high subscription price and limited market penetration.

Library Web Chic

Karen A. Coombs
www.librarywebchic.net/wordpress

"Resources for librarians who are interested in the application of web design and technologies in libraries" (Figure 2.14).

Working from various Apple devices

Right now my Apple devices make my life so much easier. In ways that I often take for granted and forget. It sort of smacked me in the face this afternoon I was sitting in my breakfast nook working.

The day started with me working on my iMac with dual external (not Mac) monitor. My spouse was still sleeping so rather than reset the audio on iMac to use my headphone not nice speakers, I kicked off some music on my iPod Touch.

Later around 2pm when the upstairs of my house became unbearably hot upstairs, I grabbed the Mac Air and iPod Touch and moved to the kitchen nook. (I refuse to use AC in April, not when I can move downstairs open up the house and save on the electric bill.) Using sharing over my Airport Extreme powered network, I grabbed what needed from the iMac and/or my shared work drive. I logged into Skype on my iPod and had my weekly "phone" meeting with my boss.

Right now I'm sitting curled up writing this on the Air, listening to music on the iPod. Earlier I grabbed a backup for my husband from my 1/2 terabyte drive which is shared via the Airport Extreme and printed a recipe to a printer that I have networked using an Airport Express. Add to that the fact that VMWare gets me Windows whenever I want it. I'm pretty satisfied.

Soon we'll have an iPad at my house and I'm curious to see how my husband (who ordered it) likes it. I'm tempted, really, but I want to know all its little warts before I shell out.

I suppose I sound like an Apple evangelist. But I have two PCs in my house too and using Bonjour they can print and share with the Macs easily. Really what people choose to buy and use is their personal choice. For me Apple products have worked really well. Stuff just works and I like that.

A Library Writer's Blog

Corey Seeman

librarywriting.blogspot.com

"Have writer's block? Hopefully this resource will help librarians identify publishing and presentation opportunities in library & information science, as well as other related fields. I will include calls for papers, presentations, participation, reviewers, and other notices that I find on the web" (Figure 2.15).

CALL FOR SPEAKERS - CUBL Breakfast
@ SLA 2010 in New Orleans

We are currently planning the annual College and University Business Libraries (CUBL) Section breakfast for next year's SLA Annual Conference in New Orleans and are looking for three (3) people interested in sharing their experiences or research with their colleagues. We had an incredible turnout for our breakfast in Washington, D.C. last year and expect even more people to attend in New Orleans. Do you want to share your ideas and experiences? If so, then read on.

This year's breakfast theme will be "Advancing within the Academy: Moving on Up."

The CUBL breakfast will feature a panel discussion on advancement and promotion issues within college and university libraries, including scholarly publishing by academic librarians, tenure versus non-tenure positions and a wide range of other promotion and advancement topics.

If you are interested in speaking (15 minutes or so) on any of these topics, or if there other topics you think may be of interest to CUBL members, please let me know. You'll have to come up with your own clever presentation title, though! Please contact me no later than next Friday, November 6, 2009 if you are interested.

Figure 2.11   Librarian in Black

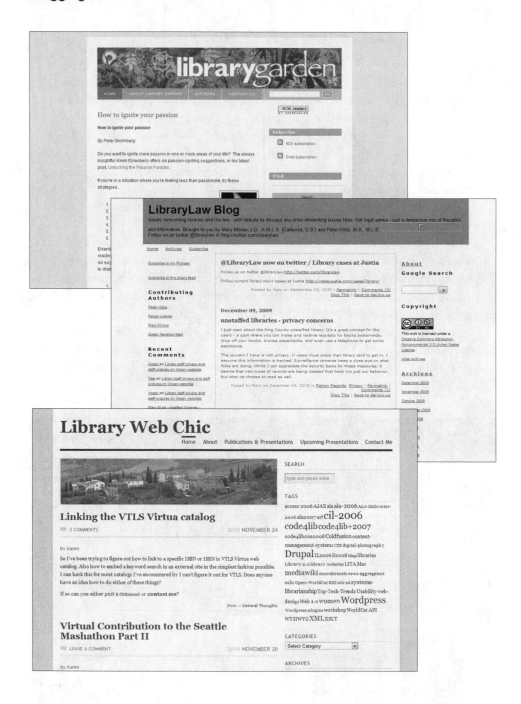

Figure 2.12   Library Garden (top)

Figure 2.13   LibraryLaw Blog (middle)

Figure 2.14   Library Web Chic (bottom)

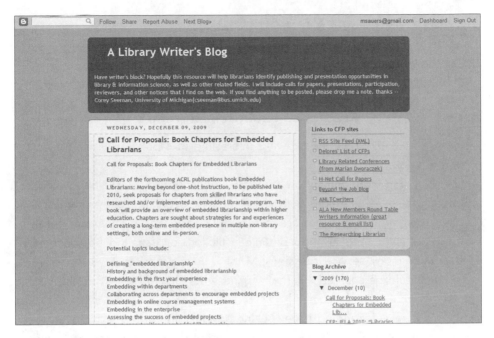

Figure 2.15   A Library Writer's Blog

LISNews

Blake Carver

www.lisnews.com

"LISNews is a collaborative weblog [aka blog] devoted to current events and news in the world of Library and Information Science. A dedicated team of international bloggers scour the World Wide Web to find stories they find interesting. You'll find links to interesting stories and websites, along with original stories, interviews and reviews. LISNews is updated frequently around the clock, usually 7 days a week. We are a non-commercial site, supported by our users" (Figure 2.16).

Overdue library books returned half century later

A high school librarian in Phoenix says a former student at the school returned two overdue books checked out 51 years ago along with a $1,000 money order to cover the fines. Camelback High School librarian Georgette Bordine says the two Audubon Society books checked out in 1959 and the money order were sent by someone who wanted to remain anonymous.

Lorcan Dempsey's Weblog (OCLC)

Lorcan Dempsey

orweblog.oclc.org

"On libraries, services, and networks" (Figure 2.17).

Reputation enhancement redux

I wrote recently about the growing interesting in reputation management on the web.

Reputation management on the web—individual and institutional—has become a more conscious activity for many, as ranking, assessment and other reputational measures are increasingly influenced by network visibility. In particular, it raises for academic institutions an issue that has become a part of many service decisions: what is it appropriate to do locally? What should be sourced externally? And what should be left to others to do? [Reputation enhancement]

This is a wide-ranging issue, pulling together in various ways overlapping issues such as individual and institutional disclosure of research and other outputs; emerging academic social networking practices; formal expertise and research output management; search engine optimization strategies; practices for improving citation, ranking and reputation measures; social reference/bibliography; and so on. I think that we will see some of this activity become more routine in organizational and operational terms over the next few years.

In this context, I was interested to see a presentation on research support by Rachel Cowan and Alex Hardman from the University of Manchester. They focus on reputation and network identity as important parts of overall research management.

MaisonBisson.com

Casey Bisson

maisonbisson.com

"This is the stuff we would have emailed you about, stuff we'll probably mention to you later. Nothing here is meant to be especially deep, and you'd probably find better, more informed stuff elsewhere. Still, we hope you enjoy it" (Figure 2.18).

iPhone's Anti-Customer Config File

In March of this year Apple applied for a patent on technology that enables or disables features of a phone via a config file. The tech is already in use: it's the carrier profiles we've been downloading recently. On the one hand this is just an extension of the parental controls that Apple has included in Mac OS X since the early days, but it also implies some rather anti-consumer thinking at the company.

One exemplar claim in the patent is that the config file can include a "blacklist of device resources to be restricted from access."

AT&T used this technology to block MMS until recently, and uses it now to block tethering, but the description given in the patent application goes much further:

For example, a carrier may wish to provide an enhanced service which utilizes the global positioning system (GPS) functionality in a mobile device. Carrier may wish to charge a premium for this service, so it may configure carrier provisioning profile to disallow third party applications from accessing the GPS functionality in device, and instead only allow applications digitally signed by carrier (or another entity affiliated with carrier) to access the GPS services in device.

Readers may remember the Trusted Computing video by Lutz Vogel and Benjamin Stephan that spotlighted the growing interest within the computing industry to impose new and artificial restrictions on the way we use the hardware and software we use daily.

Pattern Recognition

Jason Griffey

www.jasongriffey.net/wp

"I'm Jason Griffey, a librarian, technologist, writer and speaker. This is my personal blog, but I also write Perpetual Beta at American Libraries and for the ALA TechSource blog" (Figure 2.19).

Interfaces

I'm sure this isn't an original thought (so very, very few are), but it was novel enough to me that I needed to write it down ... and that's pretty much what a blog is designed for.

I've written and talked about how libraries need to become comfortable with the containers of our new digital content, as since we move into the future the containers (ereader, ipad, tablet) will be important to users. We already know, more or less, how to deal with content. I've also been thinking about the interfaces that we use to access this content, and it just hit me: Print is the only example of a media where the User Interface, Content, and Container have been, historically, the same thing. With music and video, we are completely used to the container, the content, and the user interface each being distinct: we put a tape into a player, which we control with knobs or buttons, and the content itself is ethereal and amorphous. With print, until very recently, the content, container, and interface were *all the same thing* ... a book, a magazine, a broadsheet, a newspaper. All are content, container, and interface wrapped into a single unit. This may point to one of the reasons that people seem to feel a deeper connection to print materials than to the 8mm film, or the cassette tape.

I've been thinking a lot about these distinctions between container, content, and interface ... I think that these three concepts could inform the way that libraries conceptualize what we do, and maybe find better ways to do it.

Interfaces, Part 2

This distinction from the post below, that media can either be collapsed (Content, Container, and Interface as a single piece, as a book) or expanded (each separated, as in a DVD, remote, and screen) explains a bit about why the Touch interface is so visceral. The iPad feels different from other devices when you use it, and one of the reasons that I believe it does is that it collapses what have been expanded media types. With the iPad (and to a lesser degree, the iPhone, Android devices, Microsoft Surface, etc) you directly interact with the media and information you are working with. When you watch a video on the iPad, the Content, Container, and Interface are as-a-piece, and you interact with the video by touching the video itself.

This has a lot to do with the revolutionary feel of these new touch devices...and I think it explains why previous attempts at things like Tablet PCs may have failed.

See Also ...

Steve Lawson

stevelawson.name/seealso

"A library weblog by Steve Lawson" (Figure 2.20).

Making time at the beginning for questions

One small thing seems to be working well for me in library instruction sessions lately. Instead of launching right into showing the students the library website and databases and the like, I'm starting with the projector off, and sitting down some distance from the instructor's computer and asking them questions.

I try to ask questions that I really don't know the answer to, where I'm really interested in hearing their responses. I don't quiz them. I don't ask rhetorical questions. I ask about the assignment they are working on and how they see it and what the deadlines are. I ask about what each of them are working on (if the class is small enough) or how much they have already done on the project. I ask if they are feeling good about it. And when I remember, I ask them what they want to learn more about, or how they think I might be able to help them in the next hour or two.

And so far, this has gone really well. I think it helps me build up a bit of a rapport with the class before saying stupid stuff like "OK, let's all scroll down and click the link for 'subject guides' on the library home page." I think it helps students see that I'm not a library-bot but that I am interested in talking about their work and their work habits—that I see them at least minimally as individuals with their own skill levels and motivations, and not just a class that needs to be shown how to do a search in EBSCO. I think it's more like the classroom environment they are used to.

I also think it takes me out of "performer" mode just a bit, and more into a frame of mind more common for me when I'm at the reference desk, or talking to a single student in my office. It's like a mass reference interview. It might not work if I had to talk to large lecture halls, but the biggest class I typically get has 25 people in it, so it scales well enough for me.

In fact, I first started doing this intentionally with smaller, upper-level classes, like senior seminars. I wondered if it would work with larger introductory classes. I gave it a try this morning with a class of 25 (mostly first-year students) and it seemed to work very well.

Then I had a class of about 8 juniors and seniors, and it didn't seem to help much. The class was quiet and I wasn't sure if I was getting much across.

So it's not a cure-all. But leaving some time to sit and talk helps me feel more connected to the class, and it seems to help them be a bit more receptive to what I have to say.

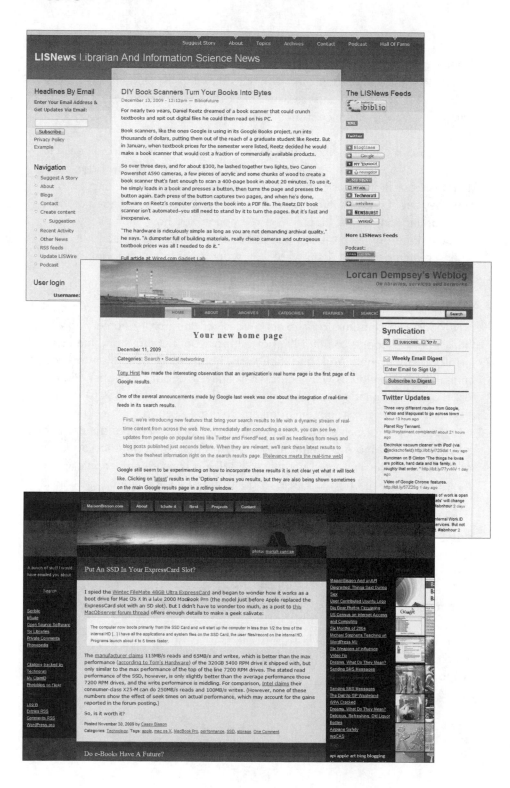

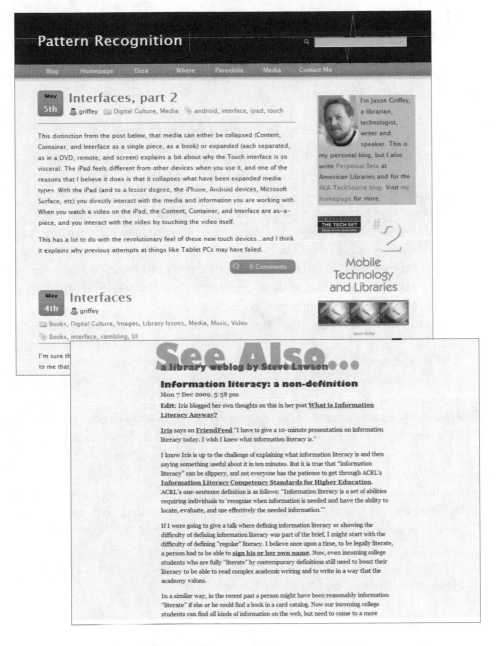

Figure 2.16   LISNews (left, top)

Figure 2.17   Lorcan Dempsey's Weblog (OCLC) (left, middle)

Figure 2.18   MaisonBisson.com (left, bottom)

Figure 2.19   Pattern Recognition (above, top)

Figure 2.20   See Also … (above, bottom)

Swiss Army Librarian

Brian Herzog

www.swissarmylibrarian.net

"Or, The Hitchhiker's Guide to Fear And Loathing at a Public Library Reference Desk" (Figure 2.21).

Withdrawing Journals: Ithaka Report

In case you missed it, Ithaka released a report in September titled "What to Withdraw: Print Collections Management in the Wake of Digitization" [pdf].

It's really geared towards academic libraries looking to achieve a balance between digitizing journals for access (and repurposing the floorspace they took up), and retaining print journals for preservation purposes.

Being a medium-size public library, our journals are mostly for popular reading, but we do keep a small magazine archive of past issues. The criteria I use on which titles are kept in the archive is basically:

Does this magazine contain information that someone will find useful in two years?

In most cases, this includes things like cooking magazines (for recipes), home improvement/craft/sport magazines (for ideas and tips), those useful for research (like *Vital Speeches of the Day*), and of course, *Consumer Reports* (we also have a large [donated] collection of *National Geographic*, dating back to 1911). But the archive has limited space, so it gets weeded every year to make room for new issues/titles.

And no discussion of digitized journals would be complete without me mentioning one of my favorite tools, the Boston Public Library's e-Journals by Title search. I make some journal collection development decisions based on what I know I can access through them, and just hope it stays that way.

For more on the Ithaka report, check out their website or Marie Newman's summary on Out of the Jungle.

Tame the Web

Michael Stephens with additional contributors

tametheweb.com

"Libraries, Technology and People" (Figure 2.22).

KGB Answers your Text Messages

No, it's not the secret service of the Soviet Union—it is, however, the commercialized reference desk. KGB, or the knowledge generation bureau as they sometimes call themselves, provides a two-way text reference service straight to mobile devices. Anywhere. Anytime. Which begs these questions: What about the reference desk? Why not ask a librarian?

You'll never hear me say or read that I think the reference desk is dead—because it's not. But I will say that we can see in the KBG that there is a niche for text message information resources and they are filling it. The question I personally wonder about is how libraries should respond.

KGB has the distinct advantage of being a company with a clear vision to provide this particular type of reference service. Libraries are obviously multifaceted in the ways they provide information resources and this dilutes, to some extent, the ability to provide a highly used text reference service.

I would venture to guess that the success depends on marketing. KGB has created a marketing campaign, traveled the country, and has a very clear brand. If libraries are to create their own "KGB" service it will all come down to how it is pushed to the user and the community the library serves.

So I ask Michael's fervid readers this: *Should libraries respond to KGB and offer their own text reference services?*

TTW Contributor: Kyle Jones

Tennant: Digital Libraries

Roy Tennant

www.libraryjournal.com/blog/1090000309.html

"Roy Tennant's news and views on digital libraries" (Figure 2.23).

The Demise of Small Screen Devices

I was just at the Computers in Libraries Conference in Crystal City, VA, which actually is still ongoing. One of the things I said at the conference was to stop worrying about recreating your web site so it would be usable on small screen mobile devices (i.e., not "smartphones" that are usually able to browse the web much better). At the time, I had almost nothing to go on but my gut, but the day after I got back I found at least some justification for my claim.

The Nielsen market research firm recently released a forecast that by some time in 2011 at least 50% of U.S. phones will be smartphones. Between the rapid expansion of the smartphone market and the meteoric rise of the tablet computer led by the iPad and similar devices, it seems clear that soon anyone on the move will have a good enough web browsing experience to interact with web sites without special accommodations. In other words, creating a "mobile-ready" web site will be but a brief technological blip.

My advice: don't bother. If you want to do something, think about creating an app for the iPhone and Android platforms, which are poised to be major players in both the smartphone and tablet markets. I'm sure there are those who would argue with my advice, so that is what the comment option is for below. Tell me I'm wrong, and why.

The Travelin' Librarian

Michael Sauers

travelinlibrarian.info

This is, of course, my blog. As with many other longtime library bloggers, I find myself posting more and more short bits of content. This is one of my more recent forays into blogging about my technology experiences (Figure 2.24).

The most beautiful book in my collection

I own a lot of limited edition books. I have one bound in tie-dyed denim, another bound in lizard skin, and one who's cover features highly polished aluminum so much so that it came with white gloves lest you leave a fingerprint on it.

However, recently I discovered Centipede Press and I must say that their books are truly works of art despite not using any particularly unique materials. My first title from them was *Slob* by Rex Miller with an introduction by Ray Garton. To say that this title is hand crafted and well bound would be an understatement.

But then I got a package in the mail yesterday. This box contained the Don Brautigam Artist Portfolio published by Centipede Press. Here's the official description:

> This large, 10 x 14 collection covers the entire artistic career of Don Brautigam. Well-known and widely acknowledged for having revolutionized paperback cover art back in the 1970s, Don passed away earlier this year. But his legacy lives on in this beautiful, oversized edition. This volume includes all of his Stephen King and Dean Koontz covers, including *Night Shift*, *The Stand*, *The Running Man*, *Dragon Tears*, *Strangers*, and a lot more. The first 30 copies are

signed by Don Brautigam and Dean Koontz. Bound in cloth with a printed front panel, and enclosed in a cloth slipcase.

My photos don't do it justice (for example. each print is on very glossy paper) but I'm at a complete loss for words beyond what you just read. Regardless, here they are and I can't say to the publisher just how proud I am to own one of these beautiful books.

Walt at Random

Walt Crawford

walt.lishost.org

"The library voice of the radical middle" (Figure 2.25).

A tiny little LITA-related post

Tiny, as in no more than ten minutes composition & posting time …

So in FriendFeed today, I got involved in a couple of discussions—one involving the worth (or otherwise) of ALA, the other involving what professional groups make sense for a systems librarian.

I'm just going to touch on the second one, where another participant said LITA was not a good choice because it was consistently five to ten years behind the times. I questioned that, and found myself defending LITA—and particularly feeling that, given LITA's bottom-up nature, something's terribly wrong if it is "five to ten years behind" (which I don't believe to be true). But then, while working on other stuff and taking a walk and doing the weekly recycling/garbage, I thought:

"Why am I defending LITA?"

There are others, who should have been aware of that thread, who are actually active in LITA—and who should be part of LITA **not** being behind the times. As noted in a number of earlier posts, I'm fairly well burned out on the organization—to the point that I'll think hard before renewing (since, given my work status, LITA costs me more than ALA does). Oh, I might still renew—as a former president, it's hard not to—but still.

It was, to some extent, a kneejerk reaction to an attack. I still don't (necessarily) agree with the attack, but as with some other areas, *it's really not my battle these days*.

If LITA is stuck behind the times, then something's terribly wrong with the IG process—or all the techies have flown the coop. I don't believe the latter, but I really don't know.

Anyway, FF friends, just a note that I probably won't be there to defend LITA next time. It's up to the **active** LITA members to do so. Or not, for that matter: I've been heard to say that it's interesting that there's no Library

Electricity Association, and these days IT is just about as omnipresent in libraries as electricity …

A Wandering Eyre

Michelle Boule

wanderingeyre.com

"Traversing life with words" (Figure 2.26).

Your Current Plan is Not a Good One

I am poking my head up because I came across some posts discussing the news that Harper Collins, Simon & Schuster, and the Hachette Book Group (of Meyer and Patterson fame) will be delaying the release of ebook formats of new releases because the hardbacks are not selling as well.

Right.

This is a great plan guys. Really. I assure you that the people that switched over to ebooks are not going to plunk down $30 for a huge book when a couple months (or some Internet searching) will get them the same book as an ebook for $10 (or free). I also assure you that a large number of the people who used to buy hardbacks now have ereaders.

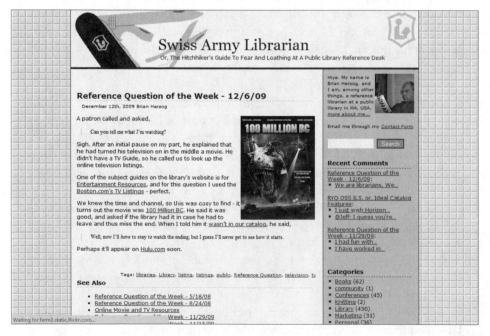

Figure 2.21   Swiss Army Librarian

I am sorry that your publishing structure is threatened by technology. Please learn to move on and adjust your company strategy or you will go drown in your own bad decisions. Pulled under by that 10 pound tome no one really wants to buy anymore.

The **Smart Bitches**, as always, have the best response.

For the record, I still buy some hardbacks, but not to read and only for authors I really love. I collect them for my shelf and there are very few I am willing to do that for anymore.

–Jane, no longer shackled to paper

Figure 2.22   Tame the Web (top)

Figure 2.23   Tennant: Digital Libraries (bottom)

Figure 2.24   The Travelin' Librarian (top)

Figure 2.25   Walt at Random (middle)

Figure 2.26   A Wandering Eyre (bottom)

Library Blogs

As I write this, there are still relatively few libraries using blog technology to enhance their websites. (I hope there will be at least one more by the time you finish the book!) Of the libraries that adopted blog technology early on, here are some of the best blogs; one or more of them might prove useful as a model for your own library blog. This is by no means an exhaustive list, though I have attempted to represent a useful range of library types and blog purposes.

Ann Arbor District Library

Ann Arbor District Library

www.aadl.org

What makes this one of the best examples online today is that this blog is also the library's home page. These librarians don't have a website and a blog—the blog is the website (Figure 2.27). Further investigation shows that the home page is not a blog itself but a collection of recent posts from the many different blogs running on the site. There is a director's blog, an events blog, a services blog, and a video blog just to name a few. (There's a complete list at www.aadl.org/services/blogs.)

Announcing the Official Book Selection of
Ann Arbor/Ypsilanti Reads 2010.

Jerry Dennis' book, *The Living Great Lakes: Searching For The Heart Of The Inland Seas* is the title selected as the focus of Ann Arbor/Ypsilanti Reads 2010. This year's theme is Michigan.

An eleven-member selection team, composed of community members, educators, students and librarians from the Ann Arbor/Ypsilanti area chose the book Wednesday night after two hours of deliberation. The other title under consideration was *Arc of Justice: Saga of Race, Civil Rights, and Murder in The Jazz Age* by Kevin Boyle.

The winner of the "Best Book of 2003" by the Outdoor Writers Association of America, The Living Great Lakes: Searching for the Heart of the Inland Seas' chronicles author Jerry Dennis' travels as a crew member on the tall-masted schooner Malabar on a four-week trip through the waters of Lakes Huron, Ontario, Michigan, Erie and Superior. The author, a resident of Traverse City, Michigan, reminisces on a lifetime spent near the lakes and interweaves his personal journey with stories from the biologists, fishermen and sailors that he met during his travels.

Ann Arbor/Ypsilanti Reads 2010 is scheduled to occur January through February 2010, with multiple opportunities for the community to become involved. For more information, visit the website.

Library of Congress Blog

Matt Raymond and Jennifer Gavin

blogs.loc.gov/loc

"Light and liberty go together" (Figure 2.28).

The Soundtrack of Our (Cartoon) Lives

A cartoon can be engaging and funny and tell a story without any audible sound at all; even newspaper cartoons of the 20th century featured characters such as Ferd'nand and The Little King, (external links) who went through their paces, frame-by-frame, with little or no dialogue to move the story along.

But sometimes, more is more, as Walt Disney found out after he created Mickey Mouse in the late 1920s and had trouble finding a home for Mickey's first two cartoons ("Plane Crazy" and "The Gallopin' Gaucho"), which were silent, before scoring a solid hit with the musical talkie "Steamboat Willie."

"You can run any of these pictures and they'd be dragging and boring, but the minute you put music behind then, they have life and vitality they don't get in any other way," Disney once said.

The Library of Congress today opens "Molto Animato!" an exhibition celebrating the winning combo of animation and music, in its Music Division Performing Arts Reading Room in the James Madison Building (101 Independence Ave., S.E., Room LM113, Washington, D.C.) The exhibition will be on view through next March 28 and will be open from 8:30 a.m. – 5 p.m. Monday through Friday.

Featured items include a pen-and-ink brush drawing of conductor Leopold Stokowski by caricaturist Miguel Covarrubias; the score from *Bambi*, with music by Frank Churchill and Edward Plumb and lyrics by Larry Morey; John Alden Carpenter's manuscript piano score for *Krazy Kat: A Jazz Pantomime*; and the movie poster for *Walt Disney Pictures Presents Aladdin*.

Also on view will be items from the Library's Art Wood Collection of Cartoon and Caricature, the David Raksin Collection of film scores (You can view excerpts, including the cartoons, from his scores for *Giddyap* and *The Unicorn in the Garden*) and the Howard Ashman Collection, including the draft script of Disney's animated film *The Little Mermaid* and audio of Howard Ashman singing Disney movie songs of his own composing.

Let's face it: sometimes silence is golden, but *Fantasia* wouldn't have been nearly as fantastic without the power of music. Here's Mickey, in

Fantasia, dressed to enact "The Sorcerer's Apprentice," a symphonic poem by composer Paul Dukas.

Library Suggestion Blog
Virginia Commonwealth University Libraries
blog.vcu.edu/libsuggest

As far as I am aware, this blog is unique in the library world. In this case, the Virginia Commonwealth University Libraries actually post the content of the comments they receive and then respond to them in this public forum. This is a great example of both conversation starting and organizational transparency (Figure 2.29).

What if a book is missing from the shelf?

How about replacing all the missing books you have? That would be a great idea. Then maybe, just maybe I wouldn't have to search through 20 books before I found ONE that was available to read.

From: a library user

Patricia Selinger, Head of Preservation replies ...

There could be several reasons why the book you are looking for is not on the shelf: someone is currently using it in the library, it is in the reshelving process, it is checked out, it is lost. For these reasons, among others, the VCU Libraries is making a significant investment in electronic books that are not subject to the circulation process and to loss, damage, and theft. The reshelving area on the 3rd floor is a good place to look if you don't find your book on the shelf. Books are picked up throughout the library during the day and brought here along with those received from Circulation. Shelves in the sorting area are labeled with call number ranges for sorting. Books are sorted into call number order onto carts. If the specific book you want is not available, we recommend Interlibrary loan.

Teresa Doherty, Head of Circulation and Information Services, adds ...

If a book is listed in the library catalog as being "available," then it should be on the shelf—not checked out to another patron, or in repair, or on order, for example. If a book isn't on the shelf where it should be, here are some suggestions:

- Check on nearby tables and photocopiers, as other patrons may have been using the book you need.

- Check the reshelving area on the third floor.

- Fill out a "Where's My Book?" tear-off sheet available on the ends of shelving units throughout the library stacks. You can drop the form off at the Circulation service desk on the first floor. Circulation staff will search for the book and let you know when it has been found.

- Patrons can borrow materials from our library consortium partners in the Richmond area. Library staff at the circulation service desk or reference desk can help you check the catalogs of these other libraries and explain how to use a RALC Borrowing Pass (Richmond Academic Library Consortium) to borrow materials from them.

- You can also use our Interlibrary Loan and Document Delivery services offered through ILLiad to borrow materials not available through VCU Libraries.

Thanks very much for taking the time to post to the Suggestion Blog. We hope that this response is helpful to you.

Marin County Free Library Blog

Marin County Free Library

www.marincountyfreelibrary.blogspot.com

"Stay up to date on what's happening at the Library, best-selling books, great websites, book clubs, author appearances, and more!" (Figure 2.30).

Out Local History Hero!

The Oct. 9–15 edition of the Pacific Sun features our California Room Librarian Laurie Thompson in their "Hero" column for "keeping Marin history alive (and) making it accessible to a broad audience by sleuthing through files, oral histories and noncirculating books." As the Pacific Sun points out, Laurie's research talents have assisted patrons and contributed to many helpful bibliographies on local history topics including Angel Island, Marin genealogy, houseboats, railroads and historic houses. To see an online sampling of oral histories, images and other resources, visit the Anne T. Kent California Room webpage today!

NCompass Blog

Nebraska Library Commission

www.nlc.state.ne.us/blogs/nlc/index.html

"The blog of the Nebraska Library Commission" (Figure 2.31).

What youth workers and volunteers bring to the library table

Youth ages 10 to 24 make up a little over one quarter (25.5%) of Nebraska's population. Members of the Millennial generation (born between 1975 and 2005) are our future workforce. And it has been shown that civic engagement in youth leads to civic engagement later on in life. A strong case could be made to draw individuals to the library profession by planting the seed and recruiting them now as volunteers, interns, and part-time staff.

Case in point, the newly available Internship Grant program is an ideal vehicle for engaging youth in library work. The Nebraska Library Association and Nebraska Library Commission will offer grants to accredited public libraries for student internships. This joint project, Cultivating Nebraska Librarians 2.0: Building 21st Century Skills, is funded through a grant from a Nebraska foundation. These internships for youth workers are a follow-up to last year's highly successful program, which was made possible through a grant from a Nebraska foundation, and a 2008–2009 program made possible through a federal grant to the Nebraska Library Commission. Internships introduce promising high school and college students to the varied and exciting work of Nebraska libraries. The internship functions as a recruitment tool, helping the participant view the library as a viable career opportunity.

Young people can be strong advocates for library services, leading by example as staff members or volunteers. What has been your experience in working with high school or college students in the library setting?

For more information on civic learning and engagement, visit CIRCLE, the Center for Information and Research on Civic Learning and Engagement, at www.civicyouth.org. Learn more about the Internship Grant program in the Internship section of NowHiringAtYourLibrary.com.

Old Bridge Library Weblog

Old Bridge Library

obpl.blogspot.com

"A regularly updated listing of news and events for patrons at the Old Bridge, NJ Public Library" (Figure 2.32).

Step Up To the Plate @ Your Library

The Old Bridge Public Library wants to know: do you know more about baseball than the librarians at the National Baseball Hall of Fame? If you think you do, then enter Step Up to the Plate @ Your Library, and show off

Figure 2.27   Ann Arbor District Library (left, top)

Figure 2.28   Library of Congress Blog (left, middle)

Figure 2.29   Library Suggestion Blog (left, bottom)

Figure 2.30   Marin County Free Library Blog (above, top)

Figure 2.31   NCompass Blog (above, bottom)

your knowledge of baseball trivia. You may win a trip to the Baseball Hall of Fame.

The American Library Association and the National Baseball Hall of Fame and Museum's Step Up to the Plate @ Your Library program teams up two American classics—baseball and libraries-to promote the importance of information literacy skills and to increase awareness of the library as an essential information resource.

People of all ages are encouraged to use the print and electronic resources available at the Old Bridge Public Library to answer a series of trivia questions designed for their age group (10 and under, 11–13, 14–17 and 18 and over). Questions are available in both English and Spanish.

Everyone who successfully completes the program will be eligible to win a trip for two to the Hall of Fame in Cooperstown, NY. The program runs from April 5 through September 4.

Unlike most contests, players are encouraged to look up the answers using both print and online sources at the Old Bridge Public Library.

Players can obtain a copy of the Step Up to the Plate questions appropriate for their age and the entry form through the library or on the program's web site at www.ala.org/baseball. Each player can enter the contest online or by sending in the entry form by mail. More information on the National Baseball Hall of Fame and Museum is available at www.baseballhall.org.

For further information about library programs, call the Adult & Information Services Department, at: 732-721-5600, ext. 5033. The Central Branch of the Old Bridge Public Library is located in the Municipal Center at the corner of Route 516 and Cottrell Road.

Topeka and Shawnee County Public Library

Topeka and Shawnee County Public Library
tscpl.org

"Your place. Stories you want, information you need, connections you seek" (Figure 2.33).

Make a Quilt Square with artist Gwen McClain

When children and adolescents experience the death of someone close to them, they grieve, just as adult do.

At Midland Care Hospice, the children's bereavement program encourages young people to share their thoughts and feelings about a loved one who has died. One way children express their feelings is through drawing

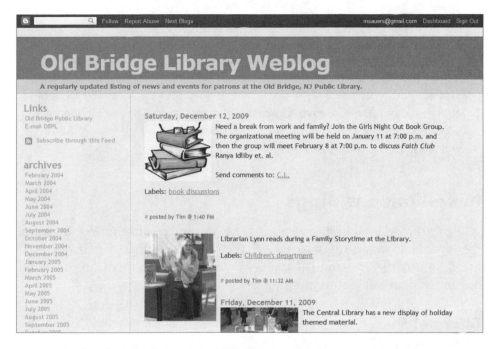

Figure 2.32   Old Bridge Library Weblog

Figure 2.33   Topeka and Shawnee County Public Library

and painting. The quilt squares may represent feelings and memories of their loved one.

Gwen Mclain has worked at Midland Care Hospice as a bereavement coordinator and art therapist for 9 years. Midland Care Hospice offers grief support to adults and children. For books about art as a way of healing, check out The Creative Connection: Expressive Arts as Healing by Natalie Rogers or The Art Therapy Sourcebook by Cathy Malchiodi. This website is also a great resource.

Miscellaneous Blogs

While the blogs listed in this section are not created by librarians or libraries, they are of potential interest to those in the LIS world. Some of them are technical; some of them are more issue-based. Take a look. Chances are you'll find one or two that will pique your interest.

Channel 9

Various Microsoft developers

channel9.msdn.com

"Channel 9 is all about the conversation. Channel 9 should inspire Microsoft and our customers to talk in an honest and human voice. Channel 9 is not a marketing tool, not a PR tool, not a lead generation tool" (Figure 2.34).

E2E: Erik Meijer and Dave Campbell: Data, Databases and the Cloud

Dave Campbell is a Technical Fellow at Microsoft and long time database architect. Today, Dave works on the hardest problems facing SQL's foray into the new world of cloud computing. His latest project in this space takes the form of SQL Azure. What is SQL Azure? What's the difference with the cloud and what we already experience with SQL server running in a clustered environment and reachable via the internet? How does this focus on cloud computing and impact the evolution of database design? What's going here? What's next? Erik Meijer, de facto E2E host and language designer, interviews Dave to get answers to some of these questions. Erik works for Dave, by the way, and as you can see that doesn't stop Erik from asking more than softball questions.

Dave will be presenting at PDC09 in the Technical Leaders track. His talk will focus on ambient data and what this means for the evolution of ways to understand and shape the data this all around us using software.

You should attend his session and come with questions if you are going to be at PDC. If you're not going to be there, then make sure to ask Dave questions when he appears on Channel 9 Live!

Enjoy!

Deeplinks

Electronic Frontier Foundation

www.eff.org/deeplinks/archive

"Noteworthy news from around the internet" (Figure 2.35).

Google Book Search Settlement Revised: No Reader Privacy Added

Late Friday night the parties to the Google Book Search class action submitted a revised settlement agreement to the federal court in New York that is hearing the case.

Unfortunately, the parties did not add any reader privacy protections. The only nominal change was that they formally confirmed a position they had long taken privately that information will not be freely shared between Google and the Registry. Our partners at the ACLU of Northern California have a blog post describing the changes we, and the authors we represent, have demanded and continuing the call for readers everywhere to let Google CEO Eric Schmidt know that reader privacy should not be left behind as books move into the digital age.

The parties also asked for truncated notice and a rushed schedule with objections and opt-outs due on January 28, 2010 and a final fairness hearing on February 18, 2010. We'll be posting more about the revised settlement and the procedures going forward.

Everything Is Miscellaneous

David Weinberger

www.everythingismiscellaneous.com

"The Power of the New Digital Disorder" (Figure 2.36).

Do-it-yourself Google Books— a million dollar idea for Amazon?

Harry Lewis has a terrific post about a $300 do-it-yourself book scanner he saw at the D is for Digitize conference on the Google Book settlement. The plans are available at DIYBookScanner.org, from Daniel Reetz, the inventor.

There are lots of personal uses for home-digitized books, so—I am definitely not a lawyer—I assume it's legal to scan in your own books. But doesn't that just seem silly if your friend or classmate has gone to the trouble of scanning in a book that you already own? Shouldn't there be a site where we can note which books we've scanned in? Then, if we can prove that we've bought a book, why shouldn't we be able to scarf up a copy another legitimate book owner has scanned in, instead of wasting all the time and pixels scanning in our own copy?

Isn't Amazon among the places that: (a) knows for sure that we've bought a book, (b) has the facility to let users upload material such as scans, and (c) could let users get an as-is scan from a DIY-er if there is one available for the books they just bought?

Gizmodo

Joel Johnson

www.gizmodo.com

"Gizmodo is a blog about gadgets and technology. Started in 2002, Gizmodo has grown to be Gawker Media's largest blog, bringing in upwards of 100 million page views a month in traffic. We post about a variety of electronics, as well as all sorts of things gadget geeks might enjoy" (Figure 2.37).

Company Claims That Its DVDs
Will Last 1,000 Years [DVDs]

A start-up by the name of Cranberry is claiming that its DiamonDisc product can last for 1,000 years without any deterioration. If true, that's great, but will you even have the equipment to read the media at that time?

Cranberry's disks are supposed to be so durable and long-lasting because they "contain no dye layers, adhesive layers or reflective materials that could deteriorate." Supposedly data is etched far more deeply into the disks than with traditional DVDs (using Cranberry's special burners, of course). You can either buy one of those burners for five grand or upload your data to the company's website and let them do the hard work for you. Either way, the longevity of these disks seems a little bit too good to be true. [Computer World via Slashdot]

Google Blog

Various Google employees

www.google.com/googleblog

This is the official blog from Google. Here's where you can get all the up-to-the-minute news of what's going on in the company (Figure 2.38).

Locking SafeSearch

When you're searching on Google, we think you should have the choice to keep adult content out of your search results. That's why we developed SafeSearch, a feature that lets you filter sexually explicit websites and images from your search results. While no filter is 100% accurate, SafeSearch helps you avoid content you may prefer not to see or would rather your children did not stumble across. We think it works pretty well, but we're always looking for ways to improve the feature.

Today we're launching a feature that lets you lock your SafeSearch setting to the Strict level of filtering. When you lock SafeSearch, two things will change. First, you'll need to enter your password to change the setting. Second, the Google search results page will be visibly different to indicate that SafeSearch is locked:

Even from across the room, the colored balls give parents and teachers a clear visual cue that SafeSearch is still locked. And if you don't see them, it's quick and easy to verify and re-lock SafeSearch.

To use SafeSearch lock, go to the "Search Settings" page on Google. For detailed instructions, check out this video.

We hope you and your family find exactly what you're looking for in Google search results—and nothing more.

IEBlog

Members of the IE team

blogs.msdn.com/ie

"The Microsoft Internet Explorer Weblog" (Figure 2.39).

Meet WOFF, The Standard Web Font Format

On April 8, 2010, Mozilla, Opera and Microsoft submitted the WOFF File Format 1.0 specification to the W3C. The submission was published on Monday, April 19 at http://www.w3.org/Submission/2010/03/.

Browser vendors and a growing number of type foundries now agree on a common encoding format for web fonts, thus closing an era of cross-browser incompatibility that began when IE4 and Netscape 4 first added support for downloadable fonts in 1997.

At the time, both Microsoft and Netscape implemented incompatible proprietary solutions. Netscape supported and later dropped Bitstream's Portable Font Resource (PFR) format. Internet Explorer's Embedded Open Type (EOT) supported the sub-setting and compression of fonts, as well as the definition of the origin policy for the font resource within the EOT file itself. Some font vendors have licensed their fonts for web use under EOT.

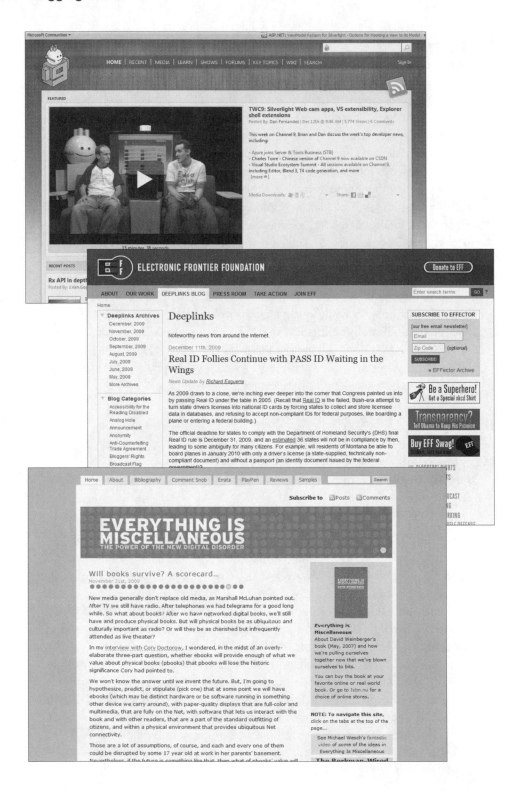

Figure 2.34   Channel 9 (left, top)

Figure 2.35   Deeplinks (left, middle)

Figure 2.36   Everything Is Miscellaneous (left, bottom)

Figure 2.37   Gizmodo (above, top)

Figure 2.38   Google Blog (above, bottom)

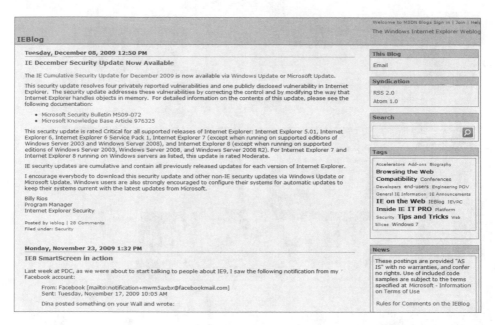

Figure 2.39   IEBlog

Ten years later, Apple added support for raw font linking to WebKit and Safari, allowing web authors to refer to raw TrueType or OpenType font files from their CSS stylesheets. Firefox and Opera followed but use of the feature was in practice limited to free fonts and specialist font obfuscation services like Typekit as font vendors were extremely reluctant to allow their intellectual property to be posted as-is on web servers. The typically large size of font files and the added practical challenges.

In March 2008, Microsoft submitted EOT for standardization to the W3C. Despite a large existing EOT-compatible IE installed base, a number of issues prevented consensus from emerging on the suitability of Microsoft's format as a web font standard. At the W3C's Technical Plenary that year, Microsoft indicated that a solution type foundries were comfortable with was essential to maximize author choice. In the summer of last year, such a solution emerged from a proposal by type designers Tal Leming and Erik van Blokland and Mozilla's Jonathan Kew. The Web Open Font Format (WOFF)—an open, compressed encoding for sfnt-based font resources—was born.

The new format's specification is a deliverable of the newly chartered Fonts Working Group on which browser vendors, type foundries and designers are represented. We are excited by some of the initial feedback to this announcement and look forward to contributing to the Working Group to advance the state of web font interoperability.

Sylvain Galineau, Program Manger

The Mozilla Blog

The Mozilla Project

blog.mozilla.com

"News, notes and ramblings from the Mozilla project" (Figure 2.40).

Celebrating Five Years of Firefox!

You say it's your birthday … Well it's our birthday too!

Five years ago today, Mozilla launched Firefox 1.0 with belief that, as the most significant social and technological development of our time, the internet is a public resource that must remain open and accessible to all. Within the first four days of launch, more than 1 million people had downloaded a brand new browsing experience.

In just five years, that number has swelled to over 330 million users worldwide; almost a quarter of internet users worldwide choose Firefox. Today, Firefox ships in more than 70 languages and offers users more than 7,000 add-ons to help customize their browsing experience.

From your desktop to your mobile device, Mozilla is committed to building an open and participatory internet. We've come so far in the past five years and we're incredibly excited about the next five. For a more comprehensive look at where we've been and where we're headed, check out Chris Blizzard's excellent post on hacks.mozilla.org.

To celebrate this milestone, Mozilla communities are hosting parties all over the globe in a special campaign called "Light the World with Firefox"— shining the Firefox logo from Tokyo to Rome, from Paris to San Francisco, and more. For full details on parties in your area or to check out other ways to join in the celebration, head to www.spreadfirefox.com/5years.

ReadWriteWeb

Richard MacManus with other members of the ReadWriteWeb team

www.readwriteweb.com

"ReadWriteWeb is a blog that provides analysis of web products and trends. One of the world's top 20 blogs, ReadWriteWeb speaks to an intelligent audience of web enthusiasts, early adopters and innovators" (Figure 2.41).

Dailyplaces: Location-Based Microblogging

We are no longer restricted by the ball and chain of desktop computers and ethernet cables. We create content from wherever we please, making location an ever increasing part of that content, and applications like Dailyplaces are helping to bring time and place to the forefront of content creation.

Dailyplaces is a location-based microblogging tool, offered as both an iPhone app and a website, that allows its users to create short posts centered around their location. According to an email from the company, the service "allows both private users and organizations as well as companies to engage in location-based, real-time communication." These users can save locations as "points of interest," tagging them with a photo and text message, as well as other contextual information, such as address, phone number, address, phone number and even website.

The thing we like about Dailyplaces is that it focuses on the importance of time and location in mobile microblogging. While Twitter offers geolocational data from both third-party clients and its website, it remains a sort of after-thought. Gowalla and Foursquare allow users to do things like create locations and add pictures and comments, but the focus remains on checking in.

Dailyplaces, on the other hand, focuses on organizing content by time and place. You can browse posts according to their relation to your location and when they were posted. Much like microblogging site Posterous, each user is given a personal page, such as my own at rwwmike.dailyplaces.net, which shows profile information, basic stats and a list of recent posts with an accompanying map.

The iPhone app lets you view posts according to who created them, when they were created and where they were created in relation to where you are. Creating a new post is as simple as tapping a button, snapping a picture and entering some text. The service can also integrate your Twitter account, posting a tweet whenever you post to Dailyplaces.

While Dailyplaces doesn't look to be the end-all of location-based microblogging, it's on the right track. We can expect to see a lot more services like this being used to create content for mobile endeavors, such as touring bands, traveling acts and even just friends on road trips that want to share their experiences. We would love to see a bit more functionality in grouping together posts, either by theme or by trip, and while the iPhone does have a camera, we're not sure that a picture should be required of each and every post. Do we really want to post pictures of black nothingness if we decide to use the service at night?

Schneier on Security

Bruce Schneier

www.schneier.com/blog

"A blog covering security and security technology" (Figure 2.42).

Beyond Security Theater

[I was asked to write this essay for the *New Internationalist* (n. 427, November 2009, pp. 10–13). It's nothing I haven't said before, but I'm pleased with how this essay came together.]

Terrorism is rare, far rarer than many people think. It's rare because very few people want to commit acts of terrorism, and executing a terrorist plot is much harder than television makes it appear. The best defenses against terrorism are largely invisible: investigation, intelligence, and emergency response. But even these are less effective at keeping us safe than our social and political policies, both at home and abroad. However, our elected leaders don't think this way: they are far more likely to implement security theater against movie-plot threats.

A movie-plot threat is an overly specific attack scenario. Whether it's terrorists with crop dusters, terrorists contaminating the milk supply, or terrorists attacking the Olympics, specific stories affect our emotions more intensely than mere data does. Stories are what we fear. It's not just hypothetical stories: terrorists flying planes into buildings, terrorists with bombs in their shoes or in their water bottles, and terrorists with guns and bombs waging a coordinated attack against a city are even scarier movie-plot threats because they actually happened.

Security theater refers to security measures that make people feel more secure without doing anything to actually improve their security. An example: the photo ID checks that have sprung up in office buildings. No-one has ever explained why verifying that someone has a photo ID provides any actual security, but it looks like security to have a uniformed guard-for-hire looking at ID cards. Airport-security examples include the National Guard troops stationed at US airports in the months after 9/11—their guns had no bullets. The US colour-coded system of threat levels, the pervasive harassment of photographers, and the metal detectors that are increasingly common in hotels and office buildings since the Mumbai terrorist attacks, are additional examples.

To be sure, reasonable arguments can be made that some terrorist targets are more attractive than others: aeroplanes because a small bomb can result in the death of everyone aboard, monuments because of their national significance, national events because of television coverage, and transportation because of the numbers of people who commute daily. But there are literally millions of potential targets in any large country (there are five million commercial buildings alone in the US), and hundreds of potential terrorist tactics; it's impossible to defend every place against everything, and it's impossible to predict which tactic and target terrorists will try next …

Wikinomics

Don Tapscott with the team at nGenera Insight
www.wikinomics.com/blog

"The Wikinomics Blog is produced by the team at nGenera Insight, a think tank headed by IT strategist, speaker, and best-selling author Don Tapscott. Since 1993 nGenera Insight has provided clients with insightful, thought-provoking analysis of emerging technology trends and their business impact. We serve as a 'strategic early warning system' for our clients, helping them discern real imperatives from all the hype and noise" (Figure 2.43).

Games, user experience, and retroactive Continuity–All enabled by platforms

Written by Jeff DeChambeau

As I may have mentioned before, Valve Software's Portal is a favorite game of mine. At our December 2009 Insight conference I profiled it as an example of a game that does an excellent job of making players feel at ease in a system that is governed by alien rules, while teaching players how to think in a new and different way—valuable lessons for enterprises that wish to help their new hires hit the ground running when dealing with specific and well-established processes.

There is more to the game than a comprehensive tutorial, there's also a sharp story, and perhaps more significantly, a robust content delivery and data-mining platform that Valve uses to update and monitor the usage of their products. Valve's content distribution platform, Steam, allows the company to apply bug-fixes and updates to games, as well as learn about how users go about playing through the games, including but not limited to the furthest level of completion, and whereabouts in the game players are most likely to meet their end.

While the ability to glean insights about how their customers use their products must be invaluable as feedback data for making better and more engaging games, it is the ability to update content seamlessly on users' computers that was a move to watch this past week.

To prepare for the upcoming release of Portal 2, Valve quietly and unceremoniously released an update to 2007's portal that changed the end of the game. The practice, known as retconning, or enforcing "retroactive continuity" is usually met with nerd-rage, but seems to have been well-received by the gaming community in this case. Thanks to their content distribution and monitoring platform, Valve has been able to take a product already in the hands of consumers, and modify it so that when their forthcoming product hits the shelves, the continuity between the first and second installments of the game's story is cohesive and correct. Not something that could be done with the game of Life or Clue.

Steam isn't the only content distribution platform that has the ability to update and change the user experience after the sale is made, Amazon's kindle had an unfortunate time with what is more or less the same story, and I'm sure that there is plenty of legal language and technical infrastructure in the iPod/Phone/Pad terms of service that allows Steve Jobs to legally annex users' first born children.

As an increasing amount of products are imbued with connectivity and access to a platform, the way that companies think about the experience they deliver to users will need to change in kind. Companies will need to find ways to cleverly leverage these platforms to make their brand experience really resonate with customers—all the while avoiding pitfalls where they may alienate users and lose their trust.

Figure 2.40   The Mozilla Blog

Figure 2.41   ReadWriteWeb (top)

Figure 2.42   Schneier on Security (middle)

Figure 2.43   Wikinomics (bottom)

Just One More

Although this is not a library or librarian blog, or even one that's LIS-related, I can't leave out the blog for the Chief of Police here in Lincoln, Nebraska. He's well spoken and a great writer, and I am including his blog here because, if nothing else, his blog is a great example of a public official blogging and organizational transparency. You may not want to read this blog in the long run, but be sure to take a look for a little inspiration.

The Chief's Corner

Tom Casady
lpd304.blogspot.com

"I'm the chief of a 425 member police force in Lincoln (population 252,000). I became an officer here in 1974, and except for a seven year detour to the Sheriff's Office, this is where I've been. I have been the chief since 1994" (Figure 2.44).

Tuesday, December 8, 2009

Dark, warm, and comfy

Yesterday was the big public hearing on City Council member John Spatz' proposed ordinance to drastically change how we handle false alarms in Lincoln. There was quite a bit of public testimony. Everyone seems to have their own idea on how the law should work in Lincoln. Personally, I favor the ordinance because it should really motivate the owners of premises with chronic repeat false alarms to do something about it. When you've got places with 10 or 20 false alarms in a given year, you wonder whether the $25 fine after the fourth free false alarm is really something they are concerned about, or whether it's more like the garbage bill—just another cost of doing business.

While delivering my testimony, the subject of the various causes of false alarms came up, and I told the following story from over the weekend, as reported in case number A9-120416 by Officer Jennifer Witzel.

At 1:37 AM on Sunday morning, officer Witzel and her colleagues were dispatched to an alarm at the clubhouse of Wilderness Ridge, where a great restaurant and nice ballroom create a prime location for wedding receptions. The alarm company reported that there were multiple drops on motion detectors—an indicator that someone or something is moving around inside. When the officers arrived, they started checking the interior of the building. Near the main entrance, they discovered the source of the alarm: a 29 year-old South Dakota man, snoozing snugly on a couch in the lobby.

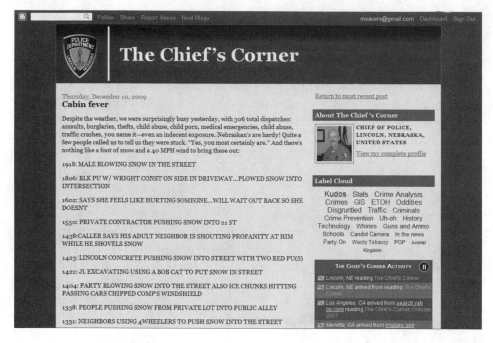

Figure 2.44   The Chief's Corner

Apparently he had grown drowsy while attending a reception, and his friends had helped him into a coat closet, where he nestled down for a short winter's nap. When he awoke and exited his comfy confines, he found that the wedding party had departed, the business had closed, and the employees had gone home. Stranded, he laid down on the sofa in his suit and tie for a little more shut-eye. We gave him a ride back to the Embassy Suites, and tucked him in.

Why, by the way, to we still refer to that rectangular plastic card as a key?

Chapter 3

The Library Blogosphere, Part 2: The Bloggers

Through my work and at conferences—notably Computers in Libraries and Internet Librarian—I've met many librarians who blog. Some of the most informative and creative among them were also very generous in taking time to be interviewed for the book. Relying mainly (but not solely) on email, I asked each individual to share his or her insights and experiences as a librarian blogger and also to tell us something about the person behind the blog. I hope you will find this behind-the-scenes look as interesting and inspiring as I did.

David Bigwood

Catalogablog
catalogablog.blogspot.com

Tell us a little about yourself, David.

I graduated in 1993 from the University of North Texas with my MLS. Libraries were a second career for me. I had been in retail management for several years after graduation from college, and I had grown very tired of that line of work and was searching for another. I was working through What Color Is Your Parachute, trying to find the right career path, when a woman I was dating opened my eyes to librarianship. It seemed a good mixture of people and tech skills. After some further investigation, I decided to pursue this career and enrolled in library school.

While still in school I found a position at the Clayton Center for Genealogical Research, part of the Houston Public Library System. My work on the reference desk there confirmed that this was a good profession for me. I then was hired by the Lunar and Planetary Institute for technical services in the library. This is where I found my passion for cataloging. Because it's a small special library, I still have reference duties, but most of my time is spent on cataloging. This is an ideal mix of tasks in a stimulating working environment. I have been here more than 20 years.

Why do you blog?

Blogging has become part of my routine. It is just as much of my professional development as reading journals, going to conferences, or giving presentations. I started blogging early in 2002 so by now it is a habit, one I still find useful.

What got you started blogging?

The main reason I started Catalogablog was to keep track of all the changes in the cataloging area of our profession. There was, and still is, lots of changes happening. There was talk of MARC leaving the communications format behind and moving to XML. AACR2 was being updated or replaced. Subject headings might be post-coordinated or replaced by tagging. Name authority files were being combined into an international virtual authority file. New metadata schemas were being discussed that were of interest to catalogers, Dublin Core, EAD, ONIX, and all the others. I needed a way to keep up with things in the profession. I'd been making bookmarks and had a stack of printouts on my desk and post-it notes stuck all over. I needed a place to easily keep track of what crossed my desk; blogging software solved that problem. It was a free and easy content management tool.

I quickly found other reasons. Writing every day, even a little bit, improves your writing skills. As I got readers, I found that there was a need for a news space. AutoCat is essential for catalogers, but much of that is discussion. Catalogablog is a place to find news and only news about what is going on in the profession. Much of it is also on AutoCat but mixed in with discussion. I have kept it going as a service to our community. I like to think it serves a need in the cataloging community.

How would you describe your blog (personal, professional, mix, etc.)?

Catalogablog is a news blog. It is not, or only very rarely, personal. It is not what I'd call professional writing. It points to requests for comments, news from important cataloging entities, and papers I find interesting. It does reflect my interests; only in that way is it personal. Lately I've been interested in the semantic web, so I point to items about linked data, RDF, OWL, microformats, and other building blocks of Web 3.0. I feel this is an area where catalogers can contribute, and should, since it will impact the future of bibliographic control.

What do you see as blogging's greatest strength?

That is a bit like asking what is the greatest strength of books. There are many; no one is overwhelming. It is very useful as a personal content management system. That is one reason I've kept it up for over seven years. It is easy to use and publish on the web. The writing tools are similar to those in a decent email client. A person can just open it up and start writing. Publishing is even easier: just hit a publish button. It is very versatile. I read many blogs; some are longer personal ruminations, some consist of snippets of code—both are possible. As a cataloger, I appreciate when the text has some semantic mark up, at least a bit. Plug-ins to popular blogging tools can add microformats, so it has even more meaning for machine processing. The automatic creation of an RSS feed is extremely important. It allows wider distribution and offers the reader the option of choosing the format in which to read the postings. Feeds can also be combined, as they are in Planet Cataloging, to create a subject portal.

What do you see as the greatest problem with blogs?

Not a problem, but a limitation: They are mainly a broadcast medium. Discussions are better as an email list or a forum. Blogs are a one-to-many (or few-to-many) publishing medium. Not a problem; nothing can serve all our communication needs. Blogs have their place along with all our other tools. Most blogs allow comments, but they are subservient to the main post and can be removed at the whim of the owner of the blog. The discussion is never on equal terms.

Why should someone start a blog and what advice would you give him or her?

Start a blog if you have something to share with the community and this way works for you. It is your professional responsibility to contribute in some way. If this is your way, get started.

Follow your passion. Don't write for readers but rather for yourself. That way even if you don't get lots of followers and become a star, you will still have something to gain from the work. Do remember that it is public—it may be found by the tenure or next search committee. However, don't let that prevent you from getting started or speaking your mind. It is an informal communication medium and some laxness in grammar is allowed. Speak with your own voice; do not write as if you were writing for a stuffy academic journal. Speak in the first person, not the academic *we*. Read Walt Crawford's *First Have Something to Say: Writing for the Library Profession.*

What are your top five favorite blogs to read?

- From the Catalogs of Babes (catalogsofbabes.wordpress.com): Thoughtful, well written with a strong personal voice.

- Thingology Blog (LibraryThing): Someone outside the cataloging profession looks at bibliographic control.

- Lorcan Dempsey's Weblog (orweblog.oclc.org): Always gives me something to consider and think about.

- Typo of the Day for Librarians (librarytypos.blogspot.com): Improves bibliographic access on a small scale five days a week.

- Librarian.net (www.librarian.net): Keeps me informed of the wider issues in the library profession.

How do you think your blogging or blogging in general has changed in the past several years?

There are now a lot more blogs. When I started in 2002, I was the only one covering cataloging. Now there is one covering FRBR, another for Dublin Core, another for typos in library catalogs, this list goes on and on. The creation of planets, like the Cataloging Planet, that combine all the postings on a topic in one place further makes a general topic blog difficult to justify. I don't think Catalogablog would be the same if I was starting today. I'd find a much smaller topic to cover.

Walt Crawford
Walt at Random
walt.lishost.org

Tell us a little about yourself, Walt.

I've been in the library field, full- or part-time, since 1968—but writing and editing even longer than that. After 38 years as a systems analyst/programmer, I'm now the Editorial Director for the Library Leadership Network as a part-time job.

Why do you blog?

Because I have things to say that don't fit neatly into one of my other writing outlets. I also use the blog to announce other publications, particularly my monthly ejournal, Cites & Insights.

What got you started blogging?

I'd been doing the ejournal, reading blogs, and increasingly using library-related blogs as source material for the ejournal for several years. Finally, I decided it would make sense to join the conversation directly, not just via comments on other blogs and commentaries in Cites & Insights.

How would you describe your blog (personal, professional, mix, etc.)?

The current tagline is "The library voice of the radical middle," and that's not a bad summary. The former tagline was "Libraries, music, net media, cruising, policy, and other stuff not quite ready for Cites & Insights." It's definitely a mix, and possibly more random than most liblogs because it's whatever I feel the urge to write about that isn't better suited to a primary outlet.

What do you see as blogging's greatest strength?

Within the library field, it's a great way to publish thoughts and even research at almost any level of formality and to engender conversations on important (and unimportant) issues. In the lead essay in the August 2007 Cites & Insights, I said "I believe that gray literature—blogs, this ejournal, a few similar publications and some lists—represents the most compelling and worthwhile literature in the library field today." I still believe that to be true. It's also the easiest way for someone new to break into library publishing—or for people to try something truly new.

What do you see as the greatest problem with blogs?

I can't answer that in the singular. Significant problems at this point:

1. It's extremely easy to start a blog. It's not so easy to keep one going.

2. Much of the conversation that used to take place in blog comments and inter-blog discussions has moved to FriendFeed and Twitter, with some dilution along the way.

3. Newcomers and some old-timers have unrealistic expectations about blogs and can become too disillusioned when they don't become rock stars.

Why should someone start a blog and what advice would you give him or her?

I think you should start a blog if you have something to say and find that a blog is the best way to say it. What you have to say doesn't necessarily have to be profound (certainly not all the time!), but it helps if you've thought it through a little bit—*purely* extemporaneous comments may fit better on Twitter and FriendFeed (and maybe Facebook).

As for advice, it relates back to the problems I cited. Don't overplan—that is, don't say "I must do a post a day, and I'd better plan to devote two hours a day to doing it right." That way lies failure for most of us. But it does help to have at least a dozen or so things before you start that you think you'll want to blog about—after all, it will take a few posts before people find you and subscribe to your feed. I don't believe in spending more energy in self-promotion than in preparing your posts, but that's just me. And don't feel bad if, after a month or even a year, you aren't seeing hundreds of page views a day or dozens of comments on each post. Finally, if you need a break, just take one (no need to announce it)—and if, after a long break, you're burned out, there's no shame in stopping.

What are your top five favorite blogs to read?

I've never been able to choose a "top five" in much of any field. I could mention Pegasus Librarian (pegasuslibrarian.com), See Also … (stevelawson.name/seealso), Information Wants to Be Free (meredith.wolfwater.com/wordpress), Blue Skunk Blog (doug-johnson.squarespace.com), and Christina's LIS Rant (christinaslibraryrant.blogspot.com), but I could just as easily mention any number of other sets of five.

How do you think your blogging or blogging in general has changed in the past several years?

I've studied how library-related blogging has changed over the past three or four years in some depth, published in two self-published books covering 607 and 521 blogs, respectively (in addition to two other books, now out of print, covering more than 200 public library blogs and academic library blogs respectively). It's too complex a picture to summarize in a few sentences, but it's clear that many blogs have somewhat fewer posts and somewhat longer posts, with a strong sense that many shorter posts have moved to so-called microblogging platforms.

My own blogging is probably as random as ever. Neither the frequency nor the average length of posts seems to have changed all that much over the past three years.

Jason Griffey

Pattern Recognition

www.jasongriffey.net/wp

Tell us a little about yourself, Jason.

I'm the Head of Library Information Technology at the University of Tennessee at Chattanooga, as well as an author, speaker, and father to the cutest 2-year-old in existence.

Why do you blog?

Because I have things to say, I suppose. When I started, it was literally to give myself an outlet to write that wasn't academic, since I started my blog while I was in graduate school. Like most early bloggers, I didn't really expect an audience—it was more about just writing. I'm a writer, it's what I do.

What got you started blogging?

It was partially peer pressure and partially a desire to try out new web tools. During grad school at UNC-Chapel Hill, I hung out with a small group of very techie types who were always trying out the newest web toys. One of them had been blogging for awhile, and I decided to give it a whirl. Early on it was the traditional "diary" style blog, but it quickly became somewhere to talk about library school topics and follow up with thoughts of my own on things in the news. Keep in mind, I started blogging in 2003, just before Google bought Blogger. It was still pretty early in the library-blog world, and I wasn't really hooked until 2004 or so when I had a post hit BoingBoing. That changed things a bit.

How would you describe your blog (personal, professional, mix, etc.)?

My blog is heavily a mix, although it's been trending more professional lately. I've split off into a handful of blogs: one for professional stuff, one for things about my daughter, yet another for ephemera that I find interesting around the web. But my "main" blog is more or less professional.

What do you see as blogging's greatest strength?

It's a direct publication medium that puts no barrier of any sort between writer and reader. No editorial hurdles to jump, no publishers telling you what to write about. Just you and people who might read you.

What do you see as the greatest problem with blogs?

The fact that it's a direct publication medium that puts no barrier of any sort between writer and reader. This means that Sturgeon's Law (90 percent of everything is crap) takes hold of the writing pretty quickly.

Why should someone start a blog and what advice would you give him or her?

Both are the same thing: First, have something to say.

What are your top five favorite blogs to read?

Well, judging from Google Reader: Lifehacker (lifehacker.com), Engadget (www.engadget.com), Smarterware (smarterware.org), Information Wants to Be Free (meredith.wolfwater.com/wordpress), and Walking Paper (www.walkingpaper.org).

Holly Hibner and Mary Kelly

Awful Library Books
awfullibrarybooks.wordpress.com

Tell us a little about yourselves, Holly and Mary.

Holly: I have worked in public libraries since 1990 and graduated from Wayne State University Library and Information Science program in 1999. I worked for 10 years as the Head of Adult Services at the Salem-South Lyon District Library. In August 2009, I became the new Adult Services Coordinator at the Plymouth District Library.

Mary: I received my MLIS from Wayne State University in 2001. I am an Adult/Teen Librarian at the Salem-South Lyon District Library, where I have worked for 11 years.

Why do you blog?

Holly: I love to write, and I love all things related to library science. Combine those two and there you have … a blog! It is a wonderful outlet for ideas that are floating around in my head.

Mary: Blogging is great way to test drive an idea with a large group of people. Librarians, especially, are all about sharing information. Getting feedback for ideas is so much easier through blogs.

What got you started blogging?

Holly: Mary and I worked side by side for 10 years. Over that decade, some interesting books crossed our desk for one reason or another. It started as a game to see who could find the most obscure, the funniest, or the oldest book, whether it was on our own library's shelves or another library's. We became kind of obsessed with the idea of collection quality, and we kept thinking that other librarians might find these books interesting too. We spoke at a library conference in early 2009 on the subject of collection quality, and we scrolled some pictures of book covers we had found as part of our presentation. The response was so great from the audience that we decided to create a blog about them. Awful Library Books was born!

Mary: A combination of things. Patrons at the reference desk were asking about blogs and how they work. In order to teach others and help people, we set up a blog. Topic wasn't as important as learning the mechanics of sites like Blogger or WordPress. For Awful Library Books, we were presenting a program on collection quality and we noticed that some of our "finds" were a hit with the audience, so we started the blog.

How would you describe your blog (personal, professional, mix, etc.)?

Holly: Awful Library Books was intended as a professional blog where we talk about weeding, knowing your clientele and their needs, and general collection quality. In reality, though, both Mary and I have a personal love of old, obscure, and funny books that maybe leaks into our blog posts. Our blog presents a different title each day that is an "awful library book" for one reason or another. We do not call them awful books … but possibly awful choices for library collections.

Mary: I would call it more a professional blog since it began with the idea that librarians would find a few laughs and ideas for improving collection quality. However, a good chunk of our readers are book or nostalgia fans. One of the unanticipated benefits of the blog is starting a frank discussion on the realities of limited budgets and the different missions of many kinds of libraries and archives.

What do you see as blogging's greatest strength?

Holly: The reach of a blog is its greatest strength. We have communicated with library staff around the world. In fact, now there are a lot of layperson visitors to our site who comment on our posts too. What a great way to bring people from anywhere and everywhere together to talk about a topic we all enjoy! Also, it's never done. Unlike a book, which is done once you get to the last page, blogs can go on and on.

Mary: The immediacy, or the "right now" aspect, of the internet is very exciting and people can share information quickly. I also really enjoy connecting with other librarians who seem to share my sense of humor and philosophy of librarianship.

What do you see as the greatest problem with blogs?

Holly: There is incompleteness about blogs. Even though every post we have ever written is still available on our site, it's almost a shame that our new site visitors may never see the oldest posts and experience how the blog has progressed over time. When you write a book, people are more likely to read it from start to finish. With a blog, readers kind of pick up halfway, with the current day's post. They might read a few past posts, but after a while there are just too many. A blog like ours posts every single day; we can only hope that they will become fans from the current day forward and stumble on some of the older posts every now and then.

Mary: The greatest strength is also its greatest problem. The "right now" aspect of blogging takes away a bit of reflection from the writing.

Why should someone start a blog and what advice would you give him or her?

Holly: You have something to say that you want to share with others? Start a blog! My advice is that if you are going to start a blog you need to commit to it. You can't post once a year and expect people to remember you. Post regularly and create a more rounded story that people can get in to. Everyone is an expert at something, so keep posting and sharing what you know.

Mary: I suppose if you think you have something to say, go for it! My best advice is to have a scope or theme and try not to get off track. I also think that it helps to define the audience of your blog.

What are your top five favorite blogs to read?
  Holly:

1. Lifehacker (lifehacker.com)

2. BoingBoing (www.boingboing.net)

3. MakeUseOf.com (www.makeuseof.com)

4. Fark (www.fark.com)

5. Neatorama (www.neatorama.com)

Mary: I have lots of favorites. I have too many librarian blogs I like to even begin to start naming them. Top five "civilian" blogs (only under duress):

1. Fark (www.fark.com)

2. Oddee (www.oddee.com)

3. Listverse (listverse.com)

4. Neatorama (www.neatorama.com)

5. MakeUseOf.com (www.makeuseof.com)

How do you think your blogging or blogging in general has changed in the past several years?

Holly: When Awful Library Books first started, we didn't know it would go beyond Mary and me and a few of our co-workers. We were very wordy—lots of commentary. Now that we get thousands of hits every day, it's more about the books and less about us. We keep it short, with just a blurb about our take on the title. In general, I think blogging is more prevalent. The platforms have become so easy that truly anyone can do it.

Mary: Well, there is a lot more of it going on, and it seems like just about everything and everyone has a blog!

Sarah Houghton-Jan
Librarian in Black
librarianinblack.net/librarianinblack

Tell us a little about yourself, Sarah.

I am the digital futures manager for the San Jose Public Library. My areas of expertise are library web services, technology training, eResources, usability, and user experience. I am also a speaker, trainer, and author, and published my first book, *Technology Training in Libraries*, in 2010.

Why do you blog?

I am as much a writer as I am a librarian. I love to share, like most people who work in libraries. I used to think about information online—think about the best websites about American History as an example—as a discrete "thing" that I could learn, that if I just kept up with what was out there, I could fill my head with a list of all of the stuff out there on the web. I realized, of course, that this is not a realistic way of thinking about information. But that desire to walk the path, to find new information all the time and share it with others to help them on their own paths, has never left me.

What got you started blogging?

I started blogging to share all of the resources, news, and tools that I found that helped me in my own digital librarian job. I think I keep blogging because I have had such a good response to what I've written on my website—people say thank you a lot or give me stories of how something they read about on my website helped them in their own work, or how they were inspired to pursue library school because of an article I'd written. If I have a chance to make a positive impact, and can, I'd feel like an idiot not to do it.

How would you describe your blog (personal, professional, mix, etc.)?

Librarian In Black is a combination of resources, tools, and news that I've found help with digital library services and also includes posts about my own library's digital projects or my own ideas about technology services and issues in libraries.

What do you see as blogging's greatest strength?

Blogging's biggest strength is the democratization of information. If you have something powerful to say, people will read what you write. You don't have to have the right connections, or schmooze with the bigwigs—just be smart and relevant to people's lives. That's a power that is unique to the self-publishing nature of the web, and I love it.

What do you see as the greatest problem with blogs?

So many blogs are created and abandoned, and then left to fester in irrelevance.

Why should someone start a blog and what advice would you give him or her?

If you have something to say and are willing to commit to regular posts, start a blog. Especially if you feel that what you want to say, or the subject matter you wish to address, isn't currently out there. Chances are, if you see the gap, other people do too—which means that if you post smartly people will enjoy what you write.

What are your top five favorite blogs to read?

ReadWriteWeb (www.readwriteweb.com), Walking Paper (www.walking paper.org), Lifehacker (lifehacker.com), Emily Chang's eHub (www.myblog log. com/buzz/community/eHub), and ResourceShelf (www.resourceshelf.com).

How do you think your blogging or blogging in general has changed in the past several years?

I have been slowly blogging less in the last year or so—down from 25 posts a week to around five. I think that part of it is a time issue, but part is a technology change. So much of my life is mobile-focused now, and I still find it too cumbersome to write a lengthy blog post on my smartphone, so I've started reading and writing more in shorter chunks via tools like Twitter and Facebook. I hope to find a more mobile-friendly way to blog more soon, perhaps with some of the newer apps available. The other big change has been that I've stopped being afraid of pissing off vendors, publishers, or other organizations that may be classified as "the man." That is a privilege that comes with slowly gained street cred: the ability to post with virtual impunity, to not be afraid of getting in trouble or risking some unknown possible opportunity. Being able to write honestly without fear is an amazing privilege.

Jessamyn West

librarian.net

Tell us a little about yourself, Jessamyn.

I am a community technology librarian and a moderator of the massive group blog MetaFilter.com. I live in a rural area of central Vermont where I teach basic computer skills. I assist tiny libraries with technology planning and implementation, helping them with Wi-Fi and websites and making sense of their systems. I maintain an online presence at jessamyn.com and librarian.net and has had my address and phone number on the internet for a decade. My favorite color is orange.

Why do you blog?

When I started in 1999, it was the best way to get information that I thought was useful to the most people in the shortest time.

What got you started blogging?

I actually found the domain for my blog, librarian.net, available on a random search. I grabbed it and thought "Huh, what should I do with this?" I already had a personal blog, and this seemed to be the best place to start a more professional blog.

How would you describe your blog (personal, professional, mix, etc.)?

It's about topics of interest to librarians. As time has passed and other people have started librarian blogs, the focus has narrowed to be more about technology and politics and the digital divide.

What do you see as blogging's greatest strength?

Anyone can do it: The tools are free and relatively simple; the tools work on any internet connection; there are sharing features built in. If you can type, you can blog.

What do you see as the greatest problem with blogs?

No one reads them anymore.

Why should someone start a blog and what advice would you give him or her?

I figure if you have something to say and you're comfortable with the online world, starting a blog (or something similar, Twitter or FriendFeed or Facebook or whatever) is a good way to share your words with people. My advice is that it's easy to attract eyeballs with controversy, but I'd suggest really talking about what you care about, not just what will make people mad. Link to other bloggers and online content, and they will link back to you. Read other blogs if you're writing a blog; that's my strongest advice.

What are your top five favorite blogs to read?

I like Freedom to Tinker (www.freedom-to-tinker.com), FreeGovInfo (free govinfo.info), Modcult (modcult.org), Dawdlr (dawdlr.tumblr.com; only updates twice a year), and Swiss Army Librarian (www.swissarmylibrarian.net).

How do you think your blogging or blogging in general has changed in the past several years?

As I said, I don't think people really read personal blogs the way they used to, but now that the White House has a blog, we can pretty much stop arguing about whether blogs are "trendy" or just a good mechanism for getting information out. Back when I started my first blog, I was editing the text live on the web server and/or using ftp to move files back and forth. Now I can use slick CMS's that can display photos, have fancy plug-ins, and do a lot of the categorizing for me.

Blogging is at once useful but also can sometimes obscure the message in favor of hyping the medium, if that makes sense. It used to be that you'd have a blog because you wanted to talk about, say, ALA or something like that, and now ALA has its own blog. It's a good news/bad news situation definitely.

Chapter 4

Creating a Blog

If you want to create a blog for your library, I suggest first creating one for yourself. You don't have to keep it up, or even tell anyone about it, but you can use it to experiment and to learn (and play) without your mistakes or missteps having any permanence or public repercussion.

Why Blog?

Almost everyone seems to have something to say, yet many people either don't know how to express themselves or lack an appropriate forum. A blog offers an informal means for expressing your ideas in public without the pressures typically associated with public speaking.

Blogs help you stay on top of events. This is a reason not only to read other people's blogs but also to create your own. In order to post to your own blog regularly, you'll have to stay current on your subject.

Unfortunately, most libraries do not promote themselves effectively to their respective communities. A blog offering new and interesting information on a regular basis is a great way to promote your library and encourage repeat visits to its website.

Blogs are cheap, fast, and easy. In this chapter, you will learn how to set up a blog in less than five minutes without any budget impact other than a minimal staff investment. Posting to a blog takes no more technical know-how other than typing.

Once you've decided that a blog is the right medium for getting your ideas across, you'll want to keep the following guidelines in mind:

- *Have something to say.* In Chapter 3, you'll find profiles of some LIS bloggers. When asked what advice they would give to a novice blogger, the most common response they gave was, "Have something to say." Sarah Houghton-Jan (Librarian in Black) may have said it best in a conversation we had on this topic: "If you don't have something to say, don't start a blog. Please. I'm begging you."

- *Have something to say **regularly**.* A blogger has an idea that he or she thinks is brilliant enough that everyone should know about it. He posts it on his blog and then disappears. This happens all the time, and it doesn't encourage readers to return. If you don't post on a regular basis, no one will read your blog. Blogs need to be updated often and regularly.

- *Have something to say **responsibly**.* Blogging has raised issues of free speech when it comes to the relationship between bloggers and employers. There are documented cases of individuals being fired for the content of their blogs. If you're going to blog, especially about work-related activities, talk to your immediate supervisor or even your library director first. Make sure they're aware of what you're planning to do and why. You may not need supervisory approval for an individual blog, but it can't hurt to check first.[1]

Michael Stephens offers two excellent posts on his blog Tame the Web that deal with issues relevant to library bloggers. The first, "Ten Things a Blogging Librarian Must Do (an exercise in common sense)" (tametheweb.com/2004/ 06/ten_things_a_blogging_libraria.html), focuses on librarians who are interested in creating individual blogs. The second, "Ten Guidelines for Developing Your Internal Blog" (tametheweb.com/2004/10/23/ten-guide lines-for-developing- your-internal-blog), should be read if you're considering creating a blog to represent your library. Despite the fact that these posts were written years ago, they are just as relevant today.

Methods for Creating Your Blog

There are several possible methods for creating your blog. You can use a web-based service or server-installed software. Both have their unique advantages and disadvantages.

Web-based services have the advantage of being accessible from any internet-connected computer. Because I travel a lot and may use as many as five different computers in a single day (not counting my smartphone), the flexibility of using the same service from any location makes a web-based service my choice. The most popular web service, Blogger.com, is free and offers free hosting space on its server. (You can, however, choose to store your blog on any server to which you have access.) A disadvantage of web-based services is that they typically lack some of the advanced features available with server-based packages or client software.

Server-based packages are software programs you can download and install on your web server. Since the software resides on a server, this blogging method is similar to a web service in that it is accessible from any internet-connected computer. Movable Type (www.movabletype.org), TypePad (www.sixapart.com/typepad), and WordPress (wordpress.com) are some of the more popular programs. These programs offer a number of additional features—such as displaying an interactive calendar-based view of posts—not available in free web-based services. Significant disadvantages are that the software is typically not free, and a certain level of technical expertise is required to install it on a server. Bloggers who are on a budget or who lack technical expertise tend not to invest in this method of blog creation—at least not for personal or small library blogs.

Some of these services, such as Movable Type, offer both server-installed and web-based services. In these instances, once you've decided that you like the features offered by a particular service, you can then decide which version to use based on your level of technological know-how and access to the appropriate hardware.

Because the main purpose of this book is to help you master the basics of blogging and RSS without considerable expenditure or technical knowledge, we'll focus on Blogger.com for the rest of this chapter. Even if you switch later to a different service or product, this coverage of Blogger.com will provide you with a useful grasp of the basics.

Blogger.com, or simply Blogger, includes excellent help files for bloggers who want to use the service. Due to potential changes in the service, its help files will be more up-to-date than the instructions supplied here.

Creating Your First Blog

Creating a Blogger Account

To get started, open your web browser and go to the Blogger website (www.blogger.com). On the right side of the page is a large orange button labeled Create a Blog. Click on that button to create your Blogger account (Figure 4.1). You will not need to repeat this step in the event that you decide to create additional blogs on the site.

The Blogger service is owned by Google. If you already have an account with any other Google service, such as Gmail, Google Docs, or iGoogle, you can automatically link that account to a new Blogger account. If this applies to you, you can skip the steps in the following list and instead just click on the Sign In First link and follow the instructions. Once you've signed in to your Google account, you will find yourself on Blogger's basic setup screen. If you don't have a Google account, you will need to complete the fields in the Create a Google Account form (Figure 4.2):

- *Email address*. Enter the email address you wish to associate with your account. You will use this address to sign in to your account in the future. *Retype your email address* to confirm that you typed it in correctly the first time.

- *Enter a password*. Choose a password for your account. Passwords must be at least six characters long. *Retype the password* to confirm that you typed the desired password correctly the first time.

- *Display name*. Choose the name you want displayed to your readers. Typically, individuals use their real names, but it's up to you. Some people use a nickname; others use pseudonyms to obscure their identities.

- *Email notifications*. Check this box if you wish to receive emails from Blogger about the service itself. In the many years I've been using Blogger, I cannot recall ever receiving an email from the service, so don't worry about spam here.

- *Birthday*. Type in your birthday. (Blogger's Terms of Service state that "you must be at least thirteen (13) years of age to use the Service.")

- *Word Verification*. This is your standard CAPTCHA designed to prevent computers from setting up Blogger accounts on a mass and automatic basis. Basically, it's a test to see if you're a human.

- *Acceptance of Terms*. Check this box to accept Blogger's terms of service. (You can read the terms by clicking on the Terms of Service link.) If you do not accept, your account will not be created.

Once you've filled in all the fields, click on the Continue arrow.

Naming Your Blog

Now that you have a Blogger account (and also a Google account), you'll need to name your blog. Here you just need to fill in just two fields (Figure 4.3):

- *Blog title*. This is what you want to call your blog. It can be whatever you wish it to be. (Mine is The Travelin' Librarian.) However, you might want to do a little research first to make sure no one else is already using your brilliant idea for a title.

- *Blog address (URL)*. This is a little more complicated. When you first set up your blog, you're automatically given space on Blogger's web server (blogspot.com) to host your content. If you really do want to host it on a different server, you can, but those settings aren't available until after you have actually created your blog. So, the URL for your blog must

Figure 4.1   Blogger home page
Figure 4.2   Creating a Blogger/Google account

Figure 4.3   Naming your blog

initially be http://*something*.blogspot.com. You need to supply the *something* in that URL. Keep in mind that *something* should ideally be both relevant to your topic and memorable. It cannot include spaces and cannot have been previously used by another blog in Blogger. Lastly, it is not case sensitive, and you probably should avoid any characters other than letters and numbers. So, go ahead and enter what you think *something* should be and click the Check Availability link to see whether your choice is available. If not, try something else or pick one of the recommended alternatives.

Once you have a title and a usable URL, click the Continue arrow.

Choosing a Template

The next step is to choose a template for your blog (Figure 4.4). There are 12 different templates to choose from. If you don't like any of them, pick the one you dislike the least for now. You'll have the opportunity to choose from a larger selection of templates or to modify your initial template once this process is complete. (We'll cover this later in the chapter.)

Once you've chosen a template, click the orange Continue arrow at the bottom of the page. Blogger will take just a few moments to create your blog and will notify you when it's done.

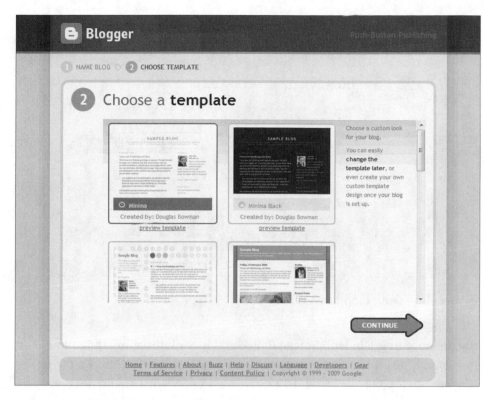

Figure 4.4   Choosing a template

At this point, if you wish to host your content on another server, you can do so by clicking on the Set Up a Custom Domain link. You can also do this at a later stage in the Settings area of your blog. I'll cover that procedure later in this chapter.

If you had a previous Blogger blog or a blog from another blogging service and wanted to import it into the one you are currently creating, you would use the Import Blog Tool here. Just click on the link and follow the steps. However, since you wouldn't be reading this book if you already had a blog, I'll skip covering this feature in detail.

Click on the Start Blogging arrow (Figure 4.5) to continue.

Using the Blogger Dashboard

You should now see a Posting interface (Figure 4.10 later in this chapter). From here, click on the Dashboard link in the upper-right corner of the screen, which brings you to Blogger's Dashboard page. The main section of

Figure 4.5   Your blog has been created!

the dashboard is labeled Manage Blogs, and it contains a link that allows you to create a new blog associated with your existing account and a list of the Blogger blogs you have access to. (You can access a blog you did not create via an invitation from that blog's creator.) The example in Figure 4.6 (from my actual account) shows that I have access to many different blogs.

You can create as many blogs as you like without having to create multiple accounts, and all the blogs you have access to are listed in reverse chronological order based on the date and time of each blog's most recent post (shown under the blog title). You are also provided with links that allow you to view the blog, create a new post, edit posts, change the blog's settings, change the blog's layout (or template), and monetize the blog. If your library creates a blog, you may want to set only one person as the blog's administrator. By giving other staff members their own Blogger accounts, you enable them to post to the library's blog but only the assigned administrator will be able to change the blog's settings. Additionally, posts by individual users will be marked with the name of the user.

Below the Blogs section are the Reading List and Other Stuff areas. These sections change often and include new posts from any blogs you're following using Blogger, as well as important news and updates from the Blogger system. I advise checking the Reading List's Blogger Buzz tab regularly, as system problems and changes in features will be reported here.

Figure 4.6   Blogger Dashboard

Also on this page are links to view your profile, edit your profile, edit your profile photo, and edit notifications. We'll be covering each of these later in this chapter.

Lastly, across the top of the page, you'll see the email address you're currently logged in under; links to the Dashboard (where you are now), your Google account, and Blogger Help; and a link to sign out. These options will appear at the top of every Blogger system page while you are logged in.

Managing Your Profile

Let's now focus on the Profile section of the Dashboard. You have four options: View Profile, Edit Profile, Edit Photo, and Edit Notifications. Take a moment to review your profile. Since you've just created your account, there won't be much to see at this point, but it will grow over time. Because I have been a Blogger member for several years, I have a relatively lengthy profile (Figure 4.7).

The Edit Profile link will lead you to the Edit User Profile interface (Figure 4.8). Complete the fields as you see fit. Beyond the first two sections, all the information requested is optional. If you feel that you need to be anonymous in your blog, you can leave the Display Name field blank or provide a pseudonym for public viewing. Even if you have supplied information, you can prevent people from viewing your profile by leaving the Share My Profile option unchecked. If you choose not to share your profile, information such as your display name will still automatically be attached to your posts, so be sure to fill in that part accordingly. When you've completed the form, click the Save Your Profile button at the bottom of the page. If you don't follow this step, your changes will not be saved.

The Edit Photo link takes you to the specific place on the Edit Profile screen that allows you to change your profile picture. Your profile picture doesn't have to be a photo—it could be your library's logo. Just be sure to pick something you feel is an appropriate pictorial representation of you and/or your library.

Clicking the Edit Notifications link takes you to a page with a single option, to subscribe or unsubscribe to the Blogger emails I mentioned previously in this chapter, under Creating Your Account (Figure 4.9).

Creating a Post in Blogger

Now that you've familiarized yourself with the Dashboard and completed your profile, you're ready to create your first post.

Head back to the Dashboard and click on the New Post link under your blog's title, and you will be taken back to the Create Post interface for your blog (Figure 4.10). Notice the four tabs under your blog's title representing the four major sections available in the Blog interface: Posting, Settings, Template, and Monetize. There is also a View Blog link that will show you your live blog as your readers see it. (We'll do this shortly.)

Below the tabs you will see links for New Post (where you are now), Edit Posts, and Comment Moderation. Below these is the interface for creating a new post.

By default, you are in the Edit Html (HyperText Markup Language) version of the Create page. (This version of post creation assumes that you have a working knowledge of HTML.) Here you are presented with a Title field and a larger body field. To create a post, first fill in the title of the post, and then type the content of the post into the larger body field. The buttons above the body field let you add formatting (bold and italics) to selected text, insert a hyperlink, set text as a block quote, perform spell-check, and insert images without using XHTML. These buttons automatically place the appropriate XHTML code into your post, although you can also choose to type your own code into both the title field and the body field.

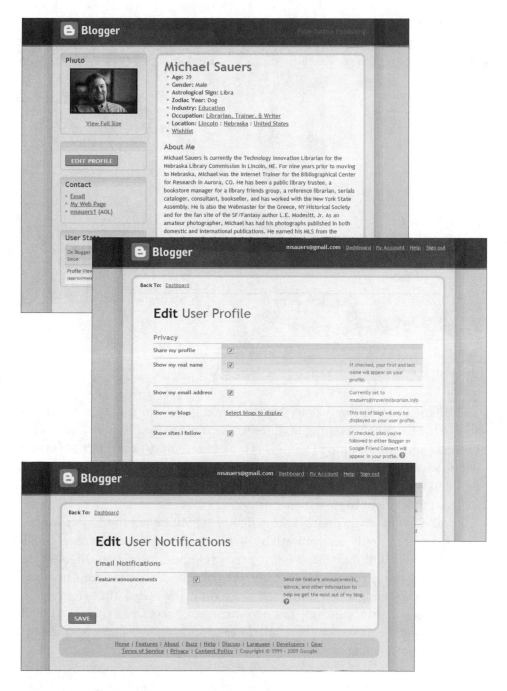

Figure 4.7   My Blogger profile (top)

Figure 4.8   Editing your user profile (middle)

Figure 4.9   Editing your user notifications (bottom)

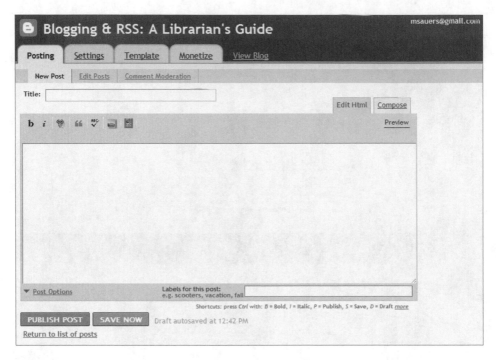

Figure 4.10   Creating a post: Edit HTML

The Post Options link below the body field gives you the opportunity to change the Comments setting to Allow or Don't Allow for this post and to edit the date and time stamp (Figure 4.11). The date and time field is set, by default, according to when you started creating the post. Later in this chapter, I will show you how to turn off comments altogether should you decide not to support them in your blog.

If you don't have a working knowledge of HTML, select the Compose tab (above the body field), and you will be taken to a WYSIWYG (What You See Is What You Get) interface for creating posts (Figure 4.12). Here, there is no assumption of or need for XHTML knowledge. You can create your posts as though you are using a standard word processing program. Editing options in the Compose interface include basic font control (face, size, color, bold, and italics), hyperlink insertion, text alignment, numbering, adding bullets or quotation marks, image insertion, and format clearing.

In either New Post interface, under the main text box, you will see a field titled Labels for This Post. Here you can add one or more (as a comma-delimited list) labels, or tags, for your post. While not required, tags can be a useful feature for your readers. For example, if you use the label *win7* on all of your posts about the newest version of Microsoft's OS, your readers will see a clickable *win7* link

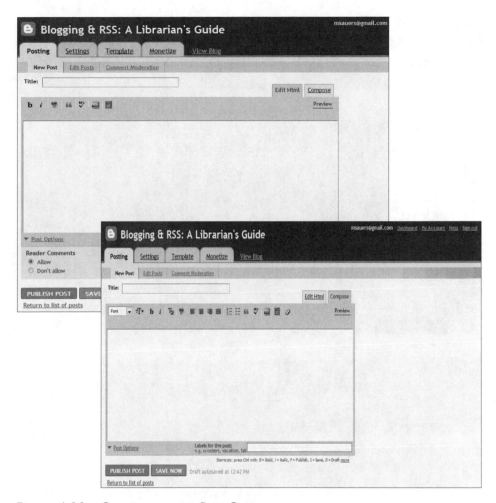

Figure 4.11   Creating a post: Post Options

Figure 4.12   Creating a post: Compose

under each of those posts. When readers click on that link, they will be presented with a page that contains just your posts with that label, allowing them
to read only what they wish to on your blog.

Blogger will remember your labels as you continue to post, so the next time
you type, the letter *w* into the labels field, for example, all of your previously
used labels starting with *w* will appear as a clickable dropdown list, as shown
in Figure 4.13.

If you need more time to compose your post or want to finish it at a later
time, click the Save Now button. This will save but not publish (i.e., make
public) your post. You can return to your post at a later time and either finish

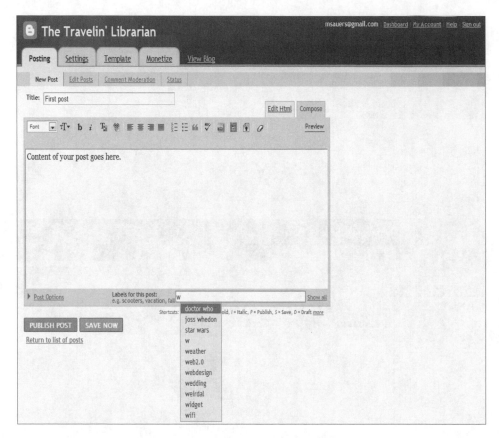

Figure 4.13   Creating a post: Labels for This Post

or delete it. (Posts are also automatically saved as drafts every few minutes. However, clicking Save Now every so often never hurt anyone.)

When you have finished writing your post, click on the Preview link to check your post for any errors (click Hide Preview to go back and make corrections). Finally, click the Publish Post button to instruct Blogger to generate a webpage based on your content and to make the page public. Depending on the size of the post, and whether you're publishing your blog on Blogger or another server, publishing a post can take anywhere from a few seconds to a few minutes. While your post is being published, you will see a status screen showing the progress of the publishing. You will be notified on screen when the publishing process has been completed successfully (Figure 4.14).

If the publishing mechanism encounters any errors, you can click on the Details link for more information. The two buttons presented to you on the Details screen—Republish Index Only and Republish Entire Blog—are typically used only if there is a temporary error and you want to try again. In such

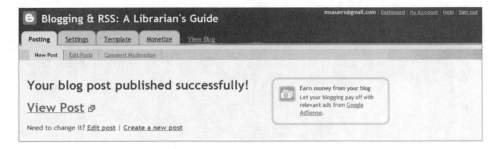

Figure 4.14   Your blog post published successfully!

cases, republishing just the index, the first page of your blog, will usually suffice. Republishing the entire blog, especially if you've been running it for any considerable period of time, is only necessary if you've made a global change to your blog (for instance, changes to the template). Larger blogs will take a while to republish; for example, my blog, with almost 2,000 posts, takes about 30 minutes to republish in its entirety.

When you're finished publishing, you can proceed to any of the other sections of the Blogger interface available via the links on the page. Don't forget that you also have the option of clicking the View Blog link if you want to see your blog live, including your new post.

To edit the post you just published, click the Edit Post link. To create another post, click Create a New Post.

Using Alternate Posting Methods

Blogger offers several alternate methods for creating new posts that do not require you to be on the New Post page in the Blogger system. You may find that one of the alternate methods is more effective for you.

Blogger for Word

In August 2005, Blogger released the Blogger add-in for Microsoft Word 2000 and 2003 (buzz.blogger.com/bloggerforword.html). Once this add-in has been downloaded and installed, you can create and edit your Blogger posts using Microsoft Word. The add-in installs an additional toolbar in Word with buttons labeled Blogger Settings (to give Word access to your blog), Open Post (to display a list of posts from your blog so you may choose which one to edit), Save as Draft (to save the current document as a draft post), and Publish (to publish the current document as a live post). Those using Word 2007 or 2010 should choose New Blog Post as a document type (Figure 4.15).

The advantage of using the Blogger add-in is that you have all of the editing capabilities and tools of Word available to you, thereby extending your options well beyond those of Blogger's built-in editing interface.

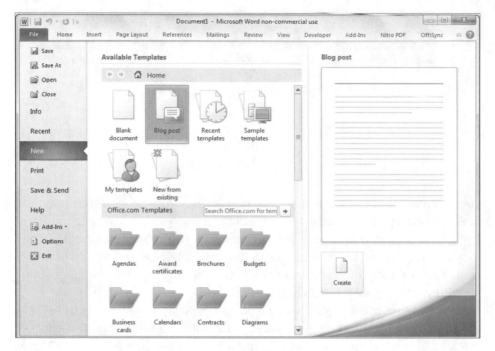

Figure 4.15   New blog post in Word 2010

BlogThis!

BlogThis! is a bookmarklet available from Blogger that allows you to automatically create a new post linking to the webpage you are visiting at the time. The bookmarklet can be found by going into Blogger Help and searching for *BlogThis!* By installing the bookmarklet, you create a new bookmark that, when selected, will open a new window containing Blogger's New Post form. The post's title is automatically filled in with the title of the webpage, and the post's body contains a link back to that page; the post is now ready for you to add whatever additional text you'd like (Figure 4.16). (If you are not logged into your Blogger account, you will be asked to enter your username and password before the form is presented to you.)

The upper-right corner of the Blog This! window displays a dropdown list of the blogs you have access to from your Google account. If you only have one blog, this is not an issue. If you have multiple blogs, be sure the blog you want to post to is selected before you click the Publish button. More than once I've created a post using BlogThis! only to discover I've published it to the wrong blog.

By default, BlogThis! uses the WYSIWYG version (labeled *Rich Text* in this window) for editing the new post. If you'd rather use the Edit HTML interface, click

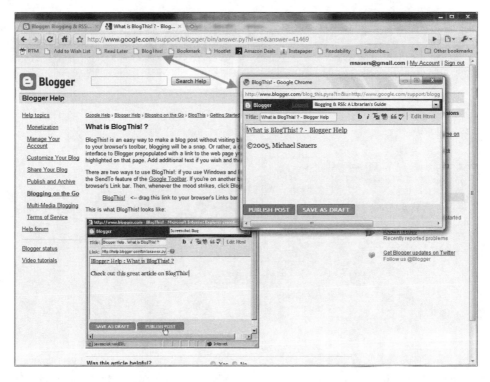

Figure 4.16   BlogThis!

on Rich Text and change to Edit HTML. BlogThis! will remember which interface you choose, so that next time you will be presented with that version first.

BlogThis! is also available as part of the Google Toolbar in Internet Explorer. Instructions for installing the Google Toolbar (along with turning on its BlogThis! button) are available on the same page as the bookmarklet.

Posting Via Email

Sometimes you may not have web access, but you can send email (for example, even if you do not have internet access on your cell phone, you may be able send email from it). As long as you can send email, you can create a blog post.

To turn on email posting for your blog, select the Settings tab in your blog and then select Email & Mobile. From the two settings available, select Email Posting Address (Figure 4.17). (We'll discuss the other setting later in this chapter.) You will be prompted to enter a secret word of at least four characters into the field. Enter your secret word and click Save Settings. You are now ready to post via email. Whatever you put in the subject line of the email will be the title of the post, and the body of the message will become the body of the post. The post may include HTML, but if you don't include any markup when emailing, you can always log in and enhance your post later.

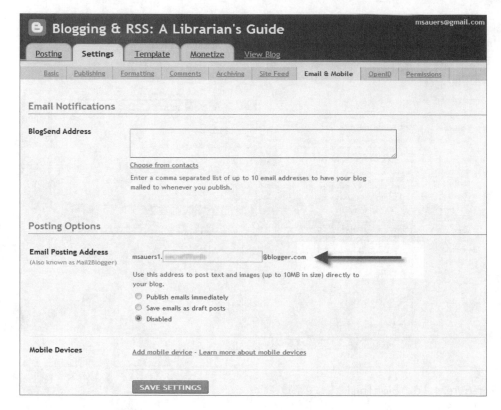

Figure 4.17   Posting via email settings

You can then choose what to do with email posts when they are received by Blogger: You can have them automatically published or saved as draft posts. You can also choose to disable this feature.

Posting Via SMS

By setting up your blog to recognize a mobile device, you can also create posts via SMS (text) messages. Just click on Add Mobile Device and you'll be instructed to send a code word via SMS to a specific number. Once that is done, your phone will be connected to your blog, and you'll be allowed to send in posts via SMS.

Posting Via Phone (Audio Posts)

If all else fails and you have no internet connectivity and absolutely must post something now, you can use the telephone. Signing up (in advance) for Gabcast (www.gabcast.com) allows you to dial a phone number, enter your blog's PIN, and record a post. The post will be published to your blog as a button (Figure 4.18) that users can click to hear your audio recording in MP3 format.

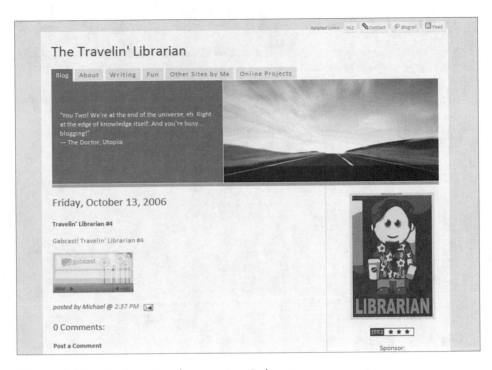

Figure 4.18   Posting via phone using Gabcast

Blog Options

Now that your blog is up and running and you've created a post or two, let's take a walk through Blogger's built-in options, which are accessible from the four tabs at the top of the main posting page.

Posting

The Posting tab offers four options: New Post, Edit Posts, Edit Pages, and Comment Moderation.

New Post

The Create Post screen (see "Creating a Post in Blogger" earlier in this chapter; see Figure 4.10) is the main interface for creating a new post or editing an existing post.

Edit Posts

The Edit Posts screen (Figure 4.19) displays a list of the most recent posts to your blog and the status of each post. The screen shows, by default, the 25 most recently created posts, regardless of status. You have access to different

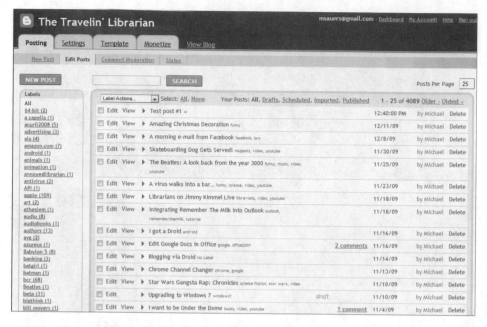

Figure 4.19   Editing posts

sets of posts through the Your Posts links, the Posts Per Page dropdown lists, and the Search box.

To the right of Your Posts are several links you can click on to see all posts, drafts, and scheduled, imported, or published posts, respectively.

The Search box allows you to perform a keyword search of all of your posts, both published and drafts, and display only those posts. For example, a search on *holiday* would display only your posts that contain the word *holiday*.

You can also view a list of your posts filtered by their labels. To do this, select one of your labels from the list on the far left side of the screen. For example, clicking on the label *win7* would show a list of only the posts with that label. Additionally, you can use the Label Actions dropdown box to apply labels to existing posts or remove them. Just select the appropriate posts using the checkboxes (or the All or None links), and select the desired action from the Label Actions dropdown list.

Also on this screen you will find a New Post button that will take you back to the Create Post screen, a Publish Selected button that will publish all selected posts, and a Delete Selected button that will delete all selected posts.

The main frame of the Edit Posts screen displays a list of either your recent posts or the posts that you have requested (by filtering or searching). For each entry in the list, there is a checkbox (previously mentioned), an Edit link, a

View link, the post's title (with a triangle icon immediately to its left—more on this shortly), and labels associated with the post, the date and time of the post, the name of the user who created the post, and a Delete link. The Edit link will take you to the composition screen pre-populated with the information from that post. This lets you edit an existing post. The View link opens a new window and shows you the post as it will be seen by your readers. The Delete link allows you to delete a post from your blog. You will be asked to confirm that you want to delete a post (Figure 4.20).

The small triangle to the left of a post's title allows you to view the full text of a post without leaving this screen (Figure 4.21). Clicking on the triangle

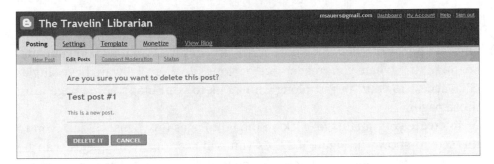

Figure 4.20　Are you sure you want to delete this post?

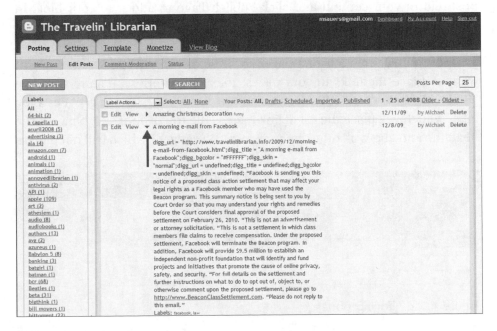

Figure 4.21　Previewing a post

toggles between viewing the post and hiding it. Any images in your post will not be displayed in this view.

Edit Pages

In 2010, Blogger introduced the ability to add "pages" to a site. You can think of pages as individual documents you might want to have as part of your blog that contain content you wouldn't necessarily want to write as a blog post. For example, in a library blog, you probably want to have a single page that lists your locations and hours; in a personal blog, you probably want a page that says something about you, including where you live, your interests, and where you work. In neither case would you necessarily want these as actual blog posts.

The other advantage to creating "pages" is that a link to the pages you create will appear on every blog post and every archived webpage on your site. So, no matter where your readers are on your site, they'll always have single-click access to your "pages" along with a link to your blog's home page from those pages.

To create your first page, click on the Edit Pages link. This will take you to the screen shown in Figure 4.22. As you will see, up to 10 "pages" can be included within your blog. To create a new page, click the New Page button.

The page creation interface is exactly the same as the one for creating a post. Fill in your content and click Publish Page to add it to your blog. In Figure 4.23, you can see that I'm creating an "About Me" page for my site, including a brief biography.

Upon publishing your first page, you'll be asked where on your site you want to place the links to your pages. Your three options (Figure 4.24) are "Blog sidebar," which will place the list of links in a sidebar gadget; "Blog tabs," which will place the list of links across the top of your site, beneath the headline and above all other content; and "No gadget," which will not place a

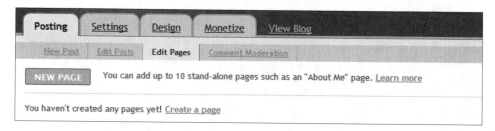

Figure 4.22   Editing pages

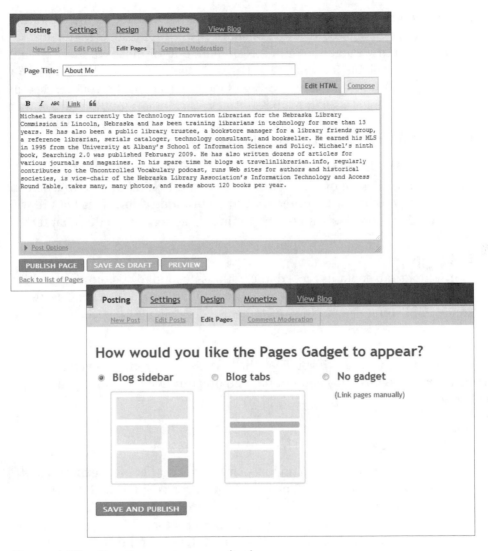

Figure 4.23   Creating a new page (top)

Figure 4.24   How would you like the Pages Gadget to appear? (bottom)

list of links anywhere. (Choosing this last option means you will need to man-ually insert hyperlinks to your pages when and where you want them.)

Make your choice and click Save and Publish. Your blog will be republished and a confirmation screen will appear just as if you'd published a blog post. If you then head back to the Edit Pages screen, you will see that you now have one page available for editing, deleting, or viewing (Figure 4.25). Figure 4.26

shows my new blog home page with the About Me link across the top of the page. Figure 4.27 shows my About Me page, also with the links at the top.

I'll be covering gadgets later in this chapter, but for those wondering what options are available for your new "Pages Gadget," click the Design tab for your blog and take a look at the Page Elements screen. As you can see in Figure 4.28, there is a section labeled Pages. Clicking on the Edit link in that area will show you options for the page (Figure 4.29), including changing both the order and style of the links to your pages.

Comment Moderation

At this point, clicking on the Comment Moderation link brings up a screen stating that you have not turned on comment moderation. This feature will be covered in more detail under the Settings heading later in this chapter.

Settings

The Settings tab contains most of the options needed to customize your blog (without needing any HTML knowledge) and is divided into nine sections: Basic, Publishing, Formatting, Comments, Archiving, Site Feed, Email and Mobile, OpenID, and Permissions.

When you change an item in the Settings section, the change will not become permanent until you click the Save Settings button. Even after you save your changes, they will not be seen on your live blog until you republish it.

Basic

The Basic screen (Figure 4.30) has several settings you can change:

- *Blog Tools.* Here you can import posts from another blog, export posts (useful for making an offline back copy of your content), or delete your blog. Just follow the simple instructions provided on the next relevant screen to complete the action. (Keep in mind that deleting a blog puts its blogspot.com URL and title back into the pool for others to use.)

- *Title.* This field contains the name of your blog that displays at the top of your blog's pages. Initially, this field will contain the title that you entered when you set up your blog.

- *Description.* This field, which is not required, should contain a brief narrative description of your blog and its purpose. The content of this field will be displayed under the blog's title if you are using any of the standard Blogger templates.

- *Add your blog to our listings?* The Blogger system has a directory of all the blogs created from within Blogger. By answering *Yes* to this question

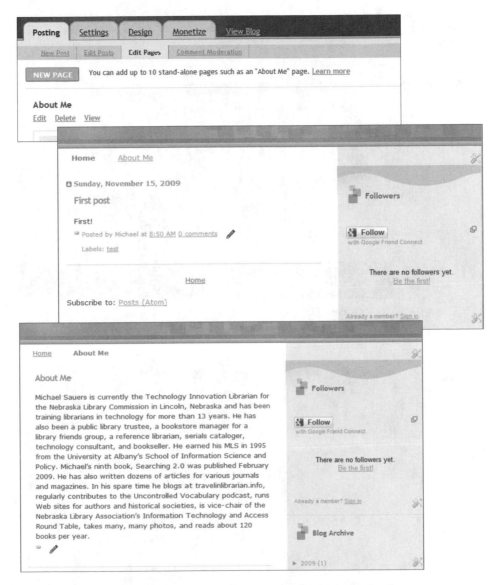

Figure 4.25   Edit Pages screen with one published screen (top)

Figure 4.26   My blog with the About Me link (middle)

Figure 4.27   About Me page on my blog (bottom)

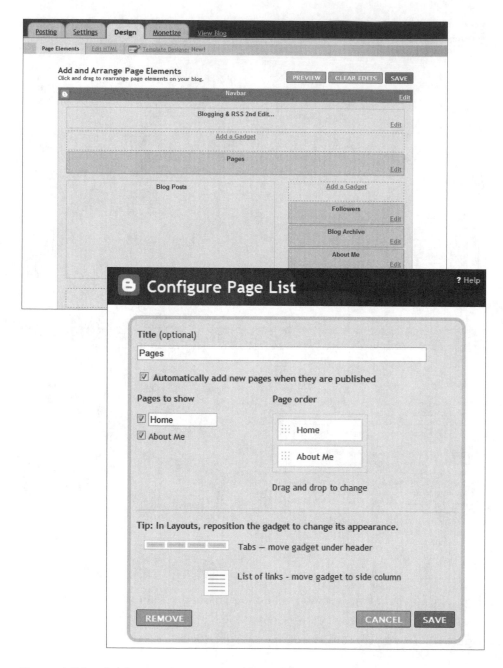

Figure 4.28   Adding and arranging page elements (top)

Figure 4.29   Configuring a page (bottom)

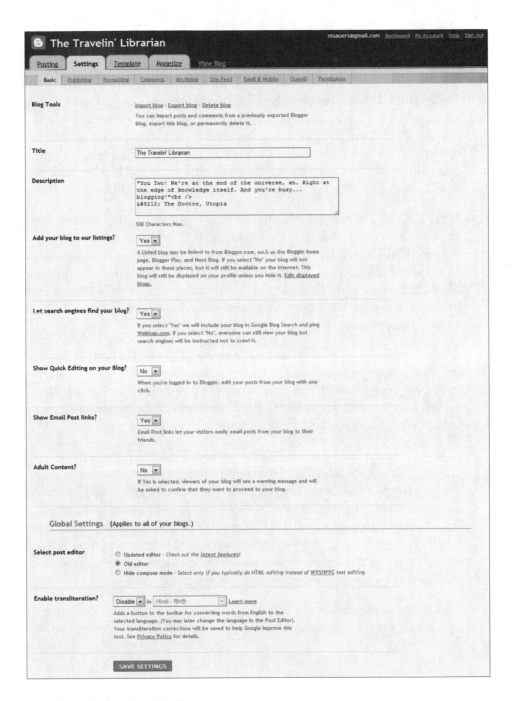

Figure 4.30   Settings: Basic

you agree to have your blog listed in that directory and also to allow your blog to appear on your user profile page should your profile also be public. Answering *No* prevents your blog from being listed in either location.

- *Show Quick Editing on your Blog?* Answering *Yes* to this question will add an Edit link (a pencil icon) after the title of each individual post (Figure 4.31). This link allows you to select a post from your blog and go directly to the editing screen for that post. This link will only appear for individuals who are logged into Blogger at the time and have permission to post and edit that blog. No one else will see this link.

- *Show Email Post links?* Answering *Yes* to this question adds another link (an envelope icon) after the title of each post. This link, visible to everyone, allows readers to email the content of a post to themselves or someone else directly from your blog (Figure 4.32). When the link is clicked, the user will be asked to enter his name and email address, the intended recipient's email address, and a note; the post will then be emailed to the specified recipient (Figure 4.33).

- *Adult Content?* If your blog contains content that you feel your readers may need to be warned about, change this option to *Yes*. When readers visit a blog marked with this option, they are presented with a warning screen and must click on an additional link accepting responsibility for viewing adult content before viewing the blog (Figure 4.34).

- *Select post editor.* Here you have three options: Updated Editor, which always contains the latest Blogger editing features; Old Editor, the more standard and less likely to change editor (the default); and Hide Compose Mode, which will turn off the WYSIWYG version of the editor and force you to enter your content with HTML markup. Choose whichever option you feel is right for you. The key difference with this feature compared to all the others on the screen is that this selection affects *all of your blogs* in the system, not just the one you're currently working on.

- *Enable transliteration?* Turn this feature on if you wish to write content in English and have Google automatically transliterate to the language you select.

Publishing

The Publishing screen has two versions. Which one you use depends on where you're publishing your blog. The blogspot.com screen is for those who are publishing their blog on Blogger's free hosting domain. Authors wishing to use their own URL to host their content will need to use the Custom Domain screen.

Figure 4.31   Edit post link (top)
Figure 4.32   Email post link (middle)
Figure 4.33   Email post to a friend (bottom)

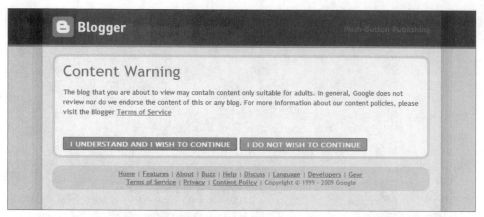

Figure 4.34   Adult content warning

On the blogspot.com screen (Figure 4.35), there are only two questions: the name of the subdomain on which you wish to publish (originally set up when you created your blog), and a CAPTCHA to prove you are human. You can of course change your URL using this screen but consider that decision carefully. If you're just now setting up your blog and no one has yet visited or bookmarked it, this shouldn't be a problem. However, further down the line, once your blog is established and has readers, changing your URL could cause confusion, to say the least, for a lot of your readers. (Never mind a potential reader's ability to find your content via a search engine or directory.)

Switching over to the Custom Domain screen makes things just a little more complicated. When you first get there, Blogger will assume that you want your site hosted on a different URL but that you don't already own that URL (Figure 4.36). In the first field, you can check availability for your desired domain name and, if available, you will be given additional steps to register and purchase that domain name. You'll also need to enter the CAPTCHA once again to prove you're human.

If you already have a domain registered and set up on a server somewhere, click Switch to Advanced Settings and enter the URL where you wish your blog to be hosted, whether you'll be using a "missing files host" and the obligatory CAPTCHA (Figure 4.37).

Since registering, purchasing, and setting up a server for your own domain is well beyond the scope of this book, I recommend that you go to your local server administrator or ISP for further assistance.

Formatting

The Formatting screen (Figure 4.38) allows you to control the look and feel of your blog (beyond the basic physical layout, which is controlled by the template, covered later in this chapter). The Formatting screen features the following settings:

- *Show.* This option allows you to set the number of posts to be displayed on your blog's home page. You can set it to show between one and 999 of either days or posts. (There is a limit of 999 posts; if you set this option to the past 100 days, but that time period includes 1,000 posts, only the first 999 will be displayed.) The typical setting for Show is the past seven days.

- *Date Header Format.* Posts are automatically grouped by day. The date header format is how you want the heading for each day to look. You have 16 different formats to choose from (Figure 4.39).

- *Archive Index Date Format.* This setting controls the format of dates for the links to your blog's archive (archives are covered later in this chapter). You have 16 different choices for how these dates are displayed (Figure 4.40).

- *Timestamp Format.* This setting controls the format of the date and time displayed on individual posts. You have seven different choices as to how this information is displayed (Figure 4.41).

- *Time Zone.* This setting tells Blogger which time zone your blog is in. All of your timestamps, by default, will be based on the time zone you set here (Figure 4.42). For example, while at a conference in Washington, D.C., I created a post at 8 AM local time. However, my time zone is set for Central Time, so the post displayed the time of 7 AM instead.

- *Language.* Your date/timestamp for individual posts can be displayed in any of almost 100 different languages. Choose the language you'd like from the dropdown list (Figure 4.43).

- *Convert line breaks.* If this is set to *No*, any use of the Enter key will be ignored when you are creating a new post. If it is set to *Yes*, when you hit the Enter key while creating a post using the Compose Version, a line break (XHTML <br/>) will be added to the post.

- *Show Title field.* Changing this to *No* removes the Title field from the Post Creation interfaces. Typically this is used by bloggers with extensive XHTML knowledge who want more precise control over how their blogs display. For most bloggers, there is no reason ever to change this setting.

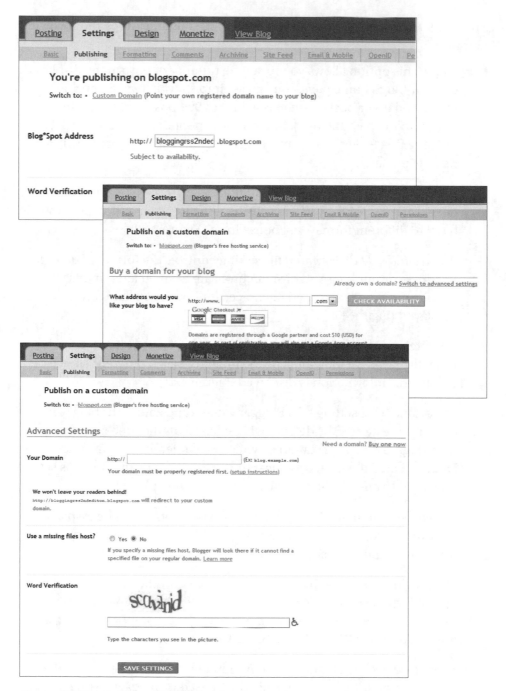

Figure 4.35   Settings: Publishing (top)

Figure 4.36   Custom domain setting (middle)

Figure 4.37   Custom domain advanced settings (bottom)

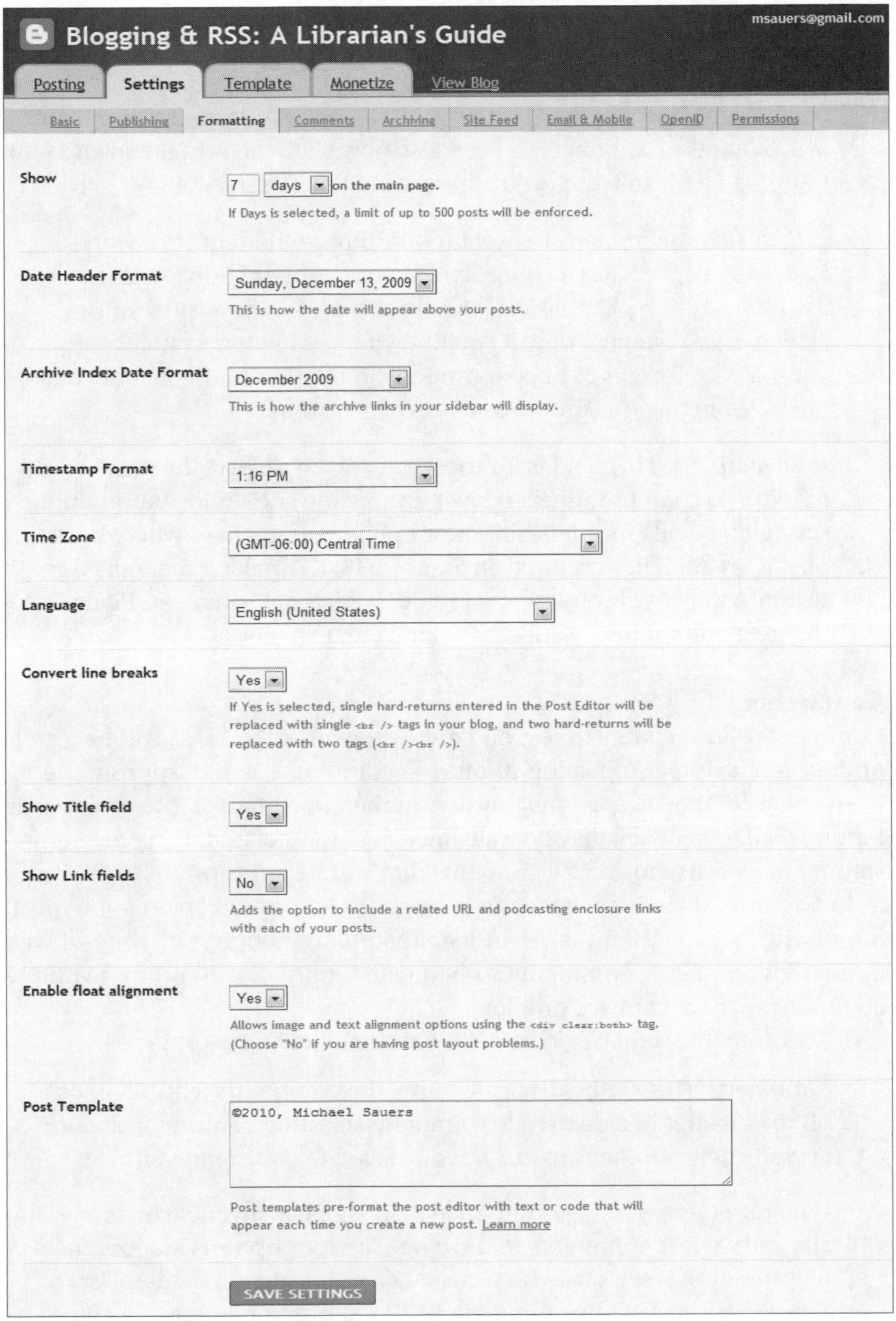

Blogging & RSS: A Librarian's Guide   msauers@gmail.com

Posting | **Settings** | Template | Monetize | View Blog

Basic | Publishing | Formatting | Comments | Archiving | Site Feed | Email & Mobile | OpenID | Permissions

Show

[7] [days ▼] on the main page.

If Days is selected, a limit of up to 500 posts will be enforced.

Date Header Format

[Sunday, December 13, 2009 ▼]

This is how the date will appear above your posts.

Archive Index Date Format

[December 2009   ▼]

This is how the archive links in your sidebar will display.

Timestamp Format

[1:16 PM   ▼]

Time Zone

[(GMT-06:00) Central Time   ▼]

Language

[English (United States)   ▼]

Convert line breaks

[Yes ▼]

If Yes is selected, single hard-returns entered in the Post Editor will be
replaced with single `<br />` tags in your blog, and two hard-returns will be
replaced with two tags (`<br /><br />`).

Show Title field

[Yes ▼]

Show Link fields

[No ▼]

Adds the option to include a related URL and podcasting enclosure links
with each of your posts.

Enable float alignment

[Yes ▼]

Allows image and text alignment options using the `<div clear:both>` tag.
(Choose "No" if you are having post layout problems.)

Post Template

```
©2010, Michael Sauers
```

Post templates pre-format the post editor with text or code that will
appear each time you create a new post. Learn more

[SAVE SETTINGS]

Figure 4.38   Settings: Formatting

- *Show Link fields.* When changed to *Yes*, this option adds a new field named Link to the post creation interfaces (Figure 4.44). This option allows bloggers with little to no XHTML experience to insert a URL that will automatically associate itself with the post's title, creating a hyperlink to another webpage. You can also now click the Add Enclosure Link to upload a file to which your title should link (Figure 4.45).

- *Enable float alignment.* To explain this fully would require a working knowledge of CSS (Cascading Style Sheets), which I don't want to assume you have. My basic advice for this option, as it says on the screen, is to change it only if you find yourself having trouble with getting your images to appear properly in relation to the text of your posts. Changing this option may solve the problem.

- *Post Template.* This field is for those who always insert the same bit of markup or content into every post. By placing such information into this field, it will automatically show up in the body field when a new post is created. For example, in Figure 4.46, I've placed the following text into the Post Template: © 2010, Michael Sauers. In Figure 4.47, that text automatically appears when I create a new post.

Comments

Comments allow readers to respond online to your posts. This can be a great option, but automatic posting of outside comments is not appropriate for every blog. If the blog is your own, whether personal or professional in nature, reader feedback may be welcomed and appreciated. For a blog representing the library, however, comments may not be appropriate.

In addition, there is the growing problem of "comment spam"—the posting of advertisements rather than legitimate commentary. In spite of this, many bloggers allow comments to be posted, only disabling the feature if comment spam becomes a problem.

The Comments screen (Figure 4.48) has the following settings:

- *Comments.* This setting basically turns the comments feature on or off. If you later decide to hide comments, existing comments are not actually deleted; they are just not displayed to your readers.

- *Who Can Comment?* This option lets the blogger specify who is actually allowed to post comments to the blog. The four options are Anyone, Registered Users, Users with Google Accounts, and Only Members of This Blog. The Anyone option allows literally anyone to post a comment to your blog. Although this option does allow for the broadest range of comments, it also significantly increases the risk of comment

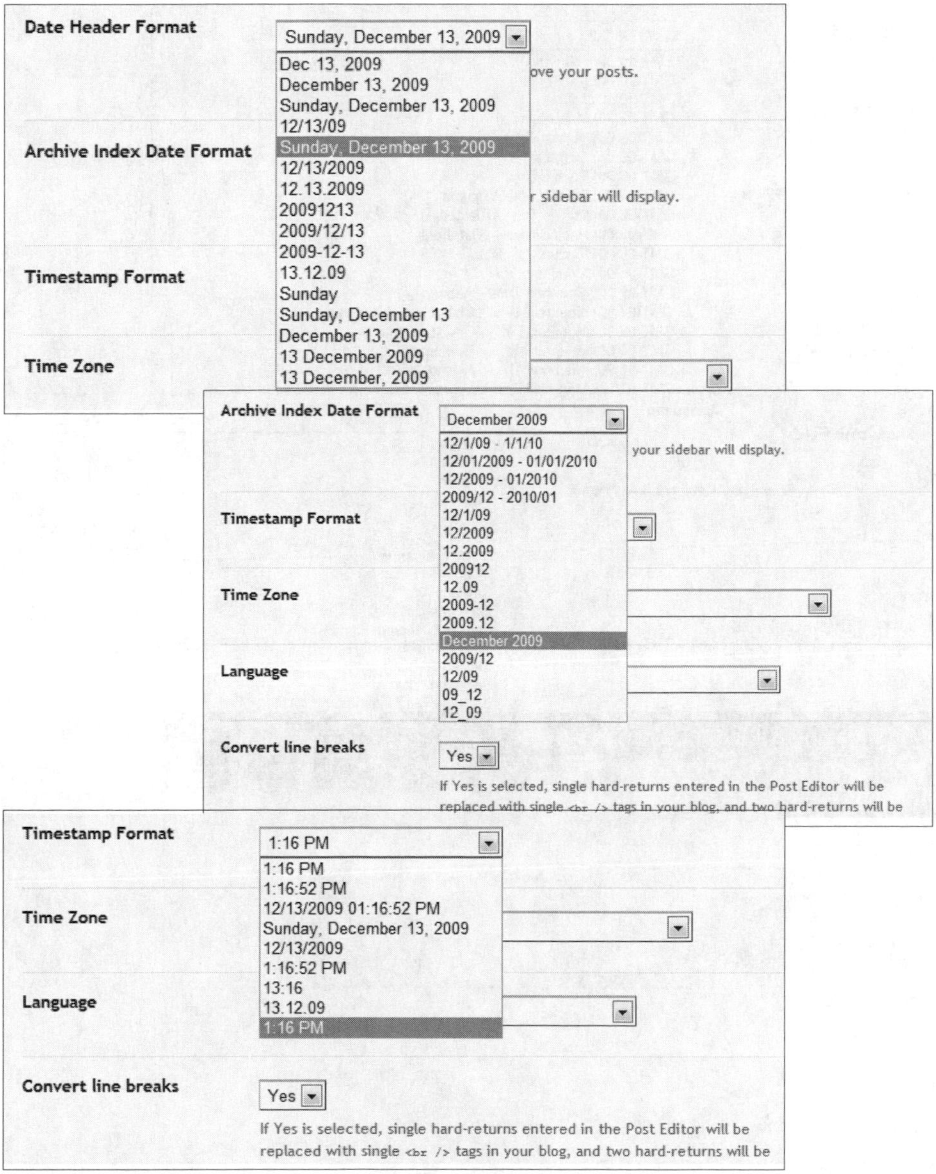

Date Header Format

Sunday, December 13, 2009

- Dec 13, 2009
- December 13, 2009
- Sunday, December 13, 2009
- 12/13/09
- Sunday, December 13, 2009
- 12/13/2009
- 12.13.2009
- 20091213
- 2009/12/13
- 2009-12-13
- 13.12.09
- Sunday
- Sunday, December 13
- December 13, 2009
- 13 December 2009
- 13 December, 2009

ove your posts.

Archive Index Date Format

r sidebar will display.

Timestamp Format

Time Zone

Archive Index Date Format

December 2009

- 12/1/09 - 1/1/10
- 12/01/2009 - 01/01/2010
- 12/2009 - 01/2010
- 2009/12 - 2010/01
- 12/1/09
- 12/2009
- 12.2009
- 200912
- 12.09
- 2009-12
- 2009.12
- December 2009
- 2009/12
- 12/09
- 09_12
- 12_09

your sidebar will display.

Timestamp Format

Time Zone

Language

Convert line breaks

Yes

If Yes is selected, single hard-returns entered in the Post Editor will be
replaced with single <br /> tags in your blog, and two hard-returns will be

Timestamp Format

1:16 PM

- 1:16 PM
- 1:16:52 PM
- 12/13/2009 01:16:52 PM
- Sunday, December 13, 2009
- 12/13/2009
- 1:16:52 PM
- 13:16
- 13.12.09
- 1:16 PM

Time Zone

Language

Convert line breaks

Yes

If Yes is selected, single hard-returns entered in the Post Editor will be
replaced with single <br /> tags in your blog, and two hard-returns will be

Figure 4.39 Date Header Format options (top)

Figure 4.40 Archive Index Date Format options (middle)

Figure 4.41 Timestamp Format options (bottom)

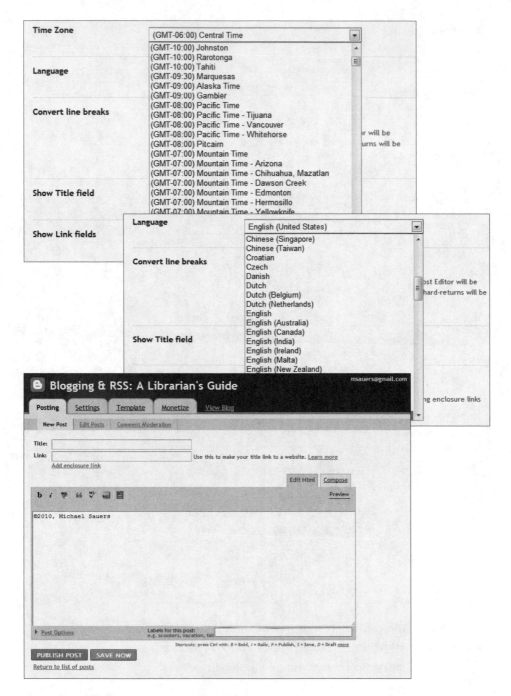

Figure 4.42 Time Zone options (top)

Figure 4.43 Language options (middle)

Figure 4.44 New post with the Link field (bottom)

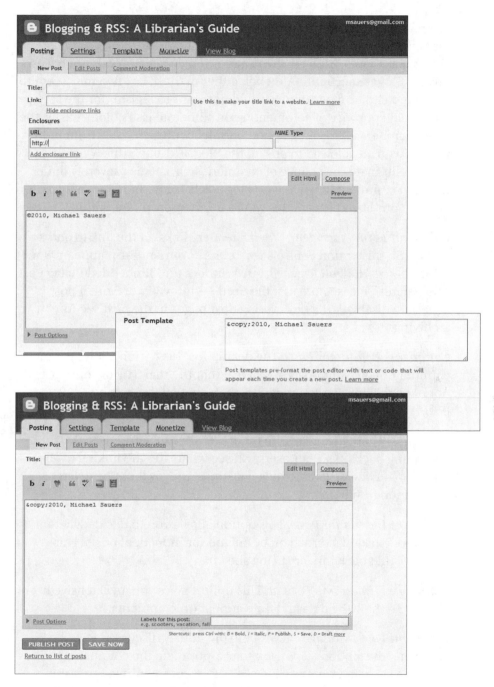

Figure 4.45 New post with Enclosures link (top)

Figure 4.46 Post Template (middle)

Figure 4.47 New post with Post Template embedded (bottom)

spam.[2] The Registered Users option allows users registered with Blogger (or OpenID) to comment. The Users with Google Accounts options allows comments by anyone who has a Google account but not necessarily a Blogger account. (Although either of these last two may seem to be a good choice, I personally would not want to register for the service for the sole purpose of commenting on someone else's blog.) Lastly, the Only Members of this Blog option permits comments only from individuals who are allowed to post to the blog. Although this will completely eliminate the chance of comment spam, it also severely limits who can comment. If you have a blog solely for exchanging information among your library's staff, this would be an appropriate option.

- *Comment Form Placement.* When a reader clicks on the link to add a comment, this option controls where the comment form appears. Your three choices are Full Page, Pop-up Window, and Embedded Below Post (the default). Please note that the third option will not work if post pages are disabled. (I'll be covering post pages in the next section on archiving.)

- *Comments Default for Posts.* The default for this option allows people to comment on all your posts. If you feel that the majority of your posts do not need to allow for commenting, then change this setting to New Posts Do Not Have Comments.

- *Backlinks.* These are links from other websites to your posts. By displaying backlinks, your users will see what sites are linking to your posts. If you decide later to hide backlinks, they will not be deleted, just hidden from view.

- *Backlinks Default for Posts.* This option allows you to decide whether you want backlinks turned on by default for individual posts. This assumes that backlinks are being shown.

- *Comments Timestamp Format.* This option gives you an extensive list of choices for how the date and time appear on comments.

- *Comment Form Message.* As with the previously discussed Post Template, this option allows you to pre-populate the comments box with text you wish your users to see before commenting. Enter that text here.

- *Comment Moderation.* Turning on this feature allows you to approve all comments before they appear on your blog for others to read. If you choose to use this feature, you should also enter an email address in the Comment Notification Email field below. This is the address where notification will be sent when a new comment is submitted and ready for approval. This feature reduces the need for you to periodically check for new comments by logging into your account. You also have the option to set comment moderation to apply only to comments on posts older than a certain number of days. This can be a good compromise if you are concerned about spam appearing on very old posts that you are no longer actively monitoring.

- *Show word verification for comments?* Selecting *Yes* forces users to enter a string of random characters to prove that the post is not being generated by a computer. I highly recommend that you turn on this feature, as it will prevent practically all comment spam.

- *Show profile images on comments?* If the person commenting has a Google account, is logged in when commenting, and has added an image to his or her profile, answering *Yes* to this option will display the image along with the posted comment.

- *Comment Notification Email.* This field allows you to enter an email address where a notification will be sent whenever a new comment is added to your blog. Personally, I find this to be a handy feature. (Assuming you have contacts listed in your Google account, you can use the Choose From Contacts link to pick an address from your Google address book, instead of typing it in.)

Once you have turned on comment moderation, the Comment Moderation link (found under the Posting tab) will provide you with additional information and options (Figure 4.49). If you have no comments waiting to be approved, the screen will say "No Unmoderated Comments Found." When there are pending comments, you will be shown a list of them. You can view the individual comments, select one or more comments using the checkboxes on the left, and then choose whether to Publish or Reject the comments. If you publish a comment, it appears on your blog for everyone to read. If you reject a comment, it is immediately deleted and will not appear on your blog.

Archiving

Archiving your blog is an important concept. If posts aren't archived, new posts will continue to be added to the top of a single webpage, making the page longer and longer, and in turn, causing increasingly long load times for readers. Archiving takes older posts and places them into their own webpages,

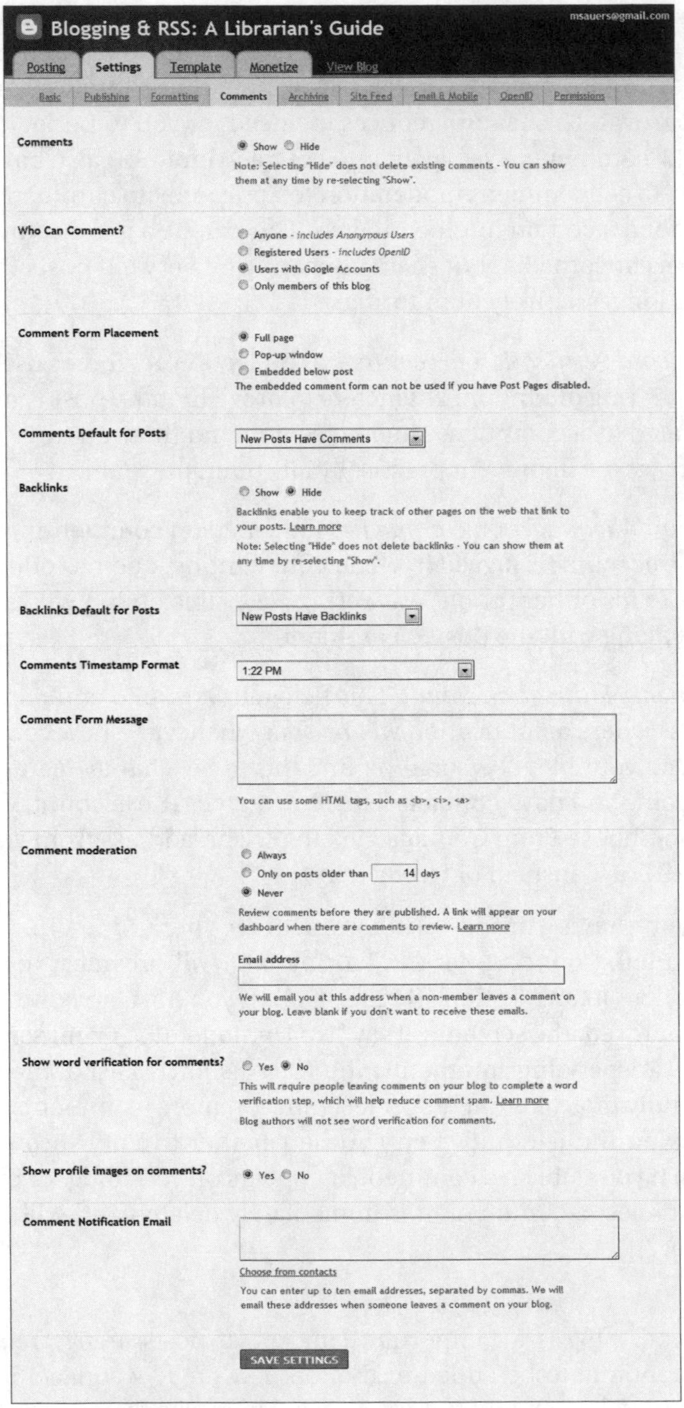

Figure 4.48 Settings: Comments

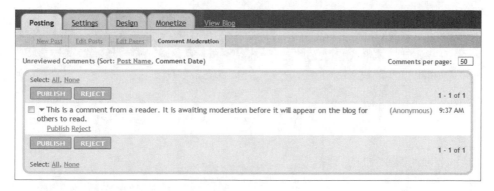

Figure 4.49 Comment Moderation

thereby allowing the most current items to load quickly but still providing links to the older material. The Archiving screen (Figure 4.50) gives the following options:

- *Archiving Frequency.* You have four choices for how often old posts should be archived. The No Archive option turns archiving off. If you choose this option, old posts not displayed on your blog's home page will not be accessible to your users. The other three choices are Daily, Weekly, and Monthly. Which one you choose should depend on how often you post and how long those posts are. You also need to keep in mind that if you choose monthly, you'll have 12 additional links on your page after a year, one for each month. If you choose weekly, you'll end the year with 52 additional links; choosing daily will net you 365 (or 366) additional links by the end of one year. Most bloggers stick to a monthly archive and a few use weekly. The only blogs I've seen with daily archives are those for conferences in which there are a lot of posts and the event only lasts a matter of days.

- *Enable Post Pages?* If this option is set to *Yes*, each post you create will not only appear on your blog's home page and in the appropriate archive, but it will also have its own unique webpage containing just that post and any associated comments. Setting this option to *No* means your posts will only appear on the home page and archive pages and will not have individual webpages. You may want to enable this option for two reasons. First, each post will have its own URL, which makes for easier bookmarking. Second, if a reader wants to link to or print out a single post, having it available on its own page (instead of as a small part of a much larger document) makes this more convenient.

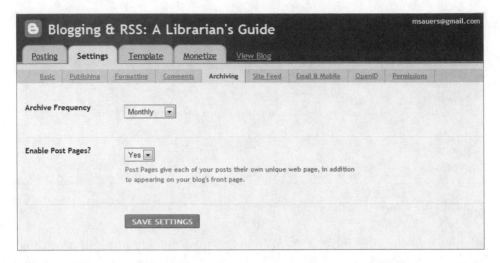

Figure 4.50 Settings: Archiving

However, there are downsides to enabling post pages. Having individual pages for each post considerably increases the size of your blog. Granted, server space is relatively inexpensive these days, but if you have a small server, you could use it up a lot sooner than expected. Using individual pages also affects the speed of publishing. With this feature turned on, creating a new post means publishing your blog's home page, the relevant archive page, *and* a new page for that particular post. These problems are not significant but you do need to be aware of them.

If you are publishing to your own server, you will have three additional fields on this screen:

- *Archive Path.* The path to the directory into which archive pages should be placed.

- *Archive URL.* Only fill in this field if the archive is being published under a different URL (domain) than the current content of your blog.

- *Archive Filename.* The filename under which all archive pages will be published.

Site Feed

The Site Feed screen allows you to control whether an RSS feed is automatically created for your blog. RSS and site feeds are covered in detail in Chapters 5–8; the Site Feed page will be covered in those chapters.

Email and Mobile

The Email and Mobile screen (Figure 4.51) gives you the option of using email as a tool in your blog. Enter up to 10 email addresses in the first field on the screen, BlogSend Address, and every time a new post is published, a copy of your blog's home page will be sent to those addresses. If you're the only person posting to your blog, this is not particularly helpful as you're already well aware of what you're posting. However, in the case of a shared blog in which multiple authors have the ability to post, it is handy to have the blog's administrator notified via email whenever someone publishes a new post. (As previously mentioned the Choose From Contacts link will allow you to pick recipients from your Google contacts.)

Filling out the Email Posting Address and Mobile Devices fields allows you to post via email (see "Using Alternate Posting Methods," earlier in the chapter).

OpenID

OpenID is a current standard for verifying your identity online. The basic premise is that you confirm your identity on one site and then reuse that establishment to authenticate you to other sites. In other words, it is a "single sign-on" system. Blogger provides you with a method for using OpenID in conjunction with your blog. If you are interested in how this works and how it might be able to benefit you, click on the Learn More About OpenID link.

Permissions

The Permissions screen (Figure 4.52) allows you to control who may post to your blog and who has administrative privileges. When you first create your blog, you will be the only person listed as allowed to post, and you will also be listed as the administrator since you're the creator and only member of the blog.

To add additional members to your blog, just click the Add Authors button and then enter the email addresses of the people you want to invite to your blog. You can also add a message to your invitation (Figure 4.53). In order to become a member of your blog, team members must either have a Blogger account already or create one for themselves. Blog members can post to a blog and can edit existing posts they have created. A blog administrator can create, edit, and delete posts, and change any of the other blog settings. Be cautious when granting administrator privileges.

Notice that there is a Remove link that allows you to delete a person's access to your blog. As usual, you will be asked to confirm this decision.

Design

Your blog's template is the XHTML and CSS that controls the overall design of your blog. It gives a consistent appearance to all of your blog's pages including

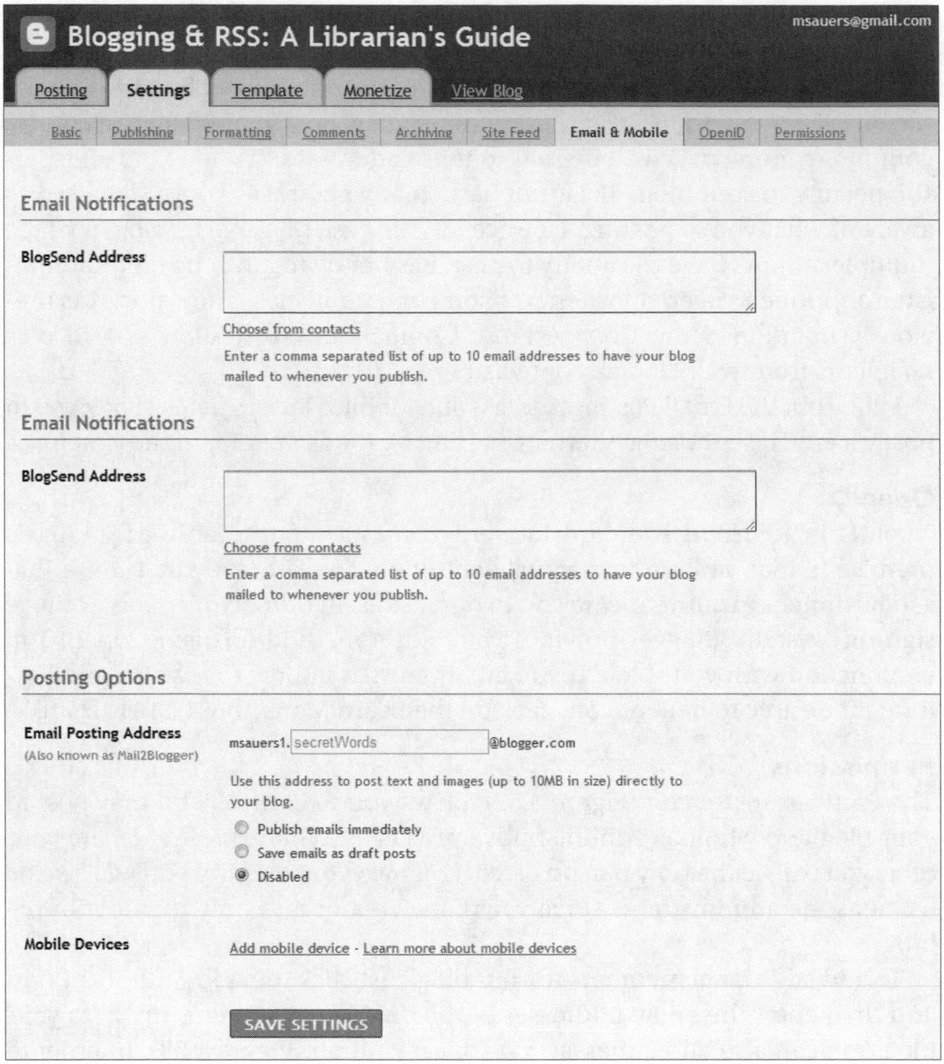

Figure 4.51 Settings: Email & Mobile

the home page, archive pages, and individual posting pages. The Layout tab offers four options: Page Elements, Fonts and Colors, Edit HTML, and Pick New Template.

Author's Note: As I said earlier in the chapter, a command of XHTML is not required to use this book and start blogging. However, while that's true, the topic cannot be avoided completely. While the information provided in this section is not something you must know in order to blog successfully, you will probably find some familiarity with XHTML useful in the long run. Even readers with

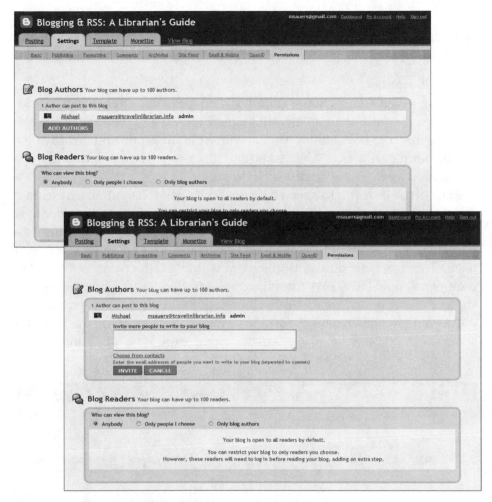

Figure 4.52 Settings: Permissions (top)

Figure 4.53 Inviting more people to write to your blog (bottom)

some webpage design experience should read this section, as it covers items specific to the Blogger system. However, understand that this is not a comprehensive review of XHTML.

In the past four years since the publication of the first edition of this book, the editing of templates is an area that has undergone significant changes and improvements in Blogger. In 2006, the only way to modify a Blogger template was to edit the XHTML and CSS directly. While that option is still available (which I'll be covering shortly), you can now use a point-and-click, drag-and-drop interface to do 99 percent of what most bloggers will want to do to their templates. You can add, move, and delete sections of your template through the Page Elements interface, and you can change the look and feel of your template (colors, fonts, etc.) through the Template Designer.

Page Elements

In the Page Elements section (Figure 4.54), you have the ability to edit particular areas of your blog template, add page elements, and rearrange page elements. While the possibilities here are almost endless and could easily be a chapter in themselves, I'll just take some time to cover enough to get you started and leave you with a few ideas to explore.

Each of the boxes on this screen is known as a page element. Each element has a name (Navbar, Blog Posts, Followers, etc.), and its position on your blog is indicated by its position on this screen. The content and/or settings of a particular page element can be edited by clicking on the Edit link. Different page elements have different options available on their edit screens. For example, Figure 4.55 shows the edit screen for Blog Posts, while Figure 4.56 shows the edit screen for a poll. To edit a page element, open its edit screen, make your changes, and click Save. To remove a page element, open its edit screen and click Remove. (Sorry, but the Navbar is the "cost" of having Blogger

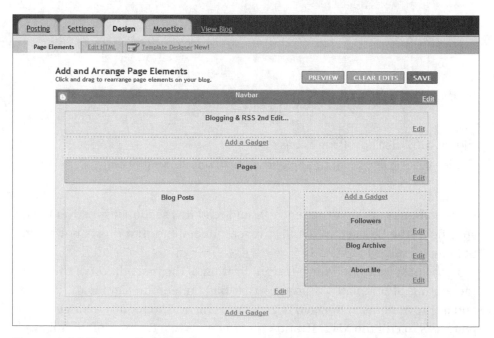

Figure 4.54 Design: Page Elements

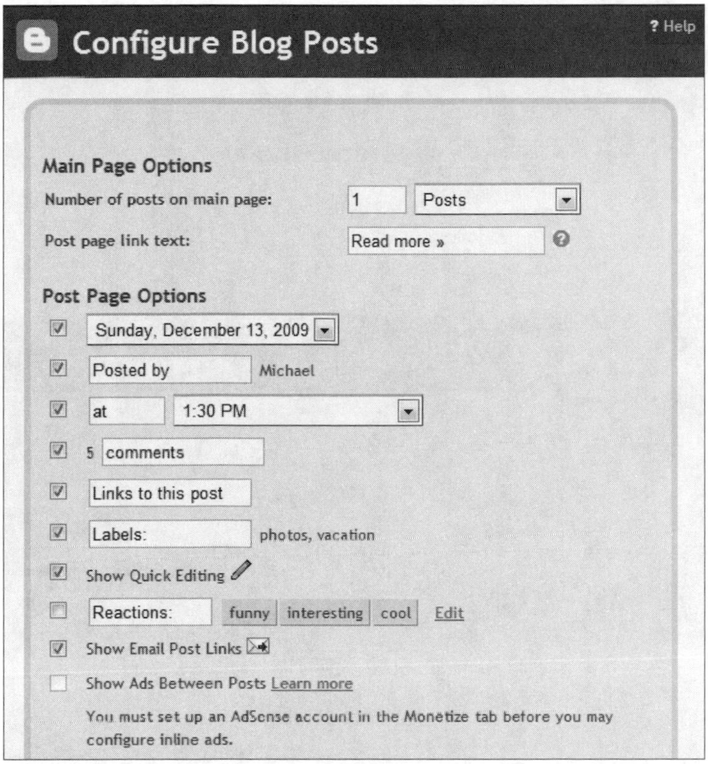

Figure 4.55 Configuring blog posts

host your content for free. Only if you publish on your own server are you given the ability to remove it.)

To add a new page element, click the Add a Gadget link on your template. (The link in the sidebar will add a gadget to the sidebar, while the one on the bottom will add a gadget to the bottom of your page.) You'll be presented with a window that offers you additional elements you can add to your page (Figure 4.57). Some of the more commonly used gadgets include Search Box, Text (for adding static text to your pages), Link List, and Poll. Choose the gadget you want and click the appropriate + icon. Once the element is added to your template, you can edit the new element through its Edit link.

Less obvious on this page is the ability to drag and drop page elements into different locations. For example, if I would like the About Me section to appear below my blog posts instead of on the right, I can just drag that element from its current location and drop it into a new spot below the Blog Posts element (Figure 4.58).

When you're all done be sure to click the Save button to commit your changes. If you feel you got something wrong, just click Clear Edits to undo

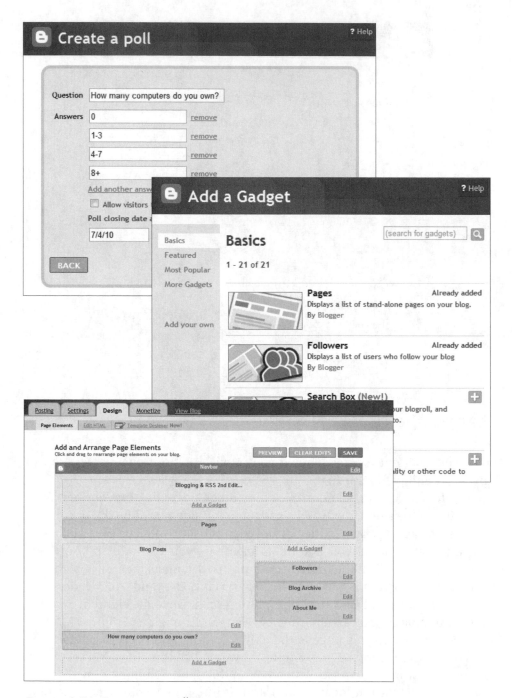

Figure 4.56 Creating a poll (top)
Figure 4.57 Adding a gadget (middle)
Figure 4.58 Moving a gadget (bottom)

any changes since your last save. If you've totally messed up and just can't recover what you want via clear edits, head on over to the Pick New Template link, which I'll discuss shortly. When you do click Save, all of your blog's pages will be republished. If you have a lot of content, it may take a few minutes for all of your pages to reflect your changes.

Template Design

Once you have all of your gadgets in place, go to the Template Designer to change simple elements, such as font, color, and background images, or to pick a completely different template. Since the possibilities are nearly endless in the Template Designer, I'll just take a few moments to highlight a few of the options you'll want to look out for.

When you open the Template Designer, your browser window will be divided into two sections. The top portion will contain the Template Designer controls and the bottom portion will contain a preview of your blog. (To temporarily remove the controls and see a full-window preview, click the Expand Preview link on the bar between the two areas. To restore the control, click the Show Controls link that appears at the top of the window.)

Any and all changes you make in the Template Designer will immediately appear in your blog preview. However, the changes will not be made permanent until you click the orange Apply to Blog button in the upper-right corner. At any point, you can abandon your changes by clicking the Back to Blogger link also in the upper-right corner of your window.

The Template Designer contains the following four sections:

- *Templates*. Here you can choose from a variety of built-in Blogger templates as a starting point for your design. There are several categories to pick from, ranging from simple to Ethereal, each with several choices within the category. To change to one of these templates, just click on it and your preview will display your selection. If you don't like it, pick another or move on to one of the other sections to tweak that design (Figure 4.59).

- *Background*. Depending on the template you chose, you may already have a default background image; with others you may not. So, if you wish to change or add a background image, use this section. Your current background image, along with overall color scheme, will be displayed (Figure 4.60). Feel free to experiment with another color scheme by clicking on one of the alternate suggestions or clicking on Main Color Theme to customize it (Figure 4.61). Clicking on Background Image brings up a new window containing hundreds of additional choices (Figure 4.62). (As far as I can tell, if you want to supply your own custom background image, you need to edit the template's code directly.) If you feel you've completely messed things up, you can always click on Use Default Background and Colors.

- *Layout.* This section has three options: Body Layout, Footer Layout, and Adjust Width. With Body Layout, you can change the location and number of your blog's sidebars from the visual choices given (Figure 4.63). (If you do make changes here, you'll most likely need to head back to Page Elements to adjust the location of your blog's gadgets.) With Footer Layout, you can change the number of sections within your blog's footers to one, two, or three (Figure 4.64). (Again, you'll want to adjust your gadgets if you make changes here.) Lastly, you can adjust the width of your template and sidebar(s) via the sliders in the Adjust Width section (Figure 4.65).

- *Advanced.* In this section, you can control the fonts and colors of the individual elements of your template, from the page text to post titles to image borders and more (Figure 4.66). To make these adjustments, choose the element from the scrolling list on the left and then choose from the options provided. In the case of colors, you can either click on a provided color swatch or provide the hexadecimal notation for the particular color you want.

When you're all done editing your design, don't forget to click the Apply to Blog button or all of your work will be lost.

Edit HTML

When you look at a Blogger template, keep in mind that a great deal of customization is possible. With a working knowledge of XHTML and CSS, you can modify colors, change fonts, reset the margins, and much more. The XHTML-savvy blogger who doesn't care for any of the supplied templates or who needs to closely pattern a blog after the library's website may decide to create a template from scratch. However, if you have no experience with XHTML and CSS and you don't wish to learn, your best bet is to try out the various Blogger templates until you find one you can live with.

Blogger has created a set of "magic elements" unique to its system that allow your content to be presented in different ways depending upon the template you choose. (In fact, each of the major blogging systems—whether web-based such as Blogger or software-based such as Movable Type—has its own set of such "magic elements.") These elements are bits of markup patterned on XHTML but are not in any XHTML specification. What they do is instruct the system (Blogger, in this case) to perform certain actions, such as put a post here, place the link to the archive here, and show the post's comments here. With Blogger, the elements are known as Blogger tags. A complete

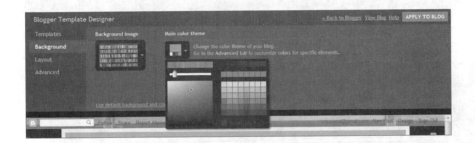

Figure 4.59 Template Design: Templates (top)

Figure 4.60 Template Design: Background (middle)

Figure 4.61 Editing the color scheme (middle)

Figure 4.62 Selecting a background (bottom)

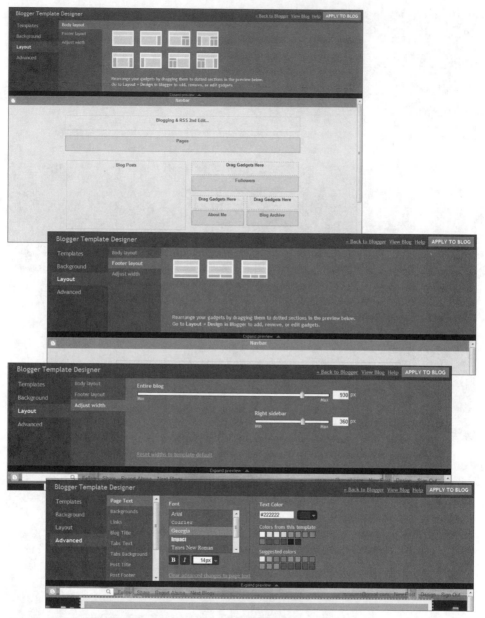

Figure 4.63 Template Design: Layout—Body (top)

Figure 4.64 Template Design: Layout—Footer (middle)

Figure 4.65 Template Design: Layout—Adjust Width (middle)

Figure 4.66 Template Design: Advanced (bottom)

list with definitions and additional information can be found on the Blogger site (www.google.com/support/blogger/bin/answer.py?hl=en&answer=46 888).

By moving the Blogger tags around or removing them altogether, you can easily change the look of your template and/or modify the features your blog offers.

On the Edit HTML page, you can also download your template for offline editing and/or backup or upload a new template that will override your current one. (Search Google for *free blogger templates* if you're looking for ideas.)

After you've made your changes to the Blogger tags, the Edit Current screen (Figure 4.67) gives you the following options in the form of three buttons at the bottom of the page:

- *Clear Edits*. This button will undo any changes you've made to your template since the last time you saved your changes. Think of it as a giant *Undo* button.

- *Preview*. If you've made some changes to your template but are not sure how they'll turn out, click this button. This option will display your blog's home page in a new window using the revised template. This version is neither saved nor is it live. If you've made mistakes, you can go back and fix them before displaying them to your readers.

- *Save Template*. Any time you've made changes to the template and want to make them permanent, you must click this button. Until you save the changes and republish your blog, the changes will not be live (seen by your readers). Republishing the entire blog is suggested at this stage to keep the template the same across your blog. Depending on the size of your blog, however, this may take several minutes. Republishing just the index is faster, but then your blog's home page will use the revised template while all of the other pages will not.

Lastly, there are three additional links at the bottom of the page:

- *Revert widget templates to default*. This resets all changes you've made to your template to their original defaults. This is one way to potentially solve the "I've totally messed everything up" problem when picking a new template doesn't solve it.

- *Revert to classic template*. Blogger used to set up its templates one way and now they set them up another way. Simply put, this link changes your template to do things the old way (i.e., the way it was done in the first edition of this book). It's your call, but if you choose this option, you'd better know HTML and CSS pretty well. You won't be able to use

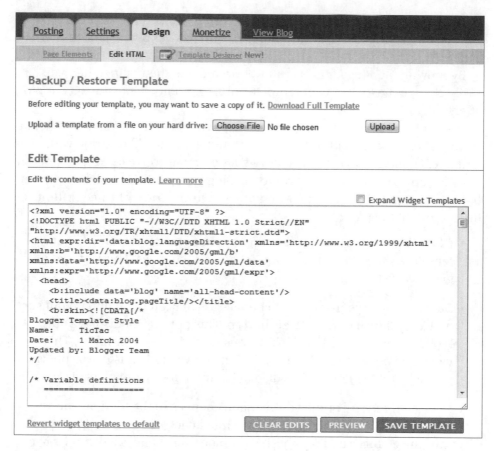

Figure 4.67 Layout: Edit HTML

the Page Elements screen or the Fonts and Color screen anymore, because they won't work under the old way of doing things.

- *View classic template.* This gives you the ability to see what the code would look like under the old way. Tread lightly if you go down this path.

Pick New Template

You can change the Blogger template at any time by selecting the Pick New link near the top of the page. You will be shown a list of all of the Blogger templates and be prompted to pick one. Many of these options will look familiar, as you picked your original template from a shortened version of this list. It's important to notice that under many of the templates listed here are additional choices that have modified color schemes.

If you change your selection, all the code in the Template field will change to match your new choice. If you've already made posts to your blog, they will be reformatted into the new template.

Monetize

This is one of the newer Blogger features, courtesy of Google. Under this tab, you can insert advertisements from the Google AdSense system into your blog. This feature will only work if you have signed up for and configured an AdSense account. Since this feature is not appropriate for libraries, I will not be going into any further detail. Those of you wishing additional information should click on the Learn More link on this page.

Blogger Help

One final note about Blogger options: There is a Help button in the upper right corner of all Blogger pages. Clicking on it will take you into the Blogger knowledgebase (Figure 4.68).

Figure 4.68 Blogger Help

Now that you have a good grasp of blog creation and related issues, let's move on to Chapter 5, where we will take a look at the other half of the equation: RSS.

Endnotes

1. Dave Taylor's excellent blog post "Who Owns Your Words, Blogger?" (www.intuitive. com/blog/who_owns_your_words_blogger.html) contains some noteworthy points regarding this issue.

2. Comment spam is any comment posted to a blog that isn't a true comment about the content of the post but instead is an attempt to get you to click on a link to another site (e.g., "Great post. Come play online poker with me."). Comment spam can be virtually eliminated by selecting the Show Word Verification for Comments option on the Comments screen.

Chapter 5

An Introduction to RSS

At this point we've covered what a blog is, looked at a number of interesting blogs (and bloggers), and reviewed the steps required to set up a blog. In this chapter, we move on to a new topic: RSS. As part of the RSS discussion, we'll also begin to explore the associated concepts of feeds and aggregators (covered in detail in Chapter 6).

What Is RSS?

Wikipedia defines RSS as "a family of web feed formats used to publish frequently updated works—such as blog entries, news headlines, audio, and video—in a standardized format. … Web feeds benefit publishers by letting them syndicate content automatically. They benefit readers who want to subscribe to timely updates from favored websites or to aggregate feeds from many sites into one place."[1]

Let's assume you recently started to read blogs. You have bookmarked several favorites and are frequently discovering and adding new ones. As you check these blogs each morning, you realize that not all of them are being posted to daily or, for that matter, on any kind of predictable schedule. As busy as you are, you begin to check these blogs for new posts less and less frequently, until one day you realize you are missing out on much of the subject-specific news and commentary that inspired you to start reading blogs in the first place.

RSS addresses this situation by helping you keep up with new and revised web-based information. It allows you to "subscribe" to a blog (or any web resource that takes advantage of RSS), letting the computer do the work of checking it regularly and notifying you when new information has been posted.

It was estimated in 2005 that approximately 8.5 percent of internet users used RSS to access information on the internet. In 2010, that number was estimated to be more than 18 percent. However, what may be more interesting is that RSS users visit three times as many websites as non-RSS users.[2] In other words, providing an RSS feed could significantly increase the likelihood that a user will visit your website.

Now that we know what RSS does, what exactly does the acronym stand for? Oddly enough, the answer to that question depends on whom you ask and which version of RSS you're talking about. RSS stands for Rich Site Summary, RDF Site Summary (just what we need—an acronym containing an acronym!), or Really Simple Syndication. The latter, which is the most descriptive of the three options and isn't based on a particular version of RSS, is currently favored by those in the know.

One wrinkle in this discussion is an RSS-like language called Atom, which works the same as RSS but was developed independently. Most people think of Atom as a version of RSS, although this is inaccurate. However, for practical purposes, the distinction is unimportant: Whether you are using RSS or Atom, you are creating what is commonly known as a *web feed*, or simply a feed. A feed is file written in "a data format used for providing users with frequently updated content. Content distributors syndicate a web feed, thereby allowing users to *subscribe* to it. … A web feed is also sometimes referred to as a syndicated feed."[3] In the pages that follow, when I am not specifically discussing RSS or Atom, I'll use *feed* as an umbrella term.

History of Feed Development

The history of feeds is a long and complicated one that has led to the current situation of multiple competing versions and formats. Following is a short version of the history of feeds, which is admittedly convoluted and a bit esoteric. Feel free to skip this section if you're not interested.

In December 1997, Dave Winer of Userland, a software development company, developed and released the scriptingNews format as a way to syndicate information on the web. Not much was made of the concept until March 1999, when Netscape developed what it dubbed RSS 0.90. Functionally similar to scriptingNews, RSS 0.90 was designed to work with Netscape's portal, my.netscape.com. In June of that same year, Winer updated scriptingNews and released version 2.0b1, incorporating the features of Netscape's RSS format and adding some new ones.

In early July 1999, Dan Libby at Netscape reworked RSS into version 0.91, incorporating the changes in scriptingNews in an attempt to establish a single format for syndicating web content. By the end of the month, Userland had agreed to adopt RSS 0.91 and officially ended development of scriptingNews. The following year, company-supported development of RSS at Netscape came to an end as the company decided to remove itself from the portal business.

In August 2000, an independent group of developers, led by Rael Dornfest, from computer book publisher O'Reilly and Associates proposed what it called RSS 1.0. This product was based on the RDF metadata format[4] and modularized most of the elements of previous RSS versions but was developed independently and thus was considered an entirely new format for syndication. RSS 1.0 was not technically an upgrade of RSS 0.91 and did not supersede the "previous" version.

There were now two different tracks under which RSS was being developed. In December 2002, Userland's Dave Winer released RSS 0.92 as a follow-up to RSS 0.91. Again, this release (which was not a significant upgrade) was not technologically related to the RSS 1.0 product. Winer released a further upgrade to the program, named RSS 2.0, in September 2002. (While in development, this upgrade was referred to as RSS 0.94, but the higher number was assigned to it on release.)

By 2003, with RSS users tired of what some referred to as the "RSS wars," a group of "leading service providers, tool vendors and independent developers" developed Atom (originally named Echo).[5] Although the end result of Atom feeds is the same as that of both RSS types, Atom was developed from scratch and, unlike either of the competing products, specifically with the needs of bloggers in mind. For example, Atom feeds have made internationalization easier through additional support for non-Latin character sets.[6]

Figure 5.1 shows the history of the development of RSS and Atom.

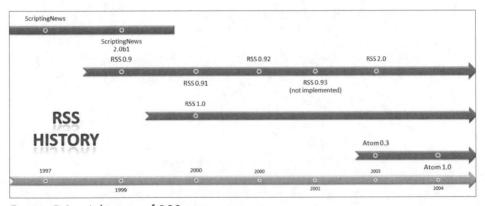

Figure 5.1   A history of RSS

What's in a Feed File?

Regardless of what they are called or the version number, feeds are all XML-based languages. That is to say, they are written to conform to the rules of XML (Extensible Markup Language). For those of you familiar with HTML

(Hypertext Markup Language), the structure of feeds will look familiar; only the terminology will be different.[7]

Rather than focus on the differences among the various feed versions, I'm going to walk you through one very basic example of an RSS file. First, take a minute to read it and see if you can figure out what each part means. Then read the explanations following the code to see how close you were.

```xml
<?xml version="1.0"?>
<rss version="0.92">
   <channel>
      <title>travelinlibrarian.info</title>
      <link>http://www.travelinlibrarian.info/</link>
      <description>The blog of Librarian, Trainer, and writer Michael P.
      Sauers</description>
      <lastBuildDate>Tue, 01 Feb 2005 13:23:02 GMT</lastBuildDate>
      <docs>http://backend.userland.com/rss092</docs>
      <managingEditor>msauers@travelinlibrarian.info (Michael
      Sauers)</managingEditor>
      <webMaster> msauers@travelinlibrarian.info (Michael Sauers)</webMaster>
      <image>
         <title>Michael in Lego</title>
         <url>http://travelinlinrarian.info/blog/lego.gif</url>
         <link>http://travelinlinrarian.info/</link>
         <width>155</width>
         <height>238</height>
         <description>Michael imagined as a Lego person. Create yours at
         http://www.reasonablyclever.com/mini/</description>
      </image>
      <item>
         <title>Firefox 1.1 Delayed</title>
         <link>http://Weblogs.mozillazine.org/ben/archives/007434.html</link>
         <description>According to Ben Godger (lead Firefox engineer) version
         1.1 of Firefox has been delayed and will not be released in March as
         originally scheduled.</description>
         <category domain="http://www.dmoz.org/">Computers: Software:
         Internet: Clients: WWW: Browsers: Firefox</category>
      </item>
   </channel>
</rss>
```

Let's look at the segments of the file one at a time, with a brief description of what the code represents:

- `<?xml version="1.0"?>`: This is the XML Prolog. It indicates that the file is in an XML version 1.0 format. At this time, there is only one version of XML.

- `<rss version="…">…</rss>`: This is the root element and contains the rest of the document. The version attribute specifies which version of RSS is being used.

- `<channel>…</channel>`: This is the channel element and contains information about the feed itself. Actual items are not included within this section.

- `<title></title>`: When appearing within the channel element, these tags indicate the title for the feed.

- `<link></link>`: When appearing within the channel element, these tags enclose the URL for the webpage associated with the feed.

- `<description></description>`: This element should contain a narrative description of the feed.

- `<lastBuildDate></lastBuildDate>`: This element contains the date and timestamp from when the file was last updated. Aggregators use this element to determine whether new items have been posted since the page was last checked.

- `<docs></docs>`: This element contains the URL of the specifications page for the RSS version used to create this file.

- `<managingEditor></managingEditor>`: This element contains the name and/or email address of the person in charge of this feed.

- `<webMaster></webMaster>`: This element contains the name and/or email address of the webmaster for the website associated with this feed. This person may or may not be the same as the managing editor.

- `<image>…</image>`: This element contains information about the image (logo) associated with the feed.

- `<title></title>`: When these tags appear within the image element, they indicate the title for the image.

- `<url></url>`: This element contains the URL of the image file.

- `<link></link>`: Within the image element, this tag indicates the URL for the webpage associated with the image.

- `<width></width>`: This element contains the width, in pixels, of the image.

- `<height></height>`: This element contains the height, in pixels, of the image.

- `<description></description>`: This item contains a brief description of the image for accessibility purposes. If the user's aggregator does not support images, the text would be displayed instead.

- `<item>...</item>`: This element contains all of the information regarding a single item within the feed. An RSS <item> is the equivalent of a blog post.

- `<title></title>`: When appearing within the item element, this is the title for the individual item.

- `<link></link>`: When appearing within the item element, this is the URL for the webpage associated with the individual item.

- `<description></description>`: Within the item element, these tags may enclose either a summary of the item or the complete content of the item.

- `<category domain="...">></category>`: This element contains the category of the item. The domain attribute contains a URL pointing to the website that establishes the category system being used.

Keep in mind that not all of the aforementioned elements will appear in all feed types or versions and that additional elements may appear. Detailed examples of the most common feed versions are shown in the Appendix.

While some individuals continue to code webpages by hand, extensive knowledge of code is not required for RSS authors because, in most cases, software generates the code automatically. So there's no need to memorize what you've just read—a basic understanding of the way the code works will serve you well.

Feed Types

I've mentioned already that there are several types of RSS and Atom feeds available. Table 5.1 lists the principal attributes of each version.[8] While I have

Table 5.1   Features of Various RSS and Atom Versions

RSS 0.90 (Superseded by RSS 0.91)	- Does not support categories on channel or item - Does not support the following elements on the channel: language, copyright, docs, lastBuildDate, managingEditor, pubDate, rating, skipDays, skipHours - Does not support item enclosures - Does not support the following elements on items: author, comments, pubDate
RSS 0.91 (Superseded by RSS 0.92, though still commonly used)	- Does not support categories on channel or item - Does not support the following elements on the channel: language, copyright, docs, lastBuildDate, managingEditor, pubDate, rating, skipDays, skipHours, generator, ttl - Does not support item enclosures - Does not support the following elements on items: author, comments, pubDate - Limited to 15 items - Channel-level metadata only
RSS 0.92 (Superseded by RSS 2.0)	- Supports categories on channel and item - Does not support the following elements on the channel: language, copyright, docs, lastBuildDate, managingEditor, pubDate, rating, skipDays, skipHours, generator, ttl - Supports item enclosures - Does not support the following elements on items: author, comments, pubDate - Unlimited number of items - Allows both channel and item metadata
RSS 2.0	- Supports categories on channel and item - Supports item enclosures - Supports all elements on the channel and items not supported by other versions - Significantly more complex than all other versions - Modularized
RSS 1.0 (Not preceded or superseded by any other RSS versions)	- Does not support categories on channel or item - Does not support the following elements on the channel: language, copyright, docs, lastBuildDate, managingEditor, pubDate, rating, skipDays, skipHours - Does not support item enclosures - Does not support the following elements on items: author, comments, pubDate - Based on RDF (Resource Description Framework) - Modularized
Atom	- Created as a "solution" to the problem of many different RSS versions. - Supports all the features of RSS 2.0 but with a more highly defined structure - Automatically generated by the Blogger system - Supported by aggregators

included all RSS versions in the table to show changes that have been made over time, RSS 2.0 and Atom are the most commonly used today.

You will find that some blogs and other sites offering syndication give you a choice of versions you can use to receive their feeds. I feel that this merely complicates matters for the user, especially when the choices are labeled with RSS version numbers. If given a choice, the only decision of real consequence (in my opinion) is whether to receive a summary feed (just the first few lines of a post) or a complete feed (the entire content of a post). That decision is yours to make; however, the anecdotal evidence that I'm aware of suggests that most users prefer full feeds to summaries when given the choice.

Identifying Feeds

Now that you have an idea of what feeds look like and how they work, how can you determine whether a particular site offers a feed you can subscribe to? Web authors use two basic methods to indicate the existence of a feed: on screen (via hyperlinks) and behind the scenes (via HTML linking).

On-Screen Feeds

The majority of websites that have publicly available feeds make an effort to publicize that fact. Typically, a hyperlink to the URL of the feed is placed on the page itself. In some cases, an author will place a Syndicate, Feed, or RSS link on the webpage. This link goes either directly to the feed or to a page that explains syndication and then provides further links to the feeds. This type of intermediary page is more typical of sites with many available feeds, such as news sites that provide different feeds for various news categories.

In most cases, a link to a feed is provided via an orange icon. There is no standard icon, however; different people and companies have created a variety of icons to represent links to feeds. Figure 5.2 shows 25 different feed icons I've found. They're all orange (you'll have to trust me on this) but vary widely in size and visual content. Some icons specify the feed version being used, while others are based on a certain company's implementation of the technology. The key is to look for a small orange icon—if you find one, chances are it's a link to a feed.

Figures 5.3 through 5.6 show various icons and links on webpages. The examples are indicated with an arrow for easier spotting. As you can see, some are text links and others are icon links, and they can appear anywhere on the page. Some offer users a choice between different versions of feeds for the same content.

When it came to dealing with all of these different feed icons, there was finally hope. In mid-2005, the Mozilla foundation decided on a new icon

(Figure 5.7) to appear in the address bar of the Firefox browser to indicate that the page being viewed had an available feed. To the surprise of many in the technology field, Microsoft announced in late 2005 that it would also use the same icon in the then-new version of Internet Explorer, IE7. With this unexpected cooperation, a movement began to use this single icon as the standard for feeds of all types. Since then, although artists have since created many variations of the feed icon (see Figure 5.3), the icon has been pretty much standardized. If you're looking for a simple place to download this icon in many different graphic formats and sizes, head on over to the Feed Icons website (www.feedicons.com).

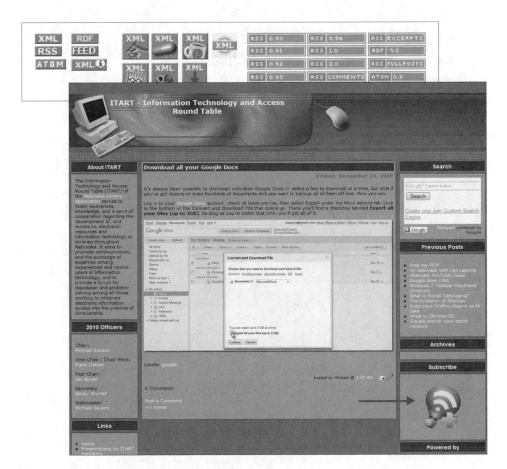

Figure 5.2   Examples of feed icons (top)

Figure 5.3   Graphical link on the ITART blog (bottom)

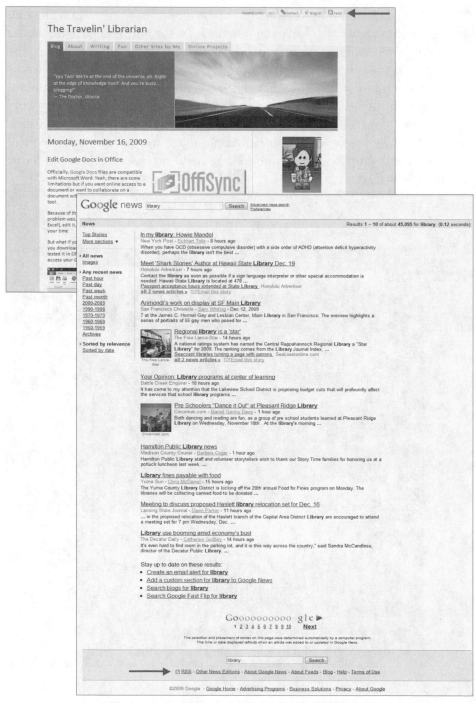

Figure 5.4   Feed link on The Travelin' Librarian blog (top)
Figure 5.5   RSS link on Google News (bottom)

Figure 5.6   XML links on Podcast Alley (top)

Figure 5.7   The standard RSS icon (bottom)

Behind-the-Scenes Feeds

An author can also create a connection between a webpage and a feed by adding some markup in the source code of the page. I call this a hidden feed because there isn't necessarily any indication of the feed on the page as viewed by the user. For example, when you do a search in the isbn.nu website for the author *koontz, dean* you receive a page of results. What you don't see is a link to a feed based on the results of that search. However, if you look at the HTML code behind the results page, you will see something similar to this following line of code near the beginning of the document:

```
<link  rel="alternate"  type="application/rss+xml"
title="RSS  2.0"  href="http://isbn.nu/97808095
52559.xml">
```

This line of code indicates to the browser that there is an "alternate" view of this page in the form of an RSS 2.0 feed. Since it's not practical to go looking for such a line in the source code of every webpage, there are a few options available to help users locate hidden feeds.

If you're a Firefox or Internet Explorer user and you get to a page with one of these links, you'll see a small orange icon in the browser's status bar (Figure 5.8). When you right-click on that icon, you'll be given the opportunity to add this feed to your browser. We'll discuss in some detail what this means to you in Chapter 6.

If you're a Google Reader user, you can copy the URL of this page and paste it into the subscribe box in Google Reader to start following the page's feed. We will cover Google Reader more fully in Chapter 6.

Figure 5.8   The RSS icon in Firefox's address bar

Finding Feeds

If you've been paying attention, you now know a feed when you see one—but poking around the web randomly hoping to spot a feed icon is not the best use of your time. The first thing you should do is check the blogs you already read to see if they have feeds. But beyond that, let's examine some efficient methods for finding useful feeds.

Mining Blogrolls

A useful technique for finding feeds is to look through the blogrolls, listings of subscribed feeds (described more fully in Chapter 6), of the authors of blogs to which you already subscribe. Chances are that authors of blogs that interest you are reading other relevant blogs. Click on some of the links and, if the blogs are of interest, see if they have feeds of their own.

Searching Via Syndic8 and Google Blogs

Syndic8 and Google Blogs are websites dedicated to indexing blogs and feeds. Syndic8 (Figure 5.9) focuses more on feeds and less on blogs and is the more searchable of the two. Google Blogs (Figure 5.10) is more blog-oriented than Syndic8, but since most blogs have associated feeds, it gets the job done. Syndic8, on the other hand, has more features to help the user discover feeds using such categories as Random Feeds, Sites We'd Like to See Syndicated, and Most Popular Feeds.

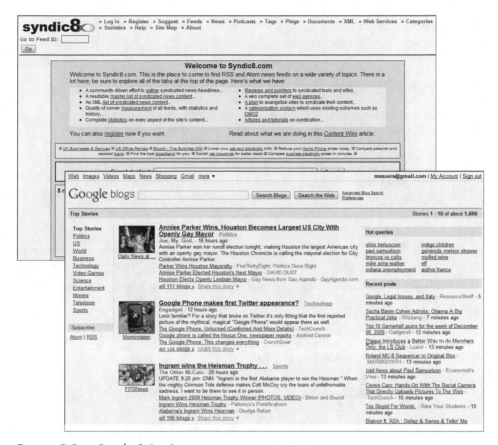

Figure 5.9   Syndic8 (top)

Figure 5.10 Google Blogs (bottom)

Figures 5.11 and 5.12 show examples of results for a search on the keyword *library* in Syndic8 and Google Blogs, respectively. As you can see, Syndic8 found 888 results, while Google Blogs found more than 82 million. (Actually this is a bit of an unfair comparison since Syndic8 is searching for feeds while Google Blogs is searching the content of blog posts, not the topics of the blogs themselves.)

Using Feeds

So, you've found a link to a feed—now, what do you do with it? First, click on the link to see what happens. Depending on your browser and the version of the feed you clicked on, you will see a page akin to one of those shown in Figures 5.13 through 5.16.

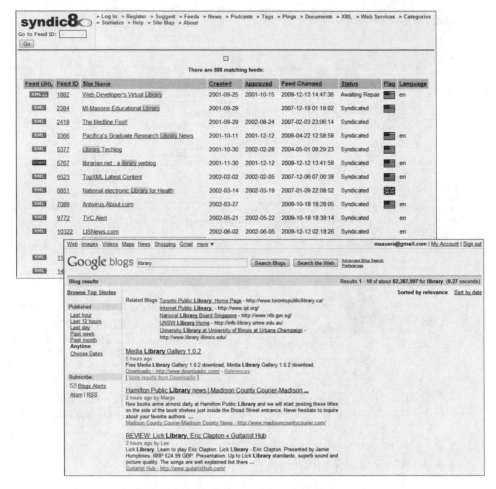

Figure 5.11   Search results for *library* on Syndic8 (top)

Figure 5.12   Search results for *library* on Google Blogs (bottom)

In the current versions of Firefox (3.5x) and Internet Explorer (8), when you click on a link to an RSS file, the browser takes over and displays a nicely formatted version of the feed's content (Figures 5.13 and 5.14 show the results).

In less recent versions of Firefox and IE, you'll probably see the raw code and content of the feed. It's readable, but it's not exactly exciting (Figure 5.15).

Sadly, in the current version of Chrome (5.0x), you'll just see the content of the feed, sans code, but without any formatting at all (Figure 5.16).

You can read the current content of a feed just by opening a link, assuming you're using an up-to-date browse. If you do just this and nothing else, however, you're missing out on the feed's greatest strength: the ability to

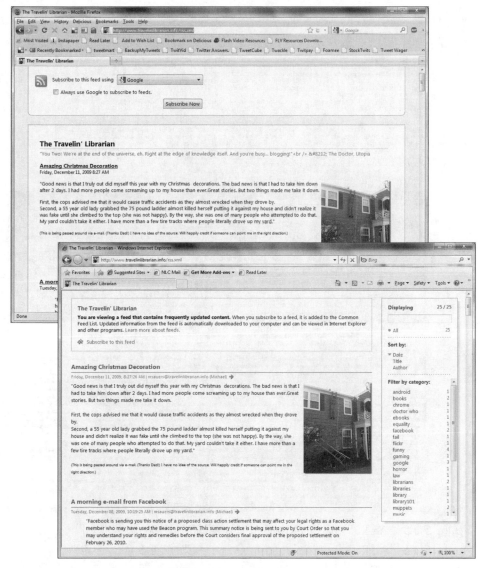

Figure 5.13   An RSS file displayed in Firefox 3.5.5 (top)

Figure 5.14   An RSS file displayed in Internet Explorer 8 (bottom)

notify you automatically of the new items and to hide the stuff you've already seen.

In order to truly take advantage of feeds, you must use a program known as an aggregator. This aggregator not only takes the code and turns it into something more reader-friendly, it also tracks the feeds, alerting you to new content on a regular basis.

Figure 5.15   An RSS file displayed in a pre-RSS era browser (top)

Figure 5.16   An RSS file displayed in Google Chrome 5.0.375.70
(bottom)

Let's move on to Chapter 6 where we will learn all about aggregators.

Endnotes

1. "RSS," Wikipedia, The Free Encyclopedia, en.wikipedia.org/wiki/RSS (accessed March 20, 2010).

2. Alex Barnett, "75 Million RSS users?" June 4, 2005, blogs.msdn.com/alexbarn/ archive/2005/06/04/425277.aspx (accessed March 20, 2010); "A brief overview of

RSS statistics," ActiveRefresh, May 26, 2010, rss-statistics.activerefresh.com/a-brief-overview-of-rss-statistics.html (accessed July 7, 2010); "RSS users visit three times as many news web sites as non-users, according to Nielsen//NewRatings," PR Newswire, September 20, 2005, www.nielsen-online.com/pr/pr_050920.pdf (accessed July 7, 2010).

3. "Web feed," Wikipedia, The Free Encyclopedia, en.wikipedia.org/w/index.php?title=Web_feed&oldid=36167370 (accessed February 4, 2006).

4. "Resource Description Framework (RDF) is a family of specifications for a meta-data model that is often implemented as an application of XML. The RDF family of specifications is maintained by the World Wide Web Consortium (W3C)." "Resource Description Framework," Wikipedia, The Free Encyclopedia, en.wikipedia.org/w/index.php?title=Resource_Description_Framework&oldid=38063891 (accessed February 4, 2006).

5. "What is Atom?" www.atomenabled.org

6. More details on the history of RSS and Atom can be found at RSS 2.0 at Harvard Law: RSS History (cyber.law.harvard.edu/rss/rssVersionHistory.html), Atom Enabled (www.atomenabled.org), The Great Syndication Wars (blog.clintecker.com/post/148426723/the-great-syndication-wars), and Six Apart: Why We Need Echo (www.sixapart.com/log/ 2003/06/why_we_need_ech.shtml).

7. Those interested in more background on exactly what XML is and does should read Peter Flynn's The XML FAQ (www.ucc.ie/xml).

8. A more complete chart can be found on the RSS.net website (www.rssdotnet.com/documents/version_comparison.html).

Chapter 6

Using an Aggregator

As we learned in Chapter 5, a feed file is made up of a lot of code that will hold little interest for most of us. What we want is the content. Now, it's true that if you open one of these files in your browser you *will* see the content, but it will be surrounded by XML markup (see "What's in a Feed File?" in the previous chapter for an example). Even if you are willing to try to read through this clutter, there's no way to determine what has been added since the last time you looked at the file. An aggregator addresses both of these issues, displaying readable text and alerting you to what's new. You will need to either install aggregator software on your computer or utilize a web-based service such as Google Reader or Bloglines before you can start reading feeds. Keep reading to find out more about your options.

What Is an Aggregator?

According to Wikipedia, "a feed aggregator, also known as a feed reader, news reader or simply aggregator, is client software or a web application which aggregates syndicated web content such as news headlines, blogs, podcasts, and vlogs in a single location for easy viewing."[1] Simply put, an aggregator is what you need to read feeds.

More specifically, an aggregator:

- Transforms XML markup into a readable and more visually appealing format

- Checks each feed periodically—once an hour, for example—for new items

- Alerts you when a feed has new items and, by default, displays only the new items from each feed

- Provides hyperlinks to original and/or related articles as provided by the feed's author

- Allows you to subscribe to multiple feeds, thus enabling you to receive all feed-based information in a single location with a single interface

These are the core functions of an aggregator, though some aggregators offer additional features, such as the ability to save, sort, and post via email.

Types of Aggregators

Currently, there are four different types of aggregators available: stand-alone clients, embedded clients, server-based, and web-based.

Stand-Alone Clients

Stand-alone clients are dedicated feed aggregating programs that are installed on a single computer. Popular stand-alone clients today include Feedreader (www.feedreader.com; Figure 6.1), FeedDemon (www.news gator.com/Individuals/FeedDemon; Figure 6.2), and NewzCrawler (www.newz crawler.com; Figure 6.3).

Stand-alone clients typically work in a three-pane environment analogous to most email clients and are easy to learn. Some, such as FeedDemon and Feedreader, are free, while others, such as NewzCrawler, are available for less than $30.

There are two downsides to this type of aggregator. The first is that this is yet another program on your computer that performs just a single function. Second, this type of aggregator locks the subscriber into reading the feeds on a single computer. If you install this type of aggregator at the office, you will not have access to your subscriptions at home or on the road. (One person I know has one aggregator installed on her office computer to handle her work-related subscriptions and another on her home computer to handle her non-work-related subscriptions. That's a great setup assuming you can clearly delineate between your "work" and "home" online sources.)

Embedded Clients

Embedded clients also require downloading and installation on a single computer. However, unlike stand-alone clients, which are dedicated to aggregating feeds, an embedded client adds aggregation functionality to a program you're already using—typically your web browser or email client. In the past, these programs needed to be literally added to existing software. Today, aggregator features have been integrated into that software.

While many users consider embedded clients to be a convenient option, as with a stand-alone client, you will be locked into reading your feeds on a

Figure 6.1   Feedreader (top)
Figure 6.2   FeedDemon (middle)
Figure 6.3   NewzCrawler (bottom)

single computer. Following are descriptions of some popular embedded clients that are available as part of widely used programs.

Outlook 2007 and 2010

If you're a committed Microsoft Outlook user and don't feel that being locked into one computer will be a problem (or you are on an Exchange server and have web-based access to your email), this aggregator can be an excellent option. Outlook's RSS reader can be found by clicking on RSS Feeds under Personal Folders in the left sidebar. Here you will see a list of any feeds you've subscribed to, and you can select and open the available items just as if you were working with an email folder (Figure 6.4).

Internet Explorer 8

Feeds in Internet Explorer 8 can be found by opening the Favorites sidebar and clicking the Feeds tab. When an individual feed is selected, its unread content will be displayed in the browser's main window (Figure 6.5). Internet Explorer feeds can be organized into folders. As browser-embedded solutions go, this one is clean and well implemented.

Firefox 3.5x

Firefox treats feeds as a bookmark folder, with each item in a feed appearing as an individual bookmark. Clicking on an item displays the content in the main browser window (Figure 6.6). Experience has taught me that the Firefox aggregator is not well implemented in comparison with Internet Explorer's RSS feature. Integrating the aggregator with bookmarks means that all a user sees of each item is its headline. To see the complete text of an item, the user must open it. Furthermore, you are not able to distinguish between unread (e.g., new) and read items.

Server-Based

Server-based aggregators are also downloaded and installed; however, unlike the two types of client programs, server-based aggregators are installed on a web server and then accessed via a web browser. Server-based options, such as Feed on Feeds (feedonfeeds.com), solve the biggest problem with client options: Since feeds are accessed via the web, the user is no longer tied to a single computer. Once the program has been installed, all you need to do is fire up a browser from any internet-connected computer and enter the URL of the aggregator (Figure 6.7).

The use of server-based aggregators does, however, pose some problems. First, you must have access to a server on which the program can be installed. Secondly, and perhaps more importantly, you need to have some technical

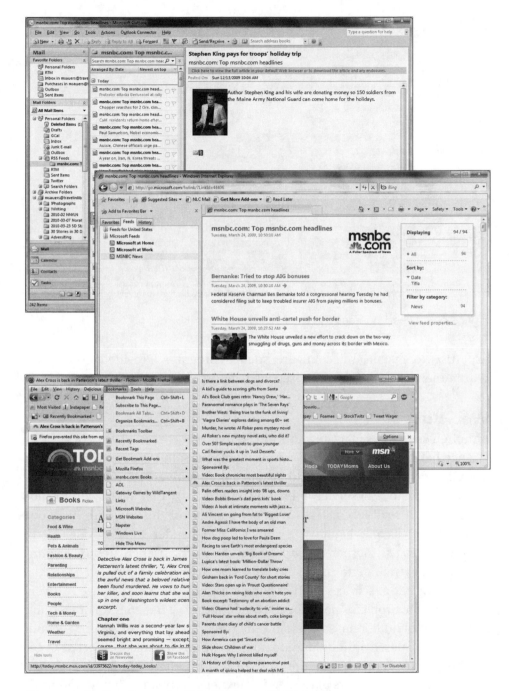

Figure 6.4   Reading a feed in Outlook 2007 (top)

Figure 6.5   Reading a feed in Internet Explorer 8 (middle)

Figure 6.6   Reading a feed in Firefox 3.5.5 (bottom)

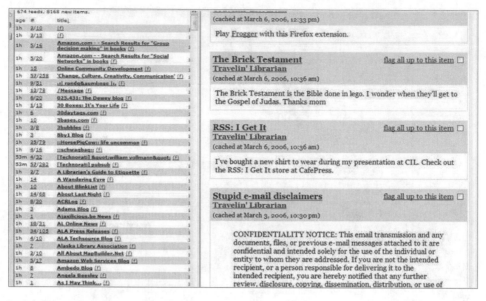

Figure 6.7   Feed on Feeds

expertise to install and configure such a program. Provided both these requirements are met, server-based aggregators may be your best option.

Web-Based

Although server-based aggregators are, in fact, web-based, there is a key difference between them and web-based aggregators: In the case of web-based aggregators, it is not necessary to install or configure any software. The web-based aggregator is a service offered by a third party that allows you to subscribe to and read feeds. The two most popular of this type are Bloglines (www.bloglines.com; Figure 6.8) and Google Reader (reader.google.com; Figure 6.9). To use these free web-based services, the user creates an account and then logs in to perform all feed-related activities.

In my opinion, services such as Bloglines and Google Reader effectively address all the problems posed by the other options. First, they do not require installation of additional software on the user's computer or server. Second, unlike server-based options, they do not require any technical expertise to get the program working. Third, the work of reading the feeds is done almost completely by the servers of the service-owner's company. Finally, and most important, web-based aggregators do not tie the user to a single computer. If you have a Google Reader account and an internet connection, you can read your feeds. For me, this is just about anywhere, as I have a web browser on my

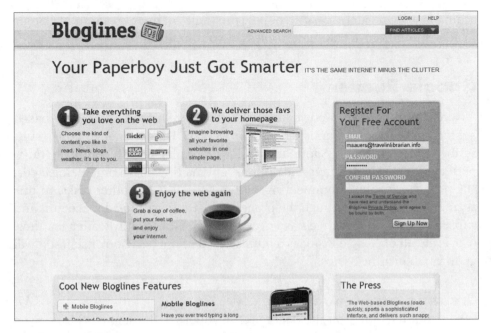

Figure 6.8   Bloglines

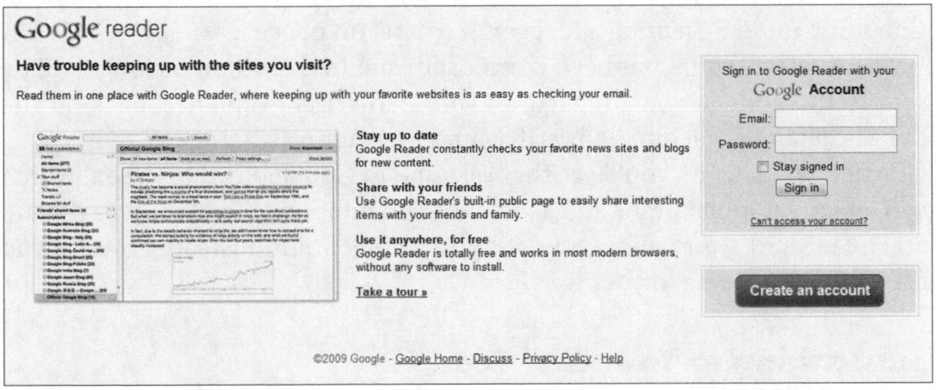

Figure 6.9   Google Reader

Droid smartphone and regularly access my Google Reader account while at
the airport waiting for a flight.[2]

Because the focus in this chapter is on how to receive and read feeds with
a minimum investment in time, effort, and expense, I'll direct your attention
to Google Reader for the rest of this chapter. Even if you believe that one of
the other options is a better solution for you, I suggest you read on or at least

scan: Most aggregators work in roughly the same manner, so a tour of Google Reader should prove helpful regardless of your final choice.

Google Reader

As already mentioned, Google Reader (Reader for short) is a free web-based aggregator that Google launched in October 2005. Reader enables you to sub-scribe to feeds in any RSS format as well as Atom feeds with complete trans-parency. It includes features and options for emailing posts, organizing feeds, "liking," sharing, and commenting, along with a host of other tasks. In this section, I'll walk you through the process of setting up a Reader account and subscribing to feeds as well as cover a number of useful Reader features. (Covering all of Google Reader's features could easily be a book itself, so I will go through just the basics.)

Creating an Account

When you first enter the site (Figure 6.10), you'll see the service's home page where you're asked to log in. If you already have an account with Google or any of its other services, you already have a Reader account. Just log in with your Google credentials and feel free to skip to the next section.

If you don't already have a Google account, you will find instructions in Chapter 4 under "Creating a Blogger Account" on page 83.

Once your account has been created, an email verification message will be sent to the address you supplied. At your earliest convenience, click on the link supplied in that email to verify your email address.

When you sign in, you'll see the Welcome to Google Reader screen, which will include popular items and a folder of recommended feed sources (Figure 6.11). Let's not worry about any of those at this point; instead, I'll walk you through subscribing to your first feed.

Subscribing to Your First Feed

As discussed in Chapter 5, there are two different ways to identify whether a site has a feed. In most cases, you'll see one of many different orange icons or a text-based hyperlink that says RSS or Syndicate This Site. Once you've found the icon or link, subscribing is easy. As an initial example, I'll have you sub-scribe to the feed for my Flickr photographs.

Open a new tab or window in your browser (CTRL-T/Command-T) and go to www.flickr.com/photos/travelinlibrarian. Scroll to the bottom of the page and find the orange icon labeled Subscribe to Travelin' Librarian's photo-stream (Figure 6.12). Right-click on the Latest link and select Copy Link

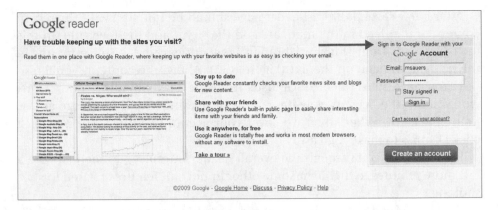

Figure 6.10   Logging into Google Reader

Figure 6.11   Welcome to Google Reader

Location (Figure 6.13). (The exact wording of the selection from this menu will vary from browser to browser.)

Now switch back to the tab or window containing Reader and click the Add a Subscription button in the upper-left corner of the page. Paste the copied URL into the empty field, then click Add (Figure 6.14).

After a few seconds, your Reader page should be updated with the recent content of that feed in the main area on the right, and the feed title (in this case, "Uploads from Travelin Librarian") will appear under Subscriptions in the navigation pane on the left (Figure 6.15). Above the content, you'll also see "You have subscribed to 'Uploads from the Travelin' Librarian'." (Don't worry about the "As you view items in your reading list ..." message at this point. We'll cover that when we cover your account settings. For now, just click Dismiss to make it go away.)

Before I walk you through the overall Reader interface, let me just take a few more minutes to highlight some other important features related to subscribing.

First is the Feed Settings button above the feed content frame (Figure 6.16). Clicking on this button provides you with the following options:

- *Sort by newest.* Choosing this option (the default, as indicated by the checkmark) displays items in reverse-chronological order.

- *Sort by oldest.* Choosing this option displays items in chronological order. This works well on feeds for comic strips where you want to be sure to read them in the order they were released.

- *Sort by magic.* According to Google, this option sorts the feeds items "based on your personal usage, and overall activity in Reader." In other words, Google is noticing things such as which items you pause on, like, share, and email to others. Based on these and other criteria, it will display the new items it thinks you will like at the top of the list. Since your account is new, you won't get much out of this feature yet. Once you've been using your account for a while, try this option and see if you think it works well for you.

- *Rename subscription.* If you don't like the name of the feed as given to you when you subscribed, feel free to click this option and rename it to something more to your liking.

- *Unsubscribe.* Click this link to unsubscribe from the feed you're currently viewing. You will be asked to confirm this choice.

- *Translate into my language.* In your Google account settings, you can pick your default language. (I'll be covering this later.) Clicking this link will automatically translate the content of this feed into the language you set. As you can expect, translation results vary widely.

- *New folder.* Reader allows you to organize your feeds into folders. With a new account, there are no folders for you to choose from; you just see the New folder option. Clicking this option will open a new small window asking "What would you like to call this new folder?" For this example, create a new folder named *Flickr* and click OK (Figure 6.17). Immediately, this feed will be placed in your newly created Flickr folder and that folder will appear in the Subscriptions list in the navigation pane. From this point forward, when you open the Feed Settings list, you will see a list of your previously created folders (in this example, just your Flickr folder) along with the New Folder option. To move a feed into an existing folder, just select the name of that folder from this list. As an example, Figure 6.18 shows a partial list of folders in my personal account.

Be aware that these options only affect the feed currently displayed in the content frame. To make global changes in your preferences across all subscribed feeds, look to the Settings link in the upper-right corner of your screen, which we'll be covering later in this chapter.

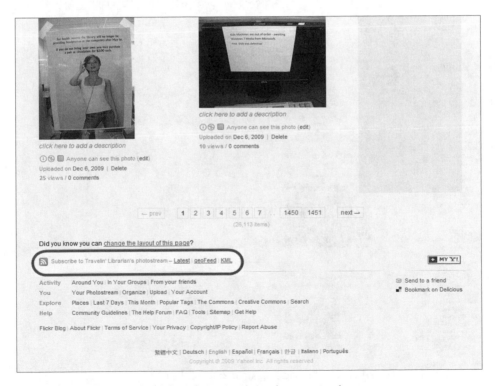

Figure 6.12 Link to feed for The Travelin' Librarian's photostream

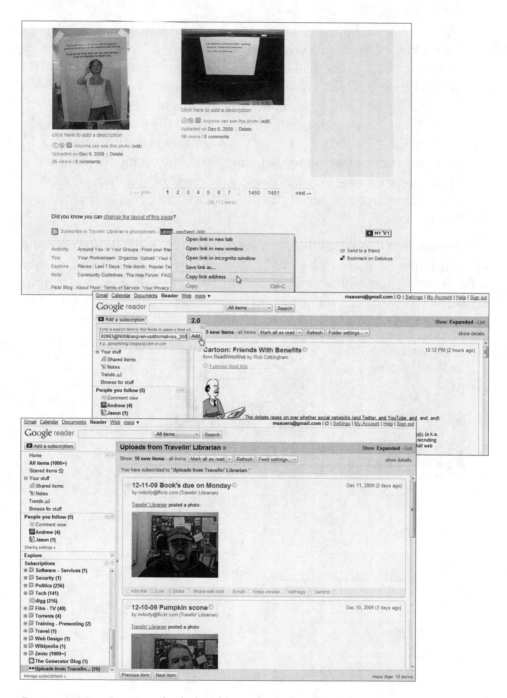

Figure 6.13   Copying the link address for a feed (top)

Figure 6.14   Adding a feed to Google Reader (middle)

Figure 6.15   Viewing the newly added feed (bottom)

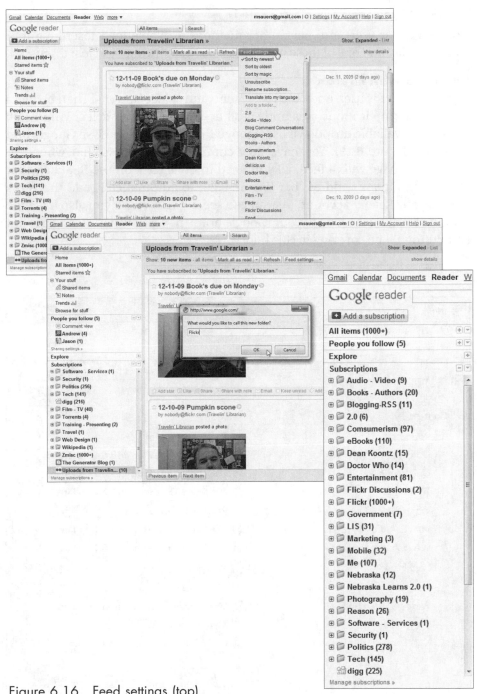

Figure 6.16   Feed settings (top)

Figure 6.17   Creating a new folder (middle)

Figure 6.18   Partial list of Google Reader folders (bottom)

Other Methods for Subscribing

Google Reader users also have other methods available for subscribing to a feed. You may find one of these methods easier than the method just discussed.

Integrate with Firefox

If you're a Firefox user, open the Help menu and select Options. Then head on over to the Applications area and scroll down the list and select Web Feed. Using the available dropdown list, change the Action field to Use Google and click OK (Figure 6.19). You have now configured Firefox so that whenever you're on a page with a feed, all you need to do is click on the RSS icon that appears in Firefox's address bar (Figure 6.20) to automatically add that site's feed to your Reader account. (As you can see in Figure 6.20, you also have the option of adding the feed to your iGoogle home page. However, iGoogle is not something I'll be covering in this book.)

Figure 6.19   Integrating Google Reader into Firefox

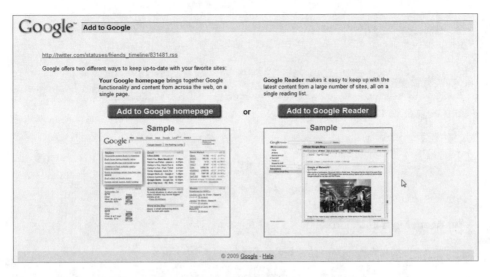

Figure 6.20   Adding a feed to Google Reader

Subscribe Bookmarklet

Bookmarklets are bookmarks you can add to your browser that, instead of pointing you back to a particular webpage, perform a command (usually written in JavaScript) to produce a desired result. Reader has a Subscribe bookmarklet that can make it easy to subscribe to feeds as you find them. To find the bookmarklet and instructions for installing it, click Settings, select Reader Settings, click on the Goodies link, and look under Subscribe As You Surf (Figure 6.21).

Now when you land on a page that has one or more feeds to subscribe to, just click on your Subscribe bookmarklet and that site's feed will automatically be added to your subscription list in your Reader account.

This is the method you need to use with Internet Explorer and, oddly enough, Google's own Chrome browser.

Add to Google

As you start looking for new feeds to subscribe to, you'll notice a link—as text, a button, or an icon—labeled + Google on some pages (Figure 6.22). This is a special link to a site's feed that automates the process of subscribing to that feed with Reader. As a Reader user, you need only click on the link to be taken to a page asking if you wish to subscribe to this feed using Reader and/or iGoogle (see Figure 6.20). Just follow the onscreen instructions for adding this feed to your Reader account. (You may have noticed that this works just as the Firefox integration does.)

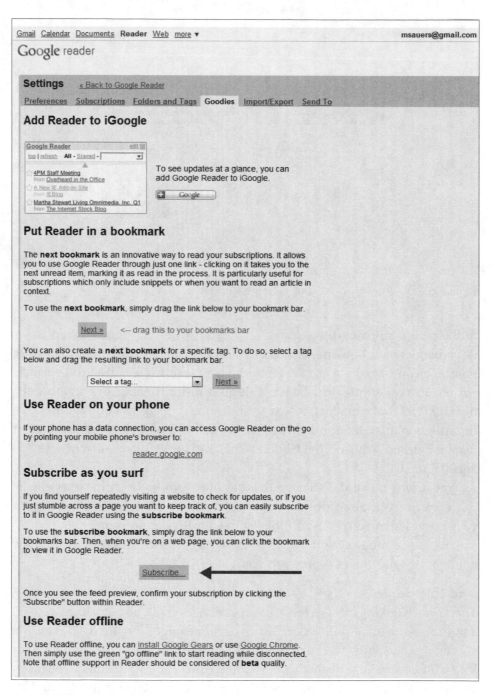

Figure 6.21   Subscribe as you surf

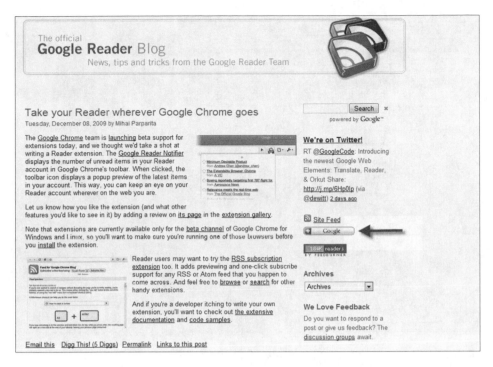

Figure 6.22   Add to Google button

If you are a blogger and want to add this feature to your own blog, follow the link labeled "Make it easier for people to discover and subscribe to your content" (www.google.com/webmasters/add.html) to find instructions on how to create the code for your button and add it to your webpage (Figure 6.23).

Reader Interface

Figure 6.24 shows my view of the Reader interface when I log into my personal account. Since I've been using it for a while, you'll notice that there is a lot more on this screen than what you see when you log into Reader. That's OK. Right now, we're less concerned about the content of the account and more about the features of Reader itself.

On the left of the screen is what's called the navigation pane. Here you can choose which content from your account you wish to view in the content area. The content area (the rest of the page to the right) will display the content you've selected in the navigation pane.

In Figure 6.25, I want to point out one important thing about what's in the content area (on the right) of this example. When you first log into your account in the future, Reader will present you with a sort of highlight reel of

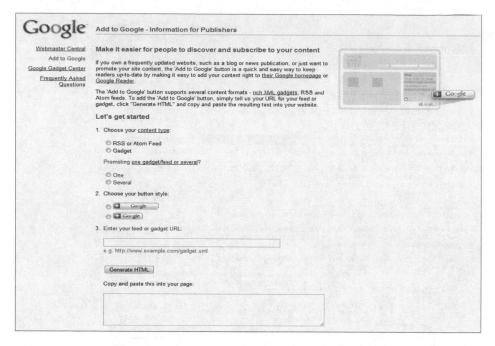

Figure 6.23   Add to Google—Information for Publishers

Figure 6.24   Google Reader home

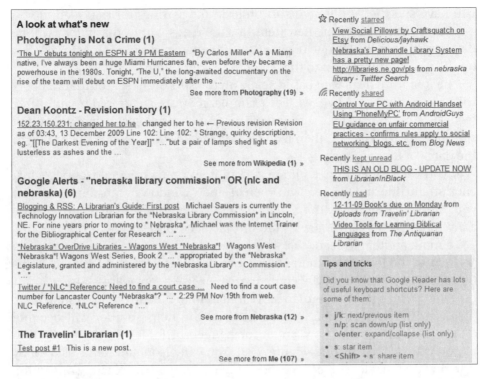

Figure 6.25 A look at what's new

what's going on with the feeds you subscribe to. It will present you with some example content from your more popular feeds (based on the same sort of criteria as the Sort by Magic feature presented earlier) along with a list of items you've recently starred, "liked," shared, or read. (We'll be covering each of these actions in turn.) You can easily jump to any of this content by clicking on the appropriate hyperlink.

Reading Feeds

In general, Reader checks feeds for new content hourly. (Feeds with fewer subscribers may not be checked as often.) When new items appear in a feed to which you subscribe, the name of that feed will appear in boldface type, and the number of new items available will be listed to the right of the title. Most of my feeds have been organized into folders. Figure 6.26 shows 31 new items in my LIS folder, which is the total number of new items for all of the feeds in that folder.

To read the new items in a single feed, click on the name of the feed in the navigation pane; the new items for that feed will be displayed in the right frame (Figure 6.27). Items will display in reverse chronological order unless you have specified a different sort order in the settings for that feed. If you click on a folder, all of the new items for the feeds within that folder will be displayed in the right frame (Figure 6.28). To open and close folders, just click on the plus or minus sign to the left of the folder name.

The items are displayed based solely on the sort order set for that folder—they are not grouped by feed. For example, if you select a folder with three feeds (A, B, and C) and the sort order is reverse-chronological, then you might see an item from feed A, then feed C, then feed A, then feed B, according to the dates of those items.

If you wish to read the entire text of an item on its original webpage, just click on the title and the item will open in a new window or tab, depending on your browser's settings. If an item includes hyperlinks, these will also be active and will open in a new window or tab accordingly.

To mark an item as read, click in that item's box, use the scrollbar to move an item to the top of the content area, use the Next Item and Previous Items buttons at the bottom of the content area, or use a keyboard shortcut (*j* for next item, *k* for previous item) to move that item to the top of the content area.

Once an item has been marked as read, the item's border will become darker, and the unread item count for its feed or folder (in the navigation pane) will decrease by one (Figure 6.29). You can also mark items as read by bringing up the relevant feed or folder and clicking on or selecting one of the options listed under the Mark All As Read button at the top of the content area. The other available options are All Items (default), Items Older Than a Day, Items Older Than a Week, or Items Older Than Two Weeks (Figure 6.30).

Once an item has been marked as read, it will no longer appear in that feed or folder. To retrieve posts you've already read, you have two options: clicking All Items for that feed/folder or performing a search. (Search will be covered later in this chapter.)

The navigation pane will update itself periodically to show you that new posts have arrived. If you get impatient, you can click on the Refresh button at the top of the content pane to check for new items in the feed or folder you're currently viewing. Alternatively, you can click on the Subscriptions heading in the navigation pane to force Reader to refresh all of your feeds and report any newly available items.

Managing Your Subscriptions

Once you've amassed a reasonably large list of subscriptions, you'll need to begin managing your feed list. You may want to give a feed a different name (one that has some meaning to you), sort your feeds alphabetically, or organize feeds into folders. There are several ways in which you can accomplish these tasks.

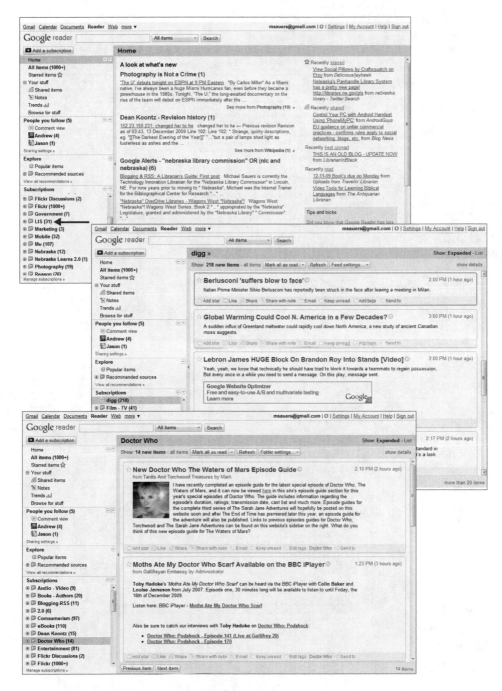

Figure 6.26   Unread items in my LIS folder (top)

Figure 6.27   Unread items from the Digg feed (middle)

Figure 6.28   Unread items from the feeds in my *Doctor Who* folder (bottom)

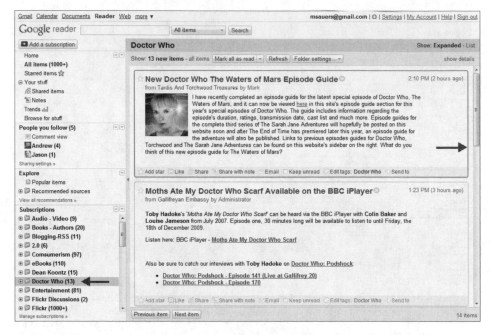

Figure 6.29   An item marked as read

Figure 6.30   Mark all as read

Feed Settings

You can manage your feeds using the Feed Settings button, which I described earlier in this chapter in the section Subscribing to Your First Feed, through a slightly hidden dropdown list in your navigation pane.

Move your mouse so that the pointer hovers over a feed name in your subscription list in the navigation pane. As you do this, you'll see a bar appear along with a down-pointing triangle to the right of the feed name. (This will also appear if you hover over a folder name.) Click on that triangle and you'll see a menu of options (Figure 6.31). These options will match the options that are available from the Feed Settings button.

If you open this menu while hovering over a folder name, you'll also see a few additional options:

- *Create a bundle.* This option allows you to create a set of feeds based on the content of that folder. This feed set bundle can then be shared as a single item, meaning that others can view or subscribe to the entire set. We'll be touching on sharing more in the "Getting Social" section later in this chapter.

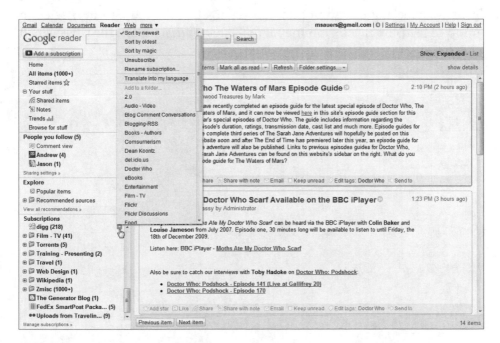

Figure 6.31   Feed options in the navigation bar

- *Delete folder*. If you delete a folder, the feeds in that folder will *not* be unsubscribed. The folder itself will be removed, but any feeds it contained will remain in your subscription list.

- *Unsubscribe from all*. Choosing this option will remove all feeds in the selected folder from your account.

Drag and Drop

Both feeds and folders can be rearranged and moved from one folder to another by simply using drag and drop. Just select the name of the item you want to move, hold down the (left) mouse button, drag it to the destination, and release the mouse button.

Managing Subscriptions Via Settings

There is an alternative interface for managing your subscriptions that is especially useful if you want to make the same changes to multiple items in a batch mode. To find this interface, click on the Settings link in the upper-right corner, then select Subscriptions (Figure 6.32).

Here you will be presented with an alphabetical list containing all of your subscriptions. You can change settings for any individual feed or group of feeds by checking the appropriate boxes to the left. You can also select a group of feeds by clicking on the All (*N*) Subscriptions, None, or Unassigned

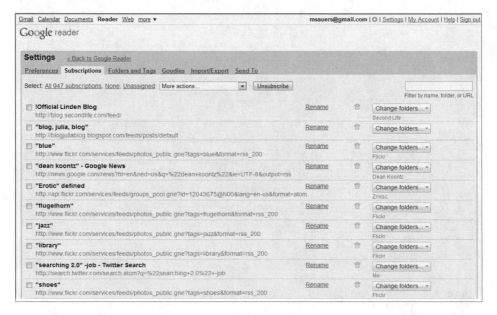

Figure 6.32   Settings: Subscriptions

links at the top of the list. Lastly, you can use the Filter by Name, Folder, or URL box in the upper-right of the page to filter the list displayed. As you type a keyword into this box, feeds or folders that do not contain that text in their title or URL will disappear from the current listing.

From this screen, you can perform the following actions:

- *Unsubscribe.* Click on the trashcan icon next to an individual feed to unsubscribe from just that feed. Use the Unsubscribe button at the top of the pane to unsubscribe from a selected batch of feeds.

- *Rename.* This link will open a small window where you can enter a different name for the feed. This will only work with individual feeds.

- *Change folders.* Use this action to add a feed to or remove it from a folder. Feeds can appear in multiple folders. Click on the triangle to pull down a list of all your folders, and select the folder or folders that you want to contain that feed. This will only work on individual feeds.

- *Add to folder.* This action (found under the More Actions dropdown list) allows you to move batches of selected feeds to the folder of your choice.

- *Remove from folder.* This action (found under the More Actions dropdown list) removes selected feeds from a folder. This will also work on batches.

All changes take effect immediately, although for some, you will first be asked to confirm the action. When you're done, click the Back to Google Reader link at the top of the page to return to reading your feeds.

Importing and Exporting Subscriptions

Also under Settings is the Import/Export link. Here you can export your subscription list as an OPML file (Outline Processing Markup Language) or import an existing OPML file into your subscription list (Figure 6.33).

Depending on your browser, clicking on the Export Your Subscriptions as an OPML File link will either open a new window in your browser containing an OPML file that lists all of your folders and feeds (which you can then save with an .xml extension), or it will automatically ask you to save that file to your computer. This is the file you can then send to others for importing into their account.

To import an OPML file, you will need to click on the Choose File button, browse for the file, and click the Upload button (Figure 6.34). All of the feeds and folders in the file will appear in your account, and you'll be subscribed to all of those feeds.

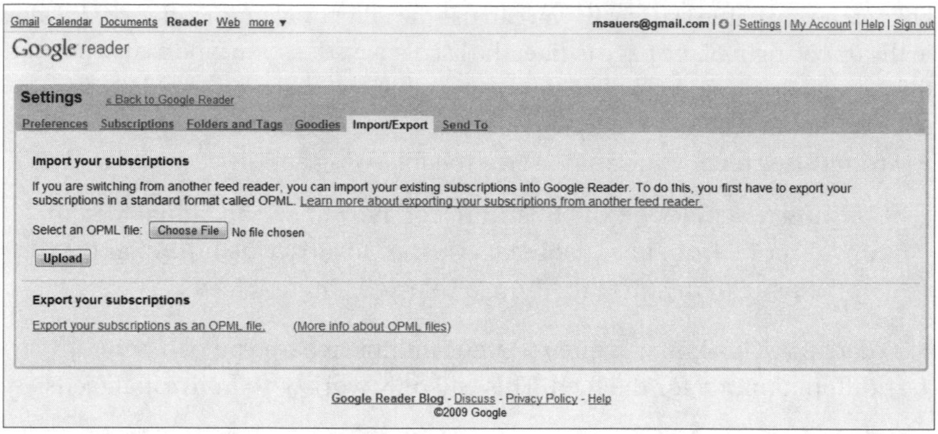

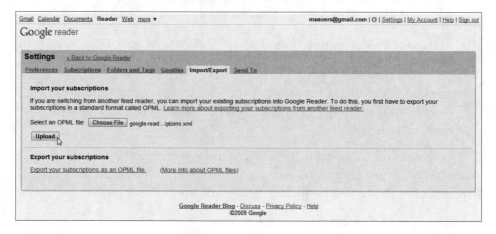

Figure 6.33   Settings: Import/Export

Figure 6.34   Importing an OPML file

Saving Posts for Later

As previously discussed, once a feed item has been marked as read, it essentially disappears from the system. Beyond searching for a past item or choosing to display all items, Reader offers four ways to store particular items more permanently for later retrieval: Add Star, Email, Keep Unread, and Send To. All of these options are available at the bottom of every post.

Add Star

Clicking Add Star will turn the star icon yellow to the left of the item's title; as a result, the link will change to Remove Star (Figure 6.35). You can think of adding a star as akin to bookmarking a webpage. To view all of your starred items, click on the Starred Items link near the top of the navigation pane, and they will be displayed in the content area of the page (Figure 6.36).

Email

Emailing a post does exactly what it implies: Reader takes the content of a post and emails it to the recipient of your choice (including yourself). By sending this email, you are, in effect, making a copy of the post to be stored outside the Reader system.

When you click a post's Email link, a sub-window will appear beneath the post (Figure 6.37). The From field will automatically be populated with the email address associated with your account, and the subject line will contain the title of the post. (The subject line can be edited.) Fill in the To field with the address to which you would like to send the email. You can enter multiple addresses, separating them with commas. (If you're a Gmail user, Google will suggest recipients based on your contact list as you type in contacts.) You can also add a note (of up to 1,000 characters) to go along with the emailed post. Lastly, check the box next to "Send me a copy of this email" to receive a copy of this message in your inbox. Click the Send button to send the message. Click the Cancel button to prevent the message from being sent.

Keep Unread

The Keep Unread checkbox (Figure 6.38) instructs Reader to leave the post in the feed indefinitely even though you've already read it. In essence, Reader will continue to consider the post "new" until the box is unchecked.

Send To

Chances are you don't have this option right now because it is turned off by default. However, if you look at Figure 6.39, I've highlighted it in my account. To turn it on, you need to access the Send To area of your account's settings, which I'll explain later in this chapter. In the meantime, let's use my account as an example of how Send To works.

The basic idea is that you might want to take the content of a particular item and send it to your account with another online service such as Delicious or Twitter. For example, I might want to bookmark an item from Reader in my Delicious account. Traditionally, I would need to open the webpage where the item originally appeared and then bookmark it in Delicious using one of the various methods available to me as a Delicious account holder. Instead, I can just click Send To and then select Delicious, and all that will be taken care of for me automatically. Or maybe I'd like to tweet about this item. Now I can just click Send To and select Twitter and off it goes.

I find this tool very useful, and I use it almost constantly. Once we get to covering the rest of your account settings, you'll see how easy this is.

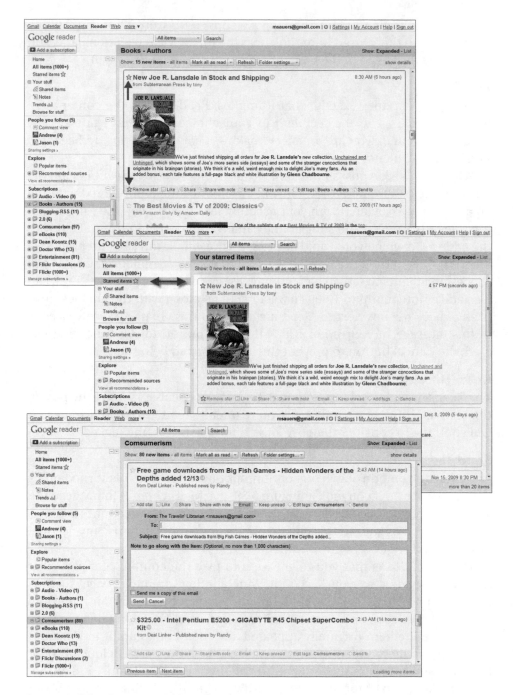

Figure 6.35   Starring an item (top)

Figure 6.36   Displaying starred items (middle)

Figure 6.37   Emailing a post (bottom)

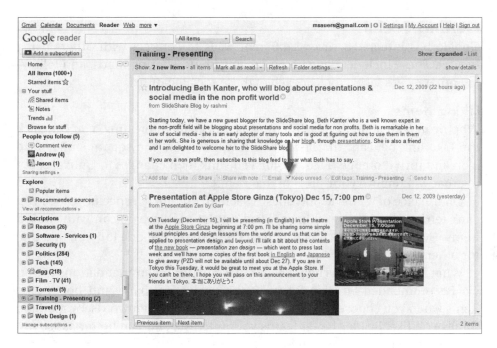

Figure 6.38   Marking a post unread

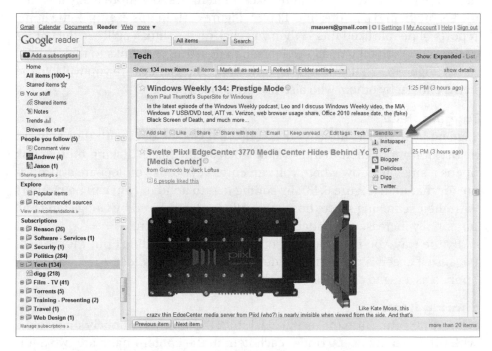

Figure 6.39   Sending an item to another account

Getting Social

Google has integrated several different ways to connect with others using Reader. These include liking items, tagging items, sharing items, and following others. Let's take a look at each of these social features.

Liking Items

When you read an item that you think is especially interesting, you can click the Like link beneath that item, which will activate the square smiley face icon and turn it orange (Figure 6.40). (The link then changes to Unlike; clicking that will remove your "like" of that item.]

On the face of it, this action doesn't seem to do much, especially since you can't retrieve the items you have "liked" in the past, as you can with starred items. However, the Like link will in fact do two things: one for you, and one for others.

What it does for you is help Reader make better recommendations to you via Recommended Sources folder in the navigation pane and better sort items when you choose the Sort By Magic option. In other words, by marking things you like, Reader better learns your interests and can better assist you in finding what you're looking for.

What it does for others is show them how many other Reader users have liked a particular item. The more Likes an item has, the more likely it is that others might find it interesting. Look at Figure 6.41. In this example, the items reports "4 people liked this." When you click on that link, you'll see the names of those users (if they've allowed this in their settings) as links to their shared items (Figure 6.42). If you liked a particular post, chances are you will like the items chosen by others who also liked that post.

Tagging Items

Tagging by itself isn't directly social but what Google does with those tags is. At the bottom of each item is a link labeled Edit Tags. Clicking on this link opens a small window where you can enter keywords you feel are appropriate for that item (Figure 6.43). By adding tags to an item, you can help others with their searching since those tags will now be indexed by Google and will potentially increase the findability of any particular item.

By the way, you may see a tag on an item that you didn't put there; that's because if a feed is placed in a folder, the name of that folder is automatically applied as a tag to all the items in that folder.

Sharing Items

Now we're getting into the really social stuff: the ability to publicly share items with other Reader users. Under each item in the content pane are two additional links: Share and Share With Note:

Figure 6.40   Liking and unliking items

- *Share.* Clicking Share will activate the orange share icon (and change the link to Unshare). (I'll let you guess what clicking Unshare does.) You can also add a brief comment about the item you are sharing by clicking on the now available Add Comment link (Figure 6.44). You can find all of your shared items by clicking on the Shared Items link in the navigation pane (Figure 6.45). Anything that you have shared will be made available to anyone who is following you in their navigation pane. (I'll be covering this in the next section.)

- *Share with note.* If you choose this link, a new window will appear containing the item along with an additional field where you can add an extended note about this item, the option to not share the item with others, and the ability to add tags to the item. Once you're done, click the Post Item button to share the item. (Clicking the Close This link will abandon the action.)

Following Others

As I've previously mentioned, whenever you share an item, it is viewable by Reader users who follow you. Conversely, you can follow others to see what they have shared. Shared items of the people you follow will appear under People You Follow in the navigation pane. As you can see in Figure 6.46, in my

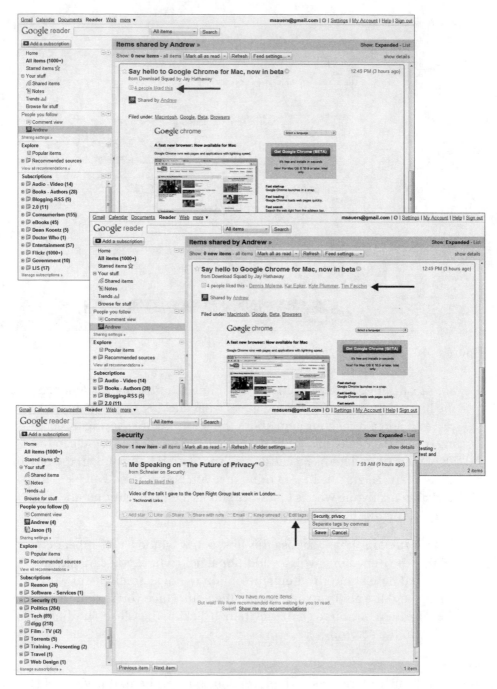

Figure 6.41   People liked this (closed) (top)

Figure 6.42   People liked this (open) (middle)

Figure 6.43   Tagging items (bottom)

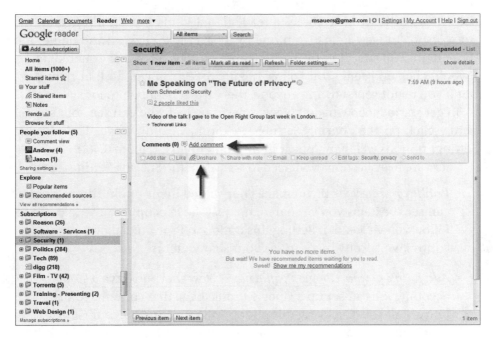

Figure 6.44   Sharing and unsharing items

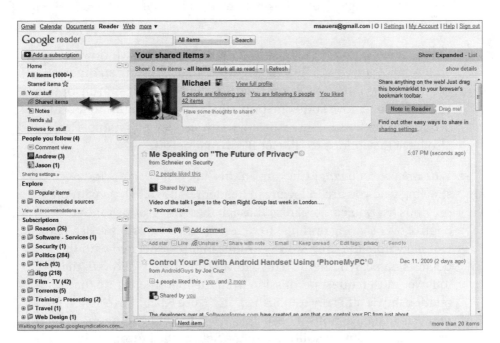

Figure 6.45   Displaying shared items

account I currently have three unread shared items from Andrew and one from Jason. To view items from one of them, I just click on the name and those items will appear in the content area. To view all of those shared items, I would click on People You Follow (Figure 6.47). You can do that right now, but if you're not yet following anyone, there won't be much to look at.

To get started following people and deciding just who can see your shared items, click on the Sharing Settings in the navigation pane. The Sharing Settings options will then appear in the content area (Figure 6.48).

There are five questions you need to answer in the Sharing Settings section:

- *Public or protected?* If you make your shared items public, then anyone can see the items you've shared, not just those people you've allowed to follow you via Reader. Setting this option to Protected allows you to control who, if anyone, can see your shared items.

- *Add a link to your Google Profile page?* Now that you have a Google account, you can set up a Google Profile page that contains information about you. Checking this option will put a link on your Google Profile page to your publicly shared items. Figure 6.49 shows the link on my Google Profile page (www.google.com/profiles/msauers). You can click on the Google Profile link here to set that up if you haven't already done so.

- *Who's following you?* Clicking on this link will open a window showing who is following you in Reader (Figure 6.50). Here you can organize your followers into groups for batch control over your sharing options. You can also remove someone from the list by clicking Unfollow in the dropdown Options menu associated with the person's name. Here you also have the options to Hide or Block that person.

- *Who are you following?* Clicking on this link will open a window showing who you are following in Reader (Figure 6.51). As with the previous list, you can organize these names into groups for batch control over sharing options. To remove someone from the list, choose Unfollow from the drop-down Options menu associated with the person's name. Whether you're following and being followed, the follower must request permission from the followee before that relationship is officially established. In Figure 6.52, I have sent a few requests that have not yet been approved. To follow someone, enter his or her name or email address into the field at the bottom of this window and Google will pass along your request. (Of course, they must also be a user of Google Reader for this to work.)

Figure 6.46   People you follow (top)

Figure 6.47   Displaying items shared by people you follow (middle)

Figure 6.48   Sharing settings (bottom)

- *Who can comment on your shared items?* Here you will see a list of your groups if you have created any. Groups, as previously mentioned, allow you to batch followers and assign permission accordingly. For example, you can create a batch named People I Know Personally and allow only those people to comment on your shared items. The creation of groups is done through Google Contacts, so I will not go into detail here.

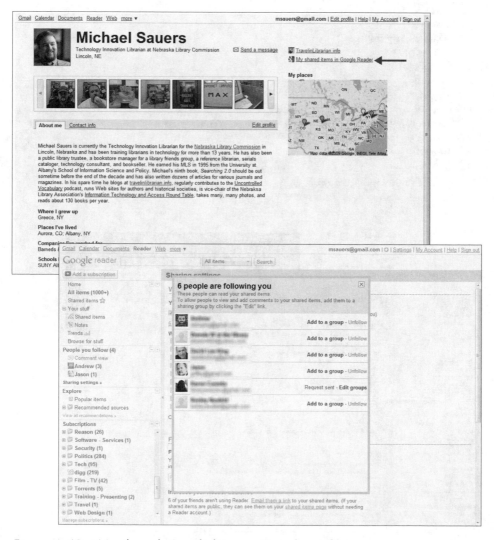

Figure 6.49   My shared items link in my Google profile
Figure 6.50   People who are following you

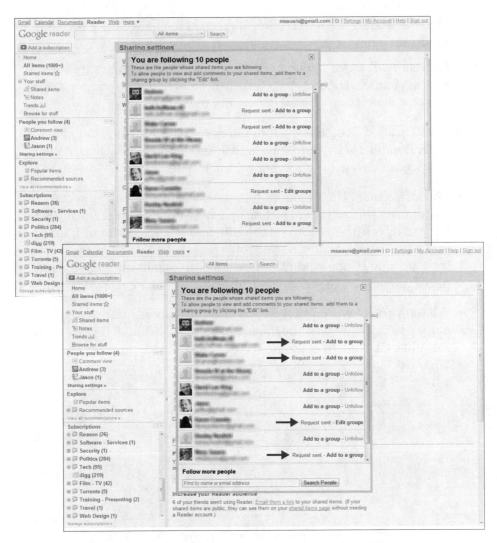

Figure 6.51   People you are following

Figure 6.52   Follow requests awaiting a response

In the Sharing Settings section, you can also find other Reader users by name or email address and send them an email request to follow them. Also, if you have friends who do not have a Reader account but you wish to allow them to see your shared items, click on Email Them a Link and supply their email address, and they'll be sent the necessary URL to view your shared items page.

Clicking on the Shared Items Page link will take you to your shared items page so you can view it as others will.

Lastly, the Sharing Settings section allows you to change the basic settings of your shared items page:

- *Preview your shared items page.* If you haven't already, click this link to look at your shared items page as others will see it. The page will open in a new window or tab based on your browser settings.

- *Choose a style.* Google offers four different styles for your shared items page: Default, Ice Cream, Ninja, and Sea. Feel free to try each of them and see which one best fits your personal style.

- *Choose a custom URL.* This option is only available if you've set up a customized URL as part of setting up your Google Profile. Once you've done that, you'll be able to set the URL for your shared items page so that it is similar to your Google Profile page URL. For example, compare the URL of my Google Profile given earlier to that of my shared items page (google.com/reader/shared/msauers).

- *Tell some friends.* As an easy way to tell others about your shared items page, you can use either the Email link to send an email (Figure 6.53) or the Add a Clip link to get some HTML code to place on your website (Figure 6.54).

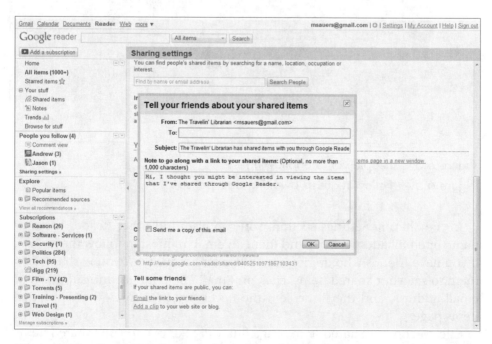

Figure 6.53 Sending an email about your shared items

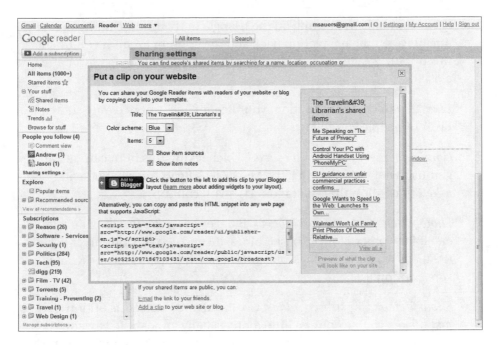

Figure 6.54   Putting a clip on your website

Managing Your Account

I've already covered two of the screens under Settings: Subscriptions and Import/Export. Now let's take a look at the rest of the settings area.

Preferences

There are eight settings under Preferences (Figure 6.55):

- *Language.* Set your default language here. This is the language that will be used if you chose Translate Into My Language earlier.

- *Start page.* This setting determines which content will be displayed when you log into your account. The default is Home, which was described earlier. The other options are: All Items, Starred Items, Posts, Links, Shared Items, People You Follow, Comment View, Popular Items, Explore, and any of the folders you have previously created.

- *Scroll tracking.* When this option is turned on (the default), an item is marked as read as long as you just scroll past it, regardless of whether you stop on that particular item.

- *Navigation pane display.* You can choose to hide the navigation pane to give you more room in which to display the item content. (This can be done manually by clicking on the triangle in the middle of the dividing line between the navigation page and the content area.) If you uncheck this option, Reader will start your sessions with the navigation pane closed.

- *Likes*. If you check this option, your Reader account will only show Likes of people you follow.

- *Confirm when marking all as read*. Unchecking this item can be dangerous. Whenever you click the Mark All as Read button, you will not be asked to confirm that operation. Use with caution.

- *Show followed blogs from Blogger*. Blogger has a feature in which you can follow other Blogger-based blogs. If you keep this option checked, the feeds from those blogs will automatically appear in your Reader subscription list.

- *Show favicons for subscriptions*. Go ahead and check this option as it just makes your account a little more visually appealing. Favicons are those customized icons a website can set up, which usually appear in your browser's address bar to the left of the URL. Checking this option instructs Reader to use the favicon for the site where the feed originates, instead of the generic RSS icon.

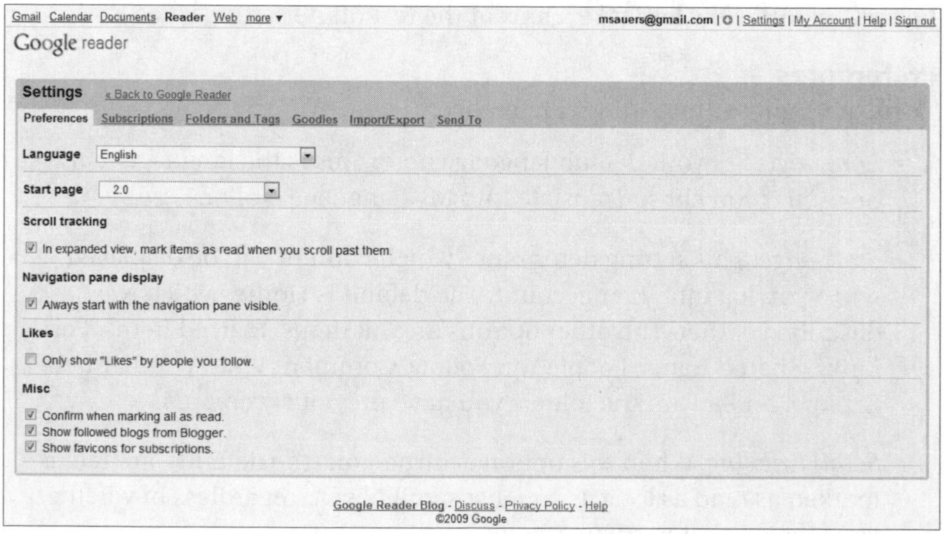

Figure 6.55   Settings: Preferences

Folders and Tags

This is another area under Settings that won't be relevant for you until you have set up some folders and tags. However, once you have, there's a lot you can do here. Again, let's use my account as an example (Figure 6.56).

Here is an alphabetical list of all the folders that I have created, with Your Starred Items and Your Shared Items at the top. As with the Subscriptions settings screen, you can perform actions on batches of folders by selecting them via the checkboxes to the left of the folder names. You can also select All *(N)* Tags, None, Public, or Private folders by clicking the appropriate link at the top of the list. Once you have made a batch selection, you can use the Change Sharing dropdown list to set all those folders to either Public or Private. Use the Delete Selected button to delete folders.

You can also perform the following actions on individual folders in the list:

- *Delete.* Click the trashcan icon next to an item to delete that folder. This option deletes only the folder and will not unsubscribe you from any feeds in that folder.

- *Make public/private.* Click on the orange icon to switch the folder between public and private.

The following options in this list will only be available for items you mark as public.

- *View public page.* Clicking this link shows you the public version of the content of the folder. This page will have the same design as your shared items page. It will not contain any information about what you have or have not read and will contain your Google Profile information if you have set that up (Figure 6.57).

- *Email a link.* Clicking this opens a new window that allows you to email a link to that folder's public page (Figure 6.58).

- *Add a clip to your site.* Clicking this link opens a new window that gives you customizable HTML that you can incorporate into your website linking back to recent items in that folder (Figure 6.59).

- *Add a blogroll to your site.* Clicking this link opens a new window that gives you customizable HTML you can incorporate into your website to display a list of links to the feeds in that folder (Figure 6.60).

Goodies

Goodies are little bonuses from Google that allow you to access certain features of Reader without necessarily having to be on the Reader page or even connected to the internet (Figure 6.61). There are five goodies available:

Figure 6.56   Settings: Folders and Tags (top)

Figure 6.57   My starred items page (closed) (middle)

Figure 6.58   Emailing friends about your shared items (open) (bottom)

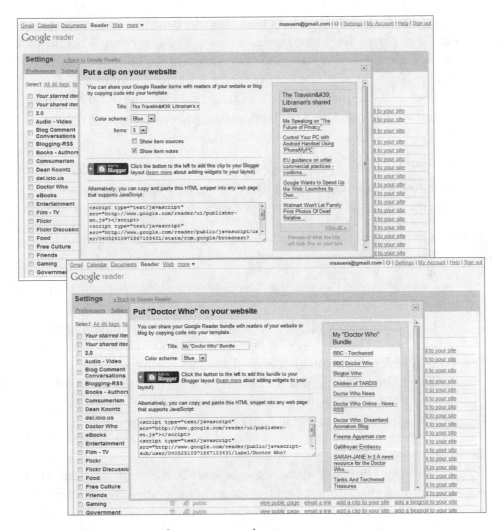

Figure 6.59   Putting a clip on your website

Figure 6.60   Putting a blogroll on your website

- *Add Reader to iGoogle*. iGoogle is a customizable Google page (www.google.com/ig). iGoogle is available through your Google account and includes the ability to add widgets (short bits of content or programming) to your page. To add the Reader widget to your iGoogle page, click the + Google button located here.

- *Put Reader in a bookmark*. This is another Reader bookmarklet. By installing this bookmarklet, you can just click it to automatically be sent to the source page of the first unread item in your Reader subscription list. That item will then be marked as read in your account. Clicking this bookmarklet again will take you to the next unread item. You can also set up a bookmarklet that does the same thing for a certain folder or tag. Select the appropriate folder or tag name from the list and then install the newly customized bookmarklet into your browser (Figure 6.62).

- *Use Reader on your phone.* This takes you to a version of Reader designed for small screens such as Windows Mobile phones, Android-based phones, and the iPhone (www.google.com/reader/m).

- *Subscribe as you surf.* This is the Subscribe bookmarklet described earlier in this chapter (see page 169).

- *Use Reader offline.* Generally Reader only works if you're connected to the internet. However, let's say you're planning on taking a flight without Wi-Fi, so you're going to be offline for several hours. To solve this problem, you can install either Google Gears or Google Chrome, both of which allow you to download all of your unread content for reading offline. Once you're back online again, your read items will be synched with your Reader account. Click the appropriate link for instructions on how to install either of these programs.

Send To

As previously mentioned, you can set up a Send To menu for each item that allows you to add functionality that sends an item's content to another service such as Delicious or Blogger. Here is where you can turn that feature on and decide which service you want available to you. Just check the boxes to select the items you wish to appear in the Send To menu. As you can see in Figure 6.63, I've selected Blogger, Delicious, Digg, and Twitter from the list provided. Choose whichever services are appropriate for you.

It is also possible to add other services that are not in this list by building your own URLs. You can see in Figure 6.64 that I've added the options to send to Instapaper and PDF. The instructions listed here aren't the greatest, but with a little practice you'll get the hang of it. To get you started, here is the URL to send to PDF:

```
http://savepageaspdf.pdfonline.com/pdfonline/pdf
online.asp?cURL=${url}
```

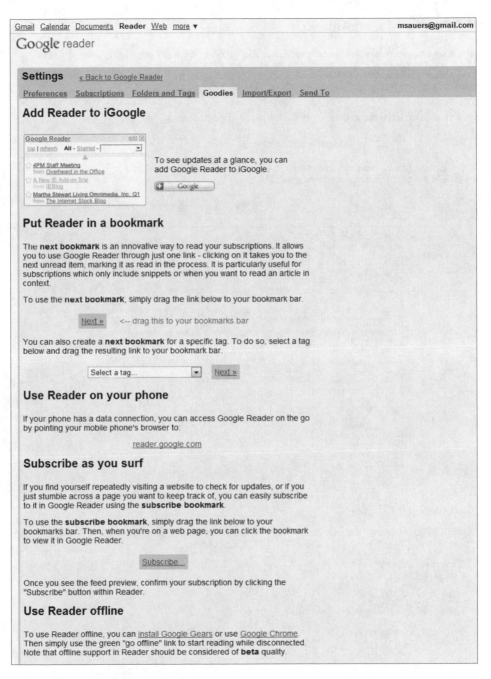

Figure 6.61   Settings: Goodies

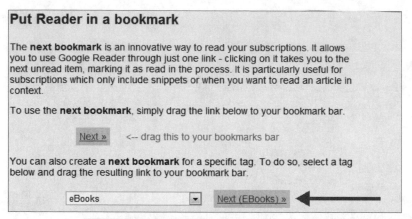

Put Reader in a bookmark

The **next bookmark** is an innovative way to read your subscriptions. It allows you to use Google Reader through just one link - clicking on it takes you to the next unread item, marking it as read in the process. It is particularly useful for subscriptions which only include snippets or when you want to read an article in context.

To use the **next bookmark**, simply drag the link below to your bookmark bar.

Next »   <-- drag this to your bookmarks bar

You can also create a **next bookmark** for a specific tag. To do so, select a tag below and drag the resulting link to your bookmark bar.

eBooks ▼   Next (EBooks) » ◄━━━━

Gmail Calendar Documents **Reader** Web more ▼   msauers@gmail.com

Google reader

Settings   « Back to Google Reader

Preferences   Subscriptions   Folders and Tags   Goodies   Import/Export   **Send To**

You can select some other sites and services to send your shared items to. Selected sites will show up in the "Send to:" menu at the bottom of each item.

Please note: For this feature to work, www.google.com needs to be on your pop-up blocker's list of allowed sites.

☑ 🅱 Blogger
☑ 🔖 Delicious
☑ 🔢 Digg
☐ 📘 Facebook
☐ 🍴 FriendFeed
☐ 📄 Instapaper
☐ 🅼 MySpace
☐ 🅿 Ping.fm
☐ 🅿 Posterous
☐ 🆁 Reddit
☐ 🆂 StumbleUpon
☐ 🆃 Tumblr
☑ 🅴 Twitter

Don't see your favorite site?

If your favorite site isn't listed above, you can add it manually. The following substitutions are applied to the URL:

Don't see your favorite site?

If your favorite site isn't listed above, you can add it manually. The following substitutions are applied to the URL:

${source} The source of the item

${title} The title of the item

${url} The URL of the item

${short-url} A shortened URL that redirects to the item

☑ 📄 Instapaper Edit | Delete
☑ 📄 PDF Edit | Delete

Create a custom link

Figure 6.62   Putting Reader in a bookmark (top)

Figure 6.63   Settings: Send to (built-in options) (middle)

Figure 6.64   Settings: Send to (adding additional options) (bottom)

To find other examples, just do a Google search for *google reader send to* and you'll find plenty more, including services such as Evernote and Wordpress.

Searching Google Reader

Searching Reader content is pretty straightforward, but it deserves a run-through since it is the best way to find those items that you remember reading last week but forgot to add a star to or email to yourself.

Reader's search box will be available to you on any Reader page (Figure 6.65) except when you're in the Settings area. Just enter your keywords into the search field, set your search limiter from the dropdown list, and click the Search button. The following limiters are available: All Items (default), Read Items, Starred Items, Shared Items, Liked Items, People You Follow, Notes, and each of your folders. Since this is in essence a Google search limited to the content of your Reader subscription, you can also use any of the regular Google Search operators (site:, link:, Boolean operators, etc.) for more specific searches.

Search results will be displayed in the content area (Figure 6.66). Each search result will include the item's title, an excerpt of the content with your keyword(s) bolded, the name of the source feed linked to that feed, the date of the item along with how long ago it was posted, and the option to star the result. A Refresh button is available to re-run the search in the event that you've searched for a hot topic that is updating constantly.

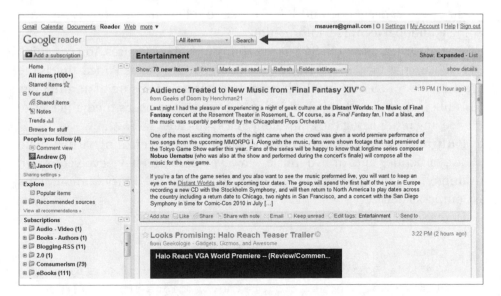

Figure 6.65   Google Reader search box

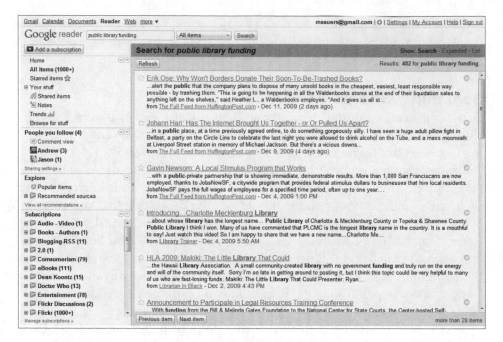

Figure 6.66   Google Reader search results

Podcasting and RSS

In Chapter 4, I introduced the concept of podcasting. Now that you have a grasp of the concepts behind RSS, I'd like to follow up on podcasting with some additional technical information.

One of the features of RSS 2.0 is the ability to add enclosures. You can think of enclosures as the RSS equivalent of attachments in email. Podcasting is the creation of an RSS feed in which each item has an enclosure of an MP3 file. This file is then downloaded and played back on the user's media player of choice, the result being the equivalent of a syndicated radio show.

Early podcasts were mostly music-related—authors creating virtual radio shows of bootleg and/or live music. However, podcasts have evolved. As an example, let's look at a podcast I produce, the Nebraska Library Commission's NCompass Podcast.

Here's some of the code for the podcast feed:

```
<item>
  <title>Episode 29: Twitter Tips & Tricks</title>
<link>http://www.nlc.state.ne.us/blogs/NLC/2009/0
9/ncompass_podcast_episode_29.html</link>
```

```
<description><p>So, you've got a Twitter
account, you post every so often and you fol-
low a few folks. But what else is there? How
can you get more out of Twitter? Join Michael
Sauers, the NLC's Technology Innovation
Librarian, as he shows you some advanced tips
and tricks that will help you use Twitter more
efficiently for your library and for yourself.
</p> <ul> <li><a href="http://delicious.com/
travelinlibrarian/twitter">Presentation
Links</a></li> <li><a href="http://www.twit-
ter.com/">Twitter</a></li> </ul></description>
<enclosure url="http://www.nlc.state.ne.us/
nlcpodcast/NCompassPodcast029.mp3"
length="56760573" type="audio/mpeg" />
<pubDate>Thu, 03 Sep 2009 12:53:13
GMT</pubDate>
<guid isPermaLink="true">NLCpodcast-2009-09-03-
12-53-13</guid>
</item>
```

The key segment of code in this example is the `<enclosure>` line, bolded in the code example. This is the link from the feed to the particular MP3 file associated with this post. If you're using a common aggregator, you'll be provided with a link to the MP3 file, which you can then download and play in any MP3-supporting media player, software, or hardware.

To be very clear, you *do not* need an iPod to take advantage of podcasting—you can use Windows Media Player, WinAmp, or any player that plays MP3 files.

If you *are* the owner of an iPod or other high-end MP3 player such as Microsoft's Zune, you can take the concept of podcasting up a level and have the MP3 files downloaded automatically into desktop software for that device, so that the next time you sync your device, the new files are transferred to it. In fact, I even have software on my Droid smartphone, Google Listen (listen.googlelabs.com), that allows me to subscribe to, download, and play podcast content directly on my phone.

Before you can subscribe to a podcast, you first need to find the URL for the feed. Many sites that offer podcasts today have icons on their pages linking to the appropriate feed file.

The Coverville webpage (www.coverville.com) shown in Figure 6.67, provides you with four different ways to subscribe to the podcast. The iTunes link will automatically launch iTunes (assuming it is installed on the computer) and subscribe you to the podcast. The Zune link will perform a similar function for Microsoft Zune owners. The RSS link works just like any other feed link and needs to be copied into an aggregator that allows for podcast subscriptions. Lastly, the Email link will take you to a page where you can enter your email address and receive links to new episodes that way.

Figure 6.68 shows the Podcast icon on the Nebraska Library Commission's website. In this case, if you are an iPod owner and would like to subscribe to the NCompass Podcast, you must perform the process manually since an automatic link is not provided. First, right-click on the Podcast link and copy the link's URL. Next, open iTunes and select Advanced and then Subscribe to Podcast from the menu (Figure 6.69). You will be shown the Subscribe to Podcast screen (Figure 6.70).

Paste the podcast's URL into the box and click OK. The new podcast, NCompass Podcast in this example, will be listed in iTunes' Podcast area, and iTunes will check the NCompass site for available episodes (Figure 6.71). In this example, there are four episodes available. The latest one (being Episode 30 here) will be automatically downloaded for you. To get additional episodes, click on the Get button to the right of the episode's title.

The small blue dot to the left of an episode title indicates that the episode has not been listened to yet. A dot to the right of a podcast's name indicates that it contains episodes that have not been listened to yet. To delete a particular episode or an entire podcast, right-click on the title and select Clear.

iTunes offers several options for managing podcast subscriptions. These options can be found by clicking the Settings button in the bottom-left corner of the screen that lists your subscribed podcasts. Here you can set how often iTunes should check for new episodes (Every hour, Every Day, Every Week, or Manually), what to download when it finds new episodes (Download All, Download Most Recent One, or Do Nothing), and which episodes to keep (All Episodes, All Unplayed Episodes, Most Recent Episodes, or the last two, three, four, five, or 10 episodes). If you check Use Default Settings for a particular podcast, some of these settings will be grayed out (Figure 6.72).

Remember, you do *not* need an iPod or iTunes to listen to podcasts, they just make it much easier.

Now that you know how to use an aggregator, let's move on to Chapter 7 where we'll take a look at some feeds to which you may want to subscribe.

Keeping all this in mind, if you don't want or need all of the features of iTunes to access podcasts, you can also use Google Reader. Just subscribe to the URL of the podcast feed as you would any text-based feed in Reader. Reader will automatically add a player widget to each episode allowing you to play and/or download each episode (Figure 6.73).

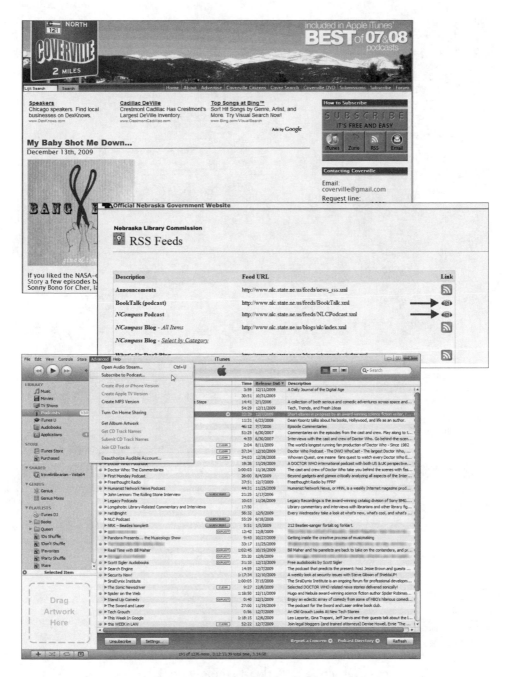

Figure 6.67   Coverville's podcast feed links (top)

Figure 6.68   The Nebraska Library Commission's podcast feed links (middle)

Figure 6.69   iTunes: Subscribe to Podcast menu item (bottom)

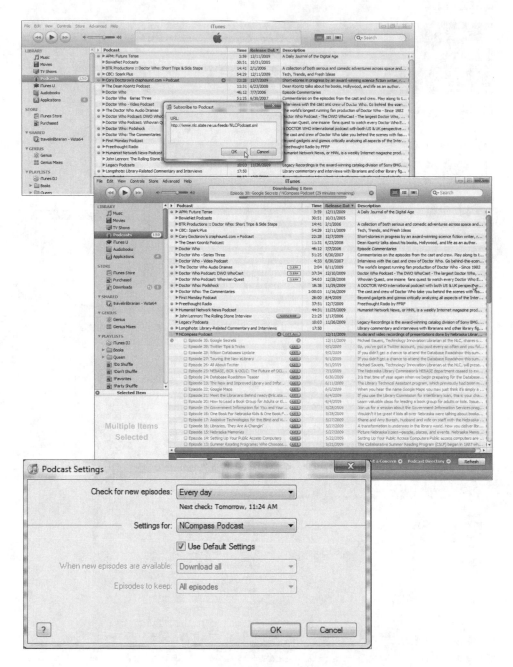

Figure 6.70   iTunes: Subscribe to Podcast window (top)

Figure 6.71   Downloading the latest episode of a podcast (middle)

Figure 6.72   iTunes: Podcast settings (bottom)

Figure 6.73   Podcast subscription displayed in Google Reader

Endnotes

1. "Aggregator," Wikipedia, The Free Encyclopedia, en.wikipedia.org/wiki/Feed_aggregator (accessed March 20, 2010).

2. A more complete list of aggregators along with links to their websites can be found on Comparison of feed aggregators page on Wikipedia (en.wikipedia.org/wiki/Comparison_of_feed_aggregators).

Chapter 7

Noteworthy Feeds

This chapter will introduce you to a number of potentially useful resources, including library, news, RSS (offering aggregated content), and miscellaneous feeds and services. Note that the library and librarian blogs covered in Chapters 2 and 3 have feeds available from their sites; these resources are not repeated in this chapter, so be sure to check them out in addition to those included here.

The URLs supplied here, in most cases, are for webpages where the relevant feeds may be found. I provide these rather than the URLs of the feeds to minimize the chance of confusion (should the URL of a feed change) and because certain sites have multiple feeds available. In the few cases where I've listed the URL of the feed itself, it is so noted.

Library and Library-Related Feeds

Hennepin County Library— Subject Guides and Search Results

www.hclib.org/pub/search/RSS.cfm

The Hennepin County Library (Minneapolis, MN) makes its subject guides available to patrons and anyone else interested in subscribing to them via RSS (Figure 7.1). As the librarians add new resources, subscribers are notified via the feeds. Subjects range from Library News to Genealogy to Jobs & Careers. There is also a comprehensive feed for those interested in being notified of all additions to every available subject.

In addition to the librarian-created subject feeds, the library offers patrons the ability to create RSS feeds based on catalog searches. A patron performs an OPAC search and receives a link to an RSS feed of those results. Figure 7.2 shows the results of my author search for *koontz, dean*. If I were to subscribe to the resulting feed, I would be notified automatically whenever a new Dean Koontz book was added to the library's collection.

Amazon.com—RSS Web Feeds for Tags

www.amazon.com/gp/help/customer/display.html?nodeId=200202840

Amazon.com currently offers many different feeds based on categories within the system (Figure 7.3). Just look for the RSS icon throughout the site. Additionally, a nearly unlimited number of feeds is offered based on the user tagging system. These feeds can cover everything from individual product tags to certain tags on products from certain users.

Nebraska Library Commission—RSS Feeds

www.nlc.state.ne.us/feeds/feeds.asp

The Nebraska Library Commission is where I currently work as the Technology Innovation Librarian so you should have seen this one coming. Here we offer feeds of our blog content, announcements, podcasts, Flickr photos, and more (Figure 7.4). We're expanding this list as often and as fast as we possibly can.

OCLC—RSS Feeds and Podcasts

www.oclc.org/rss

OCLC started offering feeds in early 2005. In May of the same year, the organization posted a single page of all its available feeds (Figure 7.5). With 20 feeds and counting, the topics range from the general (the 10 most recent OCLC news items) to specific products (WorldCat) and services (Dewey Journal: "all the latest Dewey Decimal Classification® news and announcements, DDC mappings, and tips").

Unshelved

www.unshelved.com

Welcome to the Mallville Public Library and its wonderful cast of characters created by Bill Barnes and Gene Ambaum. If you're not already reading Unshelved (Figure 7.6), shame on you. Although you can read the daily strip (and access the archives) on the website, why not make it easier on yourself and receive the comic every morning in your aggregator?

ipl2

www.ipl.org

ipl2 is a public service organization and a learning/teaching environment. To date, thousands of students and volunteer library and information science professionals have been involved in answering reference questions for the Ask an ipl2 Librarian service and in designing, building, creating, and maintaining the ipl2 collections. It is through the efforts of these students and volunteers

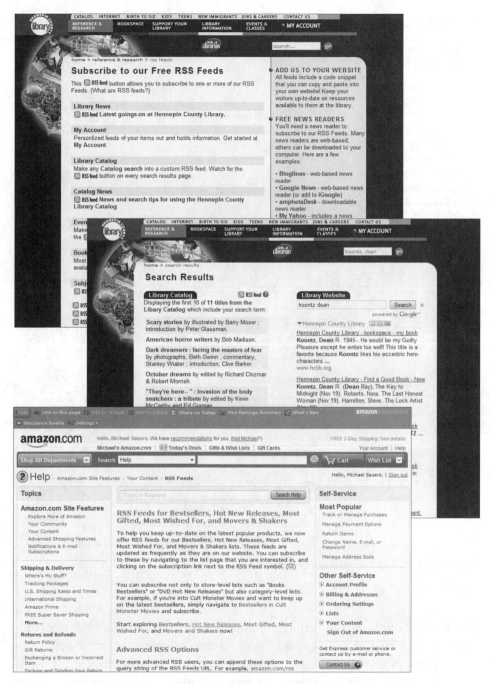

Figure 7.1   Hennepin County Library feeds page (top)

Figure 7.2   Hennepin County Library search results (middle)

Figure 7.3   Amazon.com tag feeds (bottom)

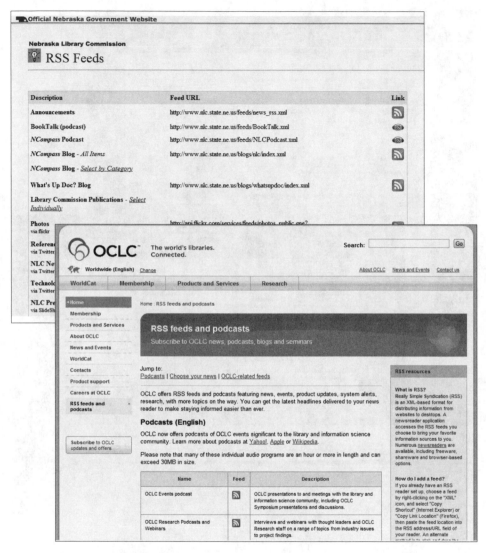

Figure 7.4 Nebraska Library Commission feeds

Figure 7.5 OCLC feeds

that the ipl2 continues to thrive. In January 2010, the website "ipl2: information you can trust" was launched, merging the collections of resources from the Internet Public Library (IPL) and the Librarians' Internet Index (LII) websites. The site is hosted by Drexel University's College of Information Science and Technology, and a consortium of colleges and universities with programs in information science are involved in developing and maintaining the ipl2 (Figure 7.7).

TOCs: Journal Tables of Contents Service
www.tictocs.ac.uk

TOCs contains a searchable database of thousands of scholarly journal tables of contents. Once you have found the journal(s) you're interested in, you can create a custom RSS feed that will send you the tables of contents from those publications as they become available (Figure 7.8).

Encyclopædia Britannica Online—Daily Content
www.britannica.com/eb/dailycontent/rss

Encyclopædia Britannica Online offers a feed for the daily content as presented on its home page (Figure 7.9). The feed typically contains links to articles on current events, "this day in history," and highlighted biographies.

University of Saskatchewan Library— Electronic Journals
library.usask.ca/ejournals/rss_feeds.php

Darryl Friesen and Peter Scott at the University of Saskatchewan Library have put together an online directory of electronic journals that provides RSS feeds (Figure 7.10), usually of their tables of contents. The directory can be sorted alphabetically by title or by publisher/source and can be searched.

WorldCat Lists
www.worldcat.org

Users of WorldCat.org can create their own lists based on subject headings and search results. These lists automatically supply RSS feeds so as new results to particular list get added you get notified. For example, see the RSS4Lib RSS list at www.worldcat.org/profiles/varnumk/lists/53691. The link to the RSS feed can be found in the upper-right corner of the page (Figure 7.11).

News Feeds

BBC—News Feeds
news.bbc.co.uk/2/hi/help/3223484.stm

At just 23 available feeds, the BBC (Figure 7.12) may not have the most comprehensive or specific list of feeds, but it is a good source for non-U.S.-centric news.

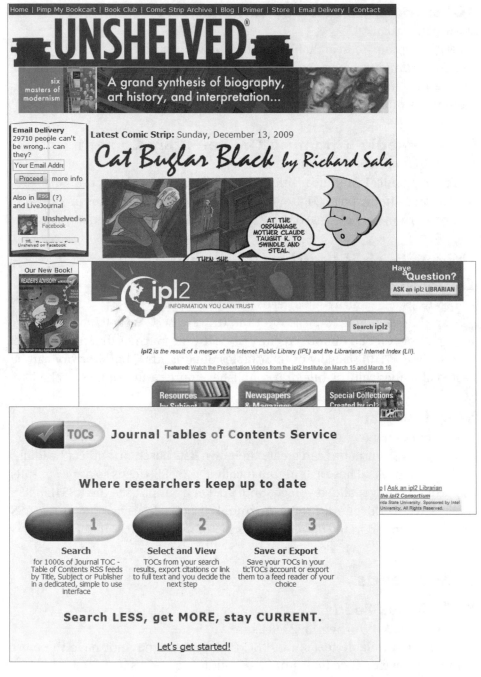

Figure 7.6   Unshelved (top)

Figure 7.7   ipl2 (middle)

Figure 7.8   Journal Tables of Contents Service (bottom)

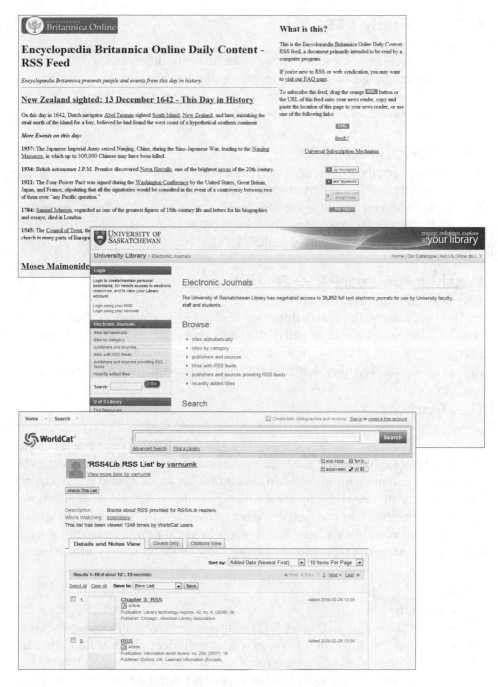

Figure 7.9   Encyclopædia Britannica Online Daily Content feed (top)
Figure 7.10   University of Saskatchewan Electronic Journals (middle)
Figure 7.11   WorldCat lists (bottom)

C|Net—Simply RSS

www.cnet.com/rss

C|Net is a well-known authoritative site for news about technology. Each of its categories contains an average of a dozen specific feeds (Figure 7.13). Anyone in charge of keeping public computers up and running smoothly will want to check out the Insecurity Complex feed.

New York Times—RSS

www.nytimes.com/services/xml/rss/index.html

With more than 100 different feeds, nearly all of the content of the New York Times online is available via RSS. Feeds range from the major news categories (with many subdivisions) to Culture & Lifestyle, as well as 40 different feeds from their opinion writers (Figure 7.14).

Washington Post—RSS Feeds

www.washingtonpost.com/wp-dyn/rss

Also with more than 100 different feeds, the Washington Post online (Figure 7.15) comes in well ahead of the pack. Its feeds cover broad categories that are also divided into narrower topics, such as discrete sports leagues, individual opinion writers, business policy, and specific geographic regions.

GovTrack.us

www.govtrack.us

The GovTrack.us website (Figure 7.16) collects legislative information from the Library of Congress and the U.S. House and Senate websites and offers it in one convenient location. You can sign up for an account and track particular subjects or use the site without an account to track all legislation. Whichever method you use, you can elect to receive a feed of current legislation showing which votes have taken place. Selecting an item within a feed sends you back to the GovTrack.us site for more detailed voting information.

Fark

www.fark.com

Drew Curtis's Fark.com (Figure 7.17) is the single largest site for news of the weird and obscure. If it's an odd news story, you'll hear about it here first. In many cases, the headlines are even funnier than the stories themselves. Note, however, that some of the stories are not appropriate for all viewers (these are marked NSFW, "Not Safe For Work").

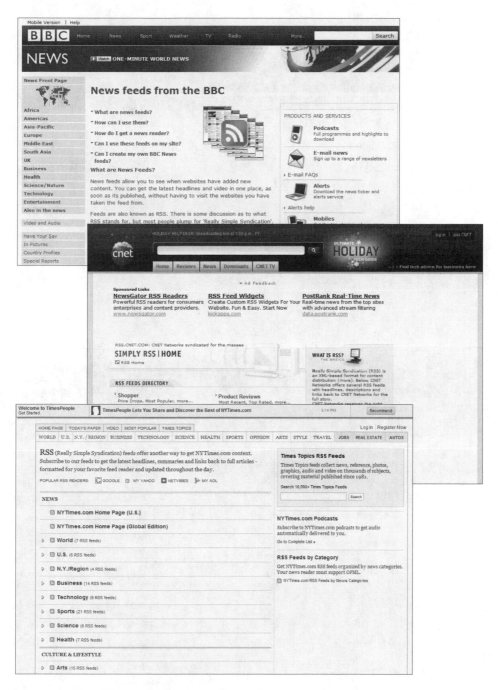

Figure 7.12 BBC news feeds (top)

Figure 7.13 CINet feeds (middle)

Figure 7.14 New York Times feeds (bottom)

Figure 7.15   Washington Post feeds

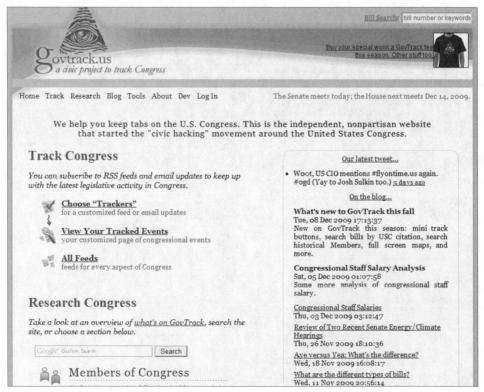

Figure 7.16   GovTrack.us

USA.gov and Pueblo—RSS Feeds

www.usa.gov/rss/index.shtml

USA.gov is the official portal for all information relating to the U.S. federal government. This page is a directory of official government RSS feeds broken down into subject categories ranging from agriculture to cybersecurity to the military. Pueblo is Federal Citizen Information Center, the publishers of those familiar government brochures you ordered from Pueblo, Colorado (Figure 7.18).

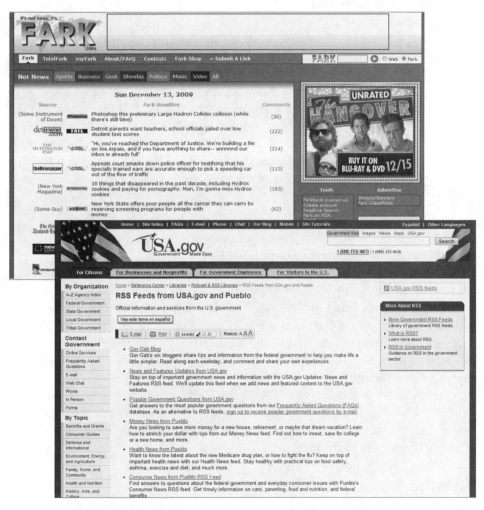

Figure 7.17   Fark.com (top)

Figure 7.18   USA.gov and Pueblo—RSS Feeds (bottom)

RSS Services

The feeds we've looked at thus far are known as static feeds—their content is written by a single individual (or organization) and then subscribed to by the reader. There arc, however, a number of RSS-based services available, many of which allow the user to perform searches across various databases with results delivered via an aggregator as an RSS feed. Although some of the listed resources may not be directly relevant to libraries, all illustrate the value of this type of service.

Google News—RSS

news.google.com

While the *New York Times* and *Washington Post* are considered the authorities in news, people are often looking for multiple viewpoints on a particular topic. This is where the Google News service can be of benefit. According to Google, "Google News gathers stories from more than 4,500 news sources in English worldwide" and is "updated nearly constantly." To take advantage of news feeds, perform a search (Figure 7.19) and then subscribe to the feed via the link at the bottom of the results page. One word of warning: I sometimes receive many duplicate results from the feed. If you're willing to overlook this flaw—which I hope will be corrected soon—this is an amazing news-based resource.

Gmail

gmail.google.com/gmail/feed/atom (feed)

If you have a Gmail account, you can choose to read your email messages in your aggregator. (You cannot, however, perform any other function such as replying or forwarding.) Any message in your Gmail inbox that is marked as unread will appear as part of the feed. Once you've logged into your Gmail account and opened a message, thereby marking it as read, it will no longer appear in the feed. This feature functions basically as an aggregator-based new mail notification.

The URL listed above is the URL of the feed itself—that is, what you subscribe to. Since each Gmail account is secured with a username and password, this service will only work with aggregators that support SSL/HTTPS and HTTP authentication (Figure 7.20).

isbn.nu

isbn.nu

isbn.nu is a service run by freelance writer Glenn Fleishman that allows users to search for books by title, author, subject, or ISBN. The results provide the prices for a given book in many different online bookstores, including Amazon.com, Barnes & Noble, Books-A-Million, Alibris, and ABEbooks. Each results page has embedded links to RSS feeds, allowing you to subscribe to those results and track changes in pricing and availability of a title.

Figure 7.21 shows Fleishman's blog post explaining how the system works (blog.glennf.com/mtarchives/004668.html) while Figure 7.22 shows a sample result. To subscribe to a feed, either perform an isbn.nu search and subscribe from the results page or build your own URL. To build your own URL, copy the URL listed for this entry and replace *isbn* with the actual ISBN of the book you want to track.

LibraryElf

www.libraryelf.com

LibraryElf may be the best current example of how RSS can and should be used in a library to the benefit of the patrons. My only disappointment is that neither a librarian nor a library vendor developed it; JANDI Enterprises Inc. ("a privately held company based in Vancouver, British Columbia") was the developer.

LibraryElf gives patrons access to notification of several events related to their library account. As a user, I'm automatically notified when a hold is ready to be picked up, when an item is due in three days, and when an item becomes overdue. What is truly amazing about this free service is that I can be notified via a feed in my aggregator *or* via email *or* via an SMS text message

Figure 7.19   Google News RSS

Figure 7.20   Gmail feed (top)

Figure 7.21   Subscribe to Book Price Changes at isbn.nu (middle)

Figure 7.22   isbn.nu result (bottom)

on my cell phone. (Personally, I find the cell phone notification to be the most useful, but I also receive RSS notifications.)

Getting LibraryElf to work with your library account is, in most cases, a two-step process. First, you create an account on the LibraryElf site, so that only you have access to your data. During this process, you set options including how you want to be notified (RSS, SMS, and/or email), when you'd like to be notified of pending due items, and how often you'd like to be notified of overdue items (Figure 7.23).

The second step, which is necessary only if you are the first person from your library to register for the service, is to add your particular library's system to the LibraryElf system. Because there are many different ILS systems comprising many different options and customizations, LibraryElf needs to be set up to work with each one individually. In my experience, this setup generally takes only one or two days. (If your library is already listed in the system, there is no need to perform this step.) After that, just sit back and wait for the notifications to arrive.

Figures 7.24 and 7.25 show sample notifications as they appear in Google Reader and as an email message, respectively.

However, library privacy advocates have expressed concerns about library patrons giving their login information to third parties (blog.librarylaw.com/librarylaw/2005/11/my_library_elf_.html). LibraryElf does clarify the risks and notes that the decision to share such information should be made by the patron rather than the library.

Miscellaneous Feeds and Services

The feeds covered in this section aren't necessarily LIS-related or of particular use to most librarians, but they are interesting or creative enough to be of note.

craigslist

www.craigslist.org

craigslist (Figure 7.26) was started in 1995 as a way for San Francisco Bay-area residents to sell and exchange items online. Since then, it has grown to include more than 500 cities in 50 countries worldwide, and includes categories for personals, "free stuff," jobs, tickets, and housing, along with many discussion forums. Each category in each city has an associated RSS feed that can be found at the bottom right-hand corner of the page.

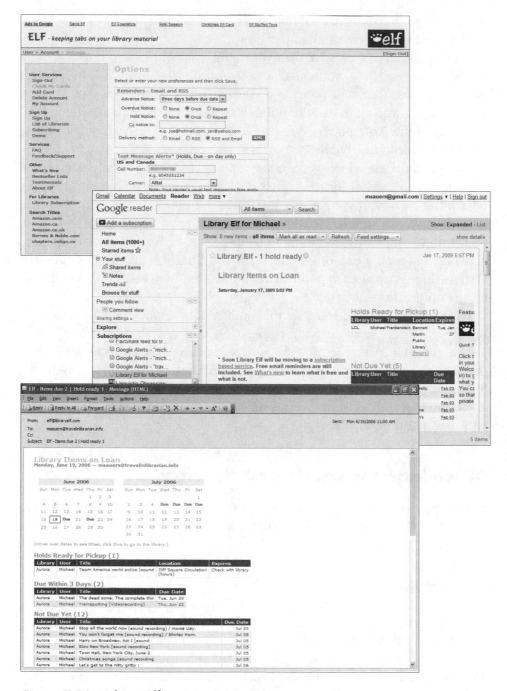

Figure 7.23   LibraryElf options (top)

Figure 7.24   LibraryElf notice via RSS (middle)

Figure 7.25   LibraryElf notice via email (bottom)

Flickr

www.flickr.com

Would you like to be notified every time I post a new photo to my Flickr account? How about every time someone posts a new photo tagged *library*? You can find RSS feeds from Flickr by heading to the bottom of either a user's photostream page or the bottom of a search results page (Figure 7.27).

Wikipedia—Changes

www.wikipedia.org

Interested in knowing whenever a specific article in Wikipedia has been edited without having to log into Wikipedia and access your watch page? Just head on over the history page for that article and look for the link to the RSS feed in the left sidebar (Figure 7.28).

eBay—Searches

www.rssauction.com

If you are a regular buyer and/or seller on eBay, you know that it's necessary to re-run your searches on a regular basis. Forgetting to run a search even one day can cause you to miss out on that perfect item you've been looking for at just the right price. With the help of the Custom eBay Searches service from Lockergnome, you can create your perfect eBay search and then subscribe to the results as an RSS feed.

Complete all the information relevant to your search and then submit it (Figure 7.29) using the Create Feed button. The service will return to you the URL for your new feed, along with HTML and JavaScript code for including it within a webpage of your own. You can then subscribe to the URL in your aggregator.

iTunes—Music Store RSS Feed Generator

ax.itunes.apple.com/rss

Every Tuesday, Apple's iTunes (Figure 7.30) service releases an electronic newsletter featuring music that is newly available through the service. Apple also provides this information via RSS. To take advantage of the feeds, you must first access the iTunes Music Store RSS Feed Generator. Select the types of music you're interested in, set a few additional options at the top, and then click the Generate button to receive the URL of the RSS feed.

Packagetrackr

www.packagetrackr.com

If you've ever tracked a package online, you know that it can be inconvenient to return to a webpage every few hours and re-enter a lengthy tracking

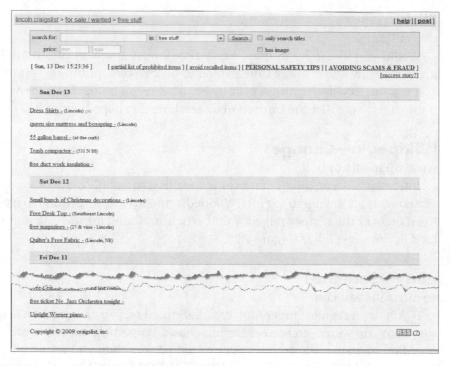

Figure 7.26   craigslist category feed

Figure 7.27   Flickr photostream feed

Figure 7.28   Wikipedia revision history feed (top)
Figure 7.29   eBay feeds (middle)
Figure 7.30   iTunes Store RSS (bottom)

number to see the status of your package. Packagetrackr is an RSS-based solution available to you.

Just create a Packagetrackr account and start entering your tracking numbers. To subscribe to the feed for a package, just copy the URL for that package's Packagetrackr page into you aggregator (Figure 7.31).

Delicious

delicious.com

Delicious is a "social bookmarks manager." It allows members to post their bookmarks and to add tags—metadata—to each posted link. Users of the site may then search through the combined collection based on the member or associated "tags" of the bookmarks. The social aspect is "its ability to let you see the links that others have collected, as well as showing you who else has bookmarked a specific site. You can also view the links collected by others, and subscribe to the links of people whose lists you find interesting." The subscription feature is why this site is listed here. Each tag and each user has an associated RSS feed to which you can subscribe, so you can receive automatic notification whenever a new bookmark relating to your topic of interest or a bookmark by a particular user is added to the system (Figure 7.32).

Topix.net

www.topix.net

Topix scours and indexes more than 10,000 news sources and organizes them into 150,000 topix.net pages. What makes Topix unique is that these pages cover "all 32,500 U.S. ZIP codes, 5,500 public company and industry verticals, 48,000 celebrities and musicians, 1,500 sports teams and personalities, and many, many more. Pretty soon, millions of people were visiting the site every month." Each one of these pages, along with search results, can be syndicated via RSS (Figure 7.33).

Traffic Conditions Data

ejohn.org/blog/traffic-conditions-data

John Resig, who created this feed service for anyone interested in traffic conditions, was "poking around the Dashboard Widget archive on the official Apple site and spotted a Yahoo! Traffic Conditions widget. This is interesting because they are somehow getting the data from their website in an easy-to-parse format. So, I peeked under the hood and, sure enough, there's an RSS feed for traffic conditions!"

Resig's blog explains how to construct a URL by hand for a feed appropriate for your area (to explain how it works to a more technical audience) and includes a form that helps you build the feed's URL automatically. Options for the feed results include setting a radius around your ZIP code area for which details are provided, and the level of severity of a given traffic condition (minor, moderate, major, or critical) (Figure 7.34).

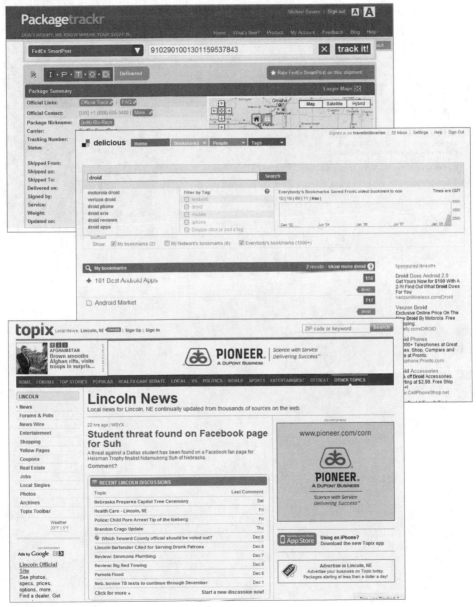

Figure 7.31   Packagetrackr (top)

Figure 7.32   Delicious (middle)

Figure 7.33   Topix (bottom)

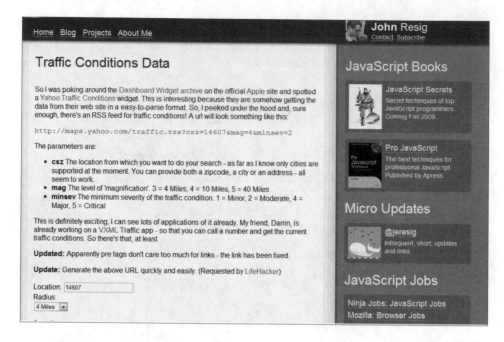

Figure 7.34   Traffic Conditions Data

Chapter 8

Creating Feeds

Feeds can be created in three ways: Hand rolling, semi-automated, or fully automated. The method you use depends largely on the source of your content: Is your feed based on a blog, in which case your content already exists, or are you creating a feed from scratch?

You may also want to consider the different feed versions available, as discussed under "Feed Types" in Chapter 5. However, before you flip back to review the features of the various versions, keep in mind that the specific software product or service you use to create your feed is unlikely to give you a choice. Each product or service supports a given feed version that you cannot change. My suggestion is not to worry about the version—just create the feed. If at some point you feel that your feed would benefit from a particular feature that your current product or service does not support, you can consider other options.

Hand Rolling

Hand rolling is writing an RSS file completely by hand. Even experienced coders don't generally hand roll feeds. If your feed is providing syndication for a blog, there is no sense in writing the feed by hand, as you will end up writing your content twice—once for the blog and once for the feed. Still, I encourage you to try hand rolling once because it will give you a greater appreciation for the code, as well as some comfort with hand editing. If you decide to hand roll a feed, these guidelines will save you some time and aggravation:

- Use copy and paste to reproduce the content of your blog entries in the RSS file instead of retyping the content.

- Set up templates. Once you've decided which version of RSS to use, create a template file that contains all of the code but none of the content. Save this file and then use it to create future feeds. Additionally, within a feed, add a mini-template for a new item. Include items such as

`<item>`, `<title>`, `<link>`, and `<description>` and place them within comment markers. Then when you want to add new items, simply make a copy of the code and add the relevant content.

Hand rolling is not a real-life solution for most of us since simple and time-efficient feed creation is our main goal.

Semi-Automated

If your RSS feed isn't blog-based, there are several programs designed to assist you in writing your code. I refer to these programs as "semi-automated" as they add the relevant code and, in some cases, even publish the feed to your server at the click of a button; however, you will still need to type the content yourself. Some of the programs available are RSS Feeds Generator (www.rss feedssubmit.com/rss-generator), Feedity (feedity.com), and Absolute RSS Editor (www.alentum.com/rsseditor). For this section, I'll be using ListGarden (www.softwaregarden.com/products/listgarden) in my examples as that's the one I've been using for several years.

ListGarden

ListGarden is a free Perl program from Software Garden (www.softwaregarden. com/products/listgarden) that allows you to create RSS 2.0 feeds without writing any code. To use ListGarden, download either the Windows or Mac client or the UNIX/LINUX server version. Which version to use depends on your environment:

- If you have a Windows-based web server, you must use the Windows client since there is no Windows server version.

- The client version is designed for use on a single machine. It is also possible to install it on a LAN and run it from multiple computers in the building. Setting up the client version on a network location will allow for multiple users but will not allow for editing outside of the LAN.

- The server version lets users access the program and edit the feeds from any internet-connected computer (when installed in the proper password-protected directory, with permissions set accordingly). Choose the server version if remote editing is a necessary feature for you.

Once the program is installed, it is a simple two-step process to access it. For the server version, enter the appropriate URL for your installation and submit the username and password as required. The client version requires that you run the program (which will place an icon in your system tray) and

Figure 8.1   The ListGarden icon in the Windows system tray

double-click the system tray icon (Figure 8.1) to open the program in your default browser (Figure 8.2).

When you first install ListGarden, there will not be any feeds available— you'll need to create one. First, select a name for your feed (from one to 10 characters in length). This is not the name your subscribers will see, but rather one that will be used by ListGarden to track your various feeds. As a demonstration, we'll create a new feed for a library's public programs called *pubprogs*, entering that title into the appropriate field and clicking the Create button (Figure 8.3).

Next, we're presented with a screen requesting the channel's basic information to be entered into the following fields:

- *Title*. In this field, enter the name of the channel the way you want your subscribers to see it. The title should be brief, yet sufficiently descriptive of the content of your channel.

- *Link*. This field should contain the URL of the webpage that corresponds to the channel of this field. If you're creating a channel based on a blog, enter the blog's URL. Otherwise, enter the URL of the corresponding webpage. For our demonstration, we'll use the URL of the page on the library's site that contains a public programs listing.

- *Description*. In this field, enter a narrative description of the content of the feed. Although you may write as much as you like, I recommend that you limit the description to a few sentences. Do be creative, however, because potential subscribers may base a decision to subscribe to your feed solely on the description.

Figure 8.4 shows the basic channel information completed for our sample feed. Once you've completed the three fields, click the Save button to create your feed. You'll be sent back to the opening page of the program where you will see the new feed listed along with any others that you may have previously created. The feed you are currently working on (*pubprogs* in this example) will be highlighted in green. To work on a different feed, click on the Select button next to the name of the feed you want.

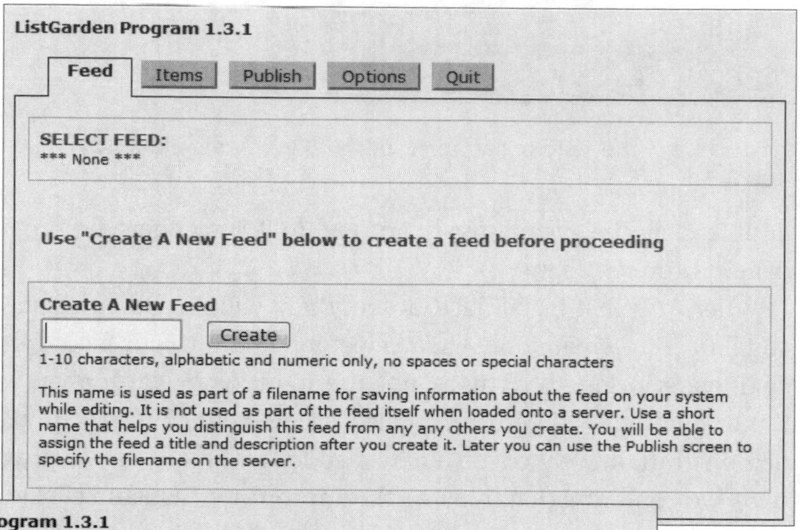

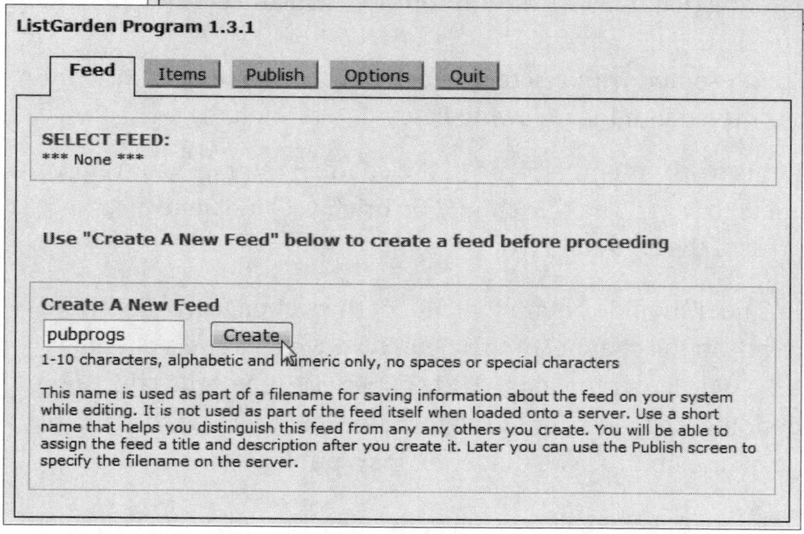

Figure 8.2   ListGarden (top)

Figure 8.3   Creating a new feed (bottom)

If at any time you want to change the title, link, or description of your feed, simply select that feed and click on the Edit button (Figure 8.5). This will take you back to the Channel Information screen.

You can also use the Channel Information screen to delete a feed. To do so, scroll down to Delete an Existing Feed, select the appropriate feed, and click the Delete button (Figure 8.6).

Once you've created your feed, you'll need to put some items into it. The most straightforward method of doing this is to click the Add button (Figure

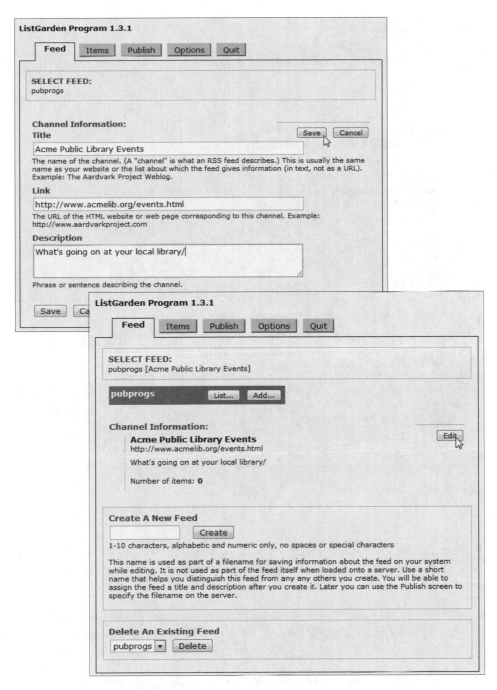

Figure 8.4   Channel information completed (top)
Figure 8.5   Edit button (bottom)

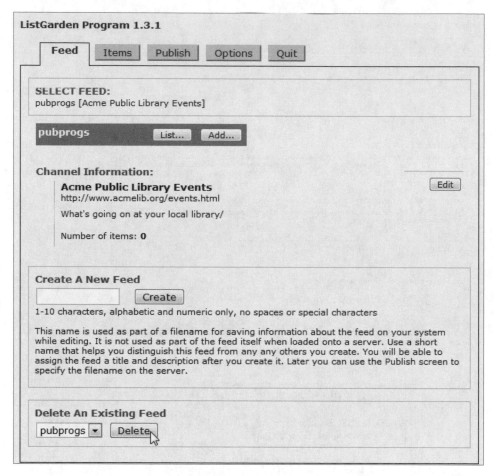

Figure 8.6   Delete button

8.7) for the feed on which you're working. You will then be taken to the Items screen (Figure 8.8), where you can add a new item to your feed. Complete the following fields:

- *Title.* Think of the title as the headline for the item. Make it concise, descriptive, and thought provoking. A great title will make the subscriber want to read the item.

- *Link.* Complete this field with the URL of the webpage that contains information about the item. This field is optional, as there may not be a webpage associated with a given item; for now, we'll work from the assumption that there is.

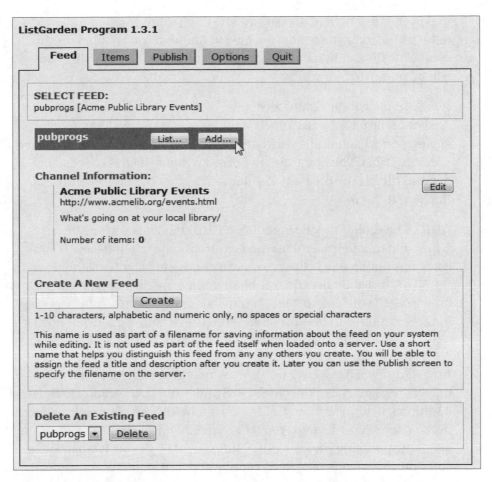

Figure 8.7   Add button

- *Description.* This field contains the narrative that will be associated with the feed. As discussed previously, some feeds provide the complete content of the item in the description while others offer only a summary. Using the Includes HTML option allows you to specify whether the Description field contains markup code. For the example feed, I'm checking this option. (If you include HTML code and do not check this box, your readers will see your code as well as your content.)

- *Enclosure.* This field allows you to add a nontext file to your item. This option is similar to attaching a file to an email message. The main reason you may wish to do this is if you're creating a podcast. In that case, you would need to browse for and select the audio file appropriate for this post. The length of the file and MIME-type information also needs to be included. If you're not sure how to find that information on your own, click the Get Info button (after selecting your file) and the fields will be populated for you.

- *PubDate.* Each item in your feed must contain a date and time stamp. This not only tells the reader when the item was posted but also allows aggregators to determine whether a particular item should be displayed to a subscriber. The option Set to Current Time (which is checked by default) directs the program to automatically set the date and time of the item to "now."

- *GUID.* The Global Unique Identifier (GUID) field lets you specify a string that uniquely identifies the item from others in the feed. If you leave this optional field blank, you can choose to have ListGarden set the GUID based on the URL specified in the Link field or create a unique GUID on its own. Since unique identifiers aren't really necessary in this example, I'll leave this item set to the default. Figure 8.9 shows how I've filled in the fields for the first event.

- *Item Additional XML.* Over the years, different vendors and software makers have extended the official RSS and Atom specification with additional fields. For example, if you want to include your podcast feed in the iTunes Store listings, you'll need to add an `<itunes:explicit>` element specifying whether your context contains explicit language. If you find yourself needing to add additional XML content to your feed, this is the field into which you enter it.

After you've filled in the fields, you will have the following options:

- *Add Item.* This button adds the item you've just created to your feed but does not publish your feed to your server. Until your feed has been published, subscribers will not see any new items.

- *Add & Publish.* This button adds the new item to your feed and immediately publishes the feed to your server.

- *Cancel.* This button allows you to stop the process and does not add the new item to your feed.

Once the item has been added, you'll be taken back to the Items screen where you will see that the feed now has a single item in it. (Figure 8.10 shows the *pubprogs* example added to the items screen.)

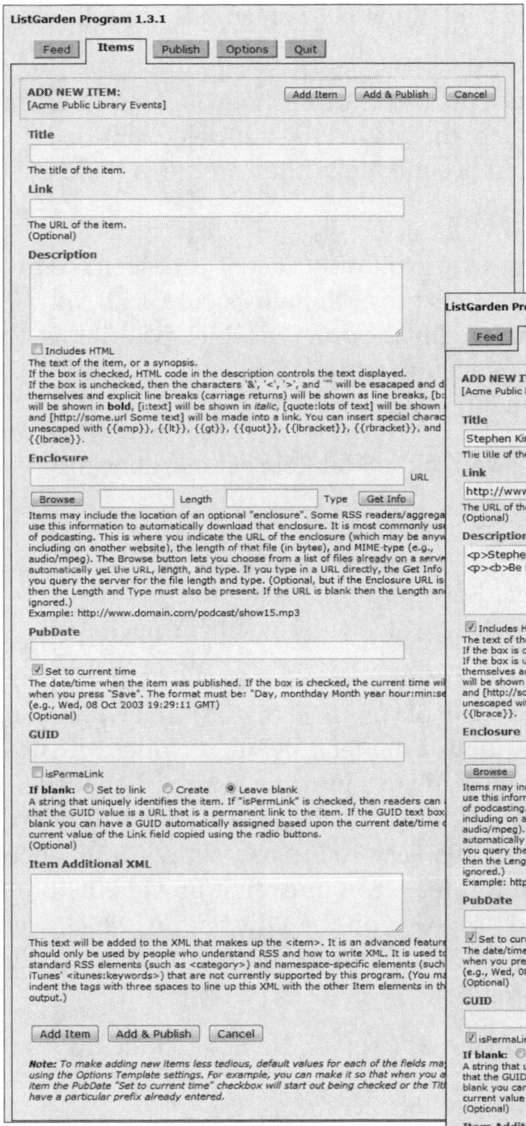

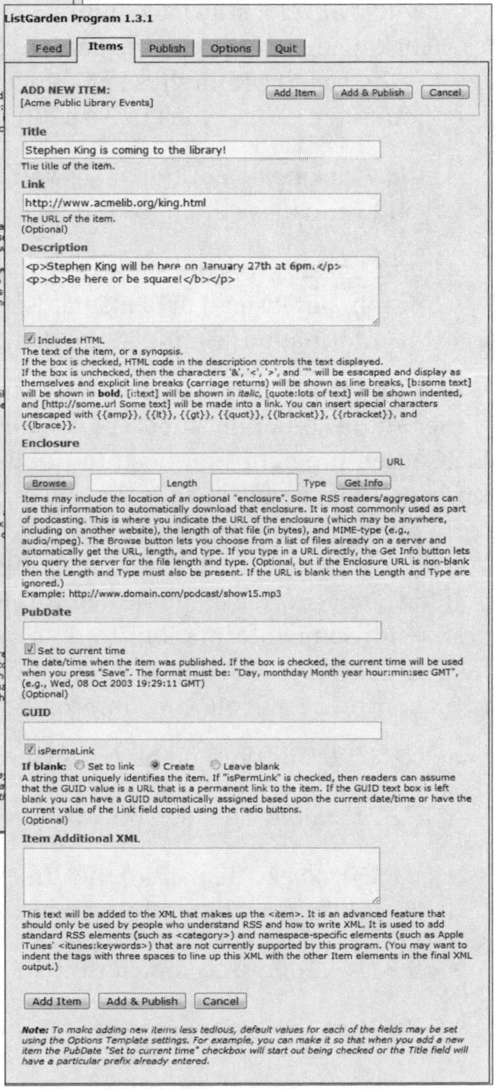

ListGarden Program 1.3.1

Feed | **Items** | Publish | Options | Quit

ADD NEW ITEM:
[Acme Public Library Events]

Add Item | Add & Publish | Cancel

Title

The title of the item.

Link

The URL of the item.
(Optional)

Description

☐ Includes HTML
The text of the item, or a synopsis.
If the box is checked, HTML code in the description controls the text displayed.
If the box is unchecked, then the characters '&', '<', '>', and '"' will be escaped and d
themselves and explicit line breaks (carriage returns) will be shown as line breaks, [b:
will be shown in *bold*, [i:text] will be shown in *italic*, [quote:lots of text] will be shown
and [http://some.url Some text] will be made into a link. You can insert special charac
unescaped with {{amp}}, {{lt}}, {{gt}}, {{quot}}, {{lbracket}}, {{rbracket}}, and
{{lbrace}}.

Enclosure

URL

Browse | Length | Type | Get Info

Items may include the location of an optional "enclosure". Some RSS readers/aggrega
use this information to automatically download that enclosure. It is most commonly use
of podcasting. This is where you indicate the URL of the enclosure (which may be anyw
including on another website), the length of that file (in bytes), and MIME-type (e.g.,
audio/mpeg). The Browse button lets you choose from a list of files already on a serva
automatically get the URL, length, and type. If you type in a URL directly, the Get Info
you query the server for the file length and type. (Optional, but if the Enclosure URL is
then the Length and Type must also be present. If the URL is blank then the Length an
ignored.)
Example: http://www.domain.com/podcast/show15.mp3

PubDate

☑ Set to current time
The date/time when the item was published. If the box is checked, the current time wil
when you press "Save". The format must be: "Day, monthday Month year hour:min:se
(e.g., Wed, 08 Oct 2003 19:29:11 GMT)
(Optional)

GUID

☐ isPermaLink
If blank: ○ Set to link   ○ Create   ● Leave blank
A string that uniquely identifies the item. If "isPermLink" is checked, then readers can
that the GUID value is a URL that is a permanent link to the item. If the GUID text box
blank you can have a GUID automatically assigned based upon the current date/time o
current value of the Link field copied using the radio buttons.
(Optional)

Item Additional XML

This text will be added to the XML that makes up the <item>. It is an advanced feature
should only be used by people who understand RSS and how to write XML. It is used to
standard RSS elements (such as <category>) and namespace-specific elements (such
iTunes' <itunes:keywords>) that are not currently supported by this program. (You ma
indent the tags with three spaces to line up this XML with the other Item elements in th
output.)

Add Item | Add & Publish | Cancel

Note: To make adding new Items less tedious, default values for each of the fields ma
using the Options Template settings. For example, you can make it so that when you a
item the PubDate "Set to current time" checkbox will start out being checked or the Titl
have a particular prefix already entered.

ListGarden Program 1.3.1

Feed | **Items** | Publish | Options | Quit

ADD NEW ITEM:
[Acme Public Library Events]

Add Item | Add & Publish | Cancel

Title

Stephen King is coming to the library!
The title of the item.

Link

http://www.acmelib.org/king.html
The URL of the item.
(Optional)

Description

<p>Stephen King will be here on January 27th at 6pm. </p>
<p><b>Be here or be square!</b></p>

☑ Includes HTML
The text of the item, or a synopsis.
If the box is checked, HTML code in the description controls the text displayed.
If the box is unchecked, then the characters '&', '<', '>', and '"' will be escaped and display as
themselves and explicit line breaks (carriage returns) will be shown as line breaks, [b:some text]
will be shown in *bold*, [i:text] will be shown in *italic*, [quote:lots of text] will be shown indented,
and [http://some.url Some text] will be made into a link. You can insert special characters
unescaped with {{amp}}, {{lt}}, {{gt}}, {{quot}}, {{lbracket}}, {{rbracket}}, and
{{lbrace}}.

Enclosure

URL

Browse | Length | Type | Get Info

Items may include the location of an optional "enclosure". Some RSS readers/aggregators can
use this information to automatically download that enclosure. It is most commonly used as part
of podcasting. This is where you indicate the URL of the enclosure (which may be anywhere,
including on another website), the length of that file (in bytes), and MIME-type (e.g.,
audio/mpeg). The Browse button lets you choose from a list of files already on a server and
automatically get the URL, length, and type. If you type in a URL directly, the Get Info button lets
you query the server for the file length and type. (Optional, but if the Enclosure URL is non-blank
then the Length and Type must also be present. If the URL is blank then the Length and Type are
ignored.)
Example: http://www.domain.com/podcast/show15.mp3

PubDate

☑ Set to current time
The date/time when the item was published. If the box is checked, the current time will be used
when you press "Save". The format must be: "Day, monthday Month year hour:min:sec GMT",
(e.g., Wed, 08 Oct 2003 19:29:11 GMT)
(Optional)

GUID

☑ isPermaLink
If blank: ○ Set to link   ● Create   ○ Leave blank
A string that uniquely identifies the item. If "isPermLink" is checked, then readers can assume
that the GUID value is a URL that is a permanent link to the item. If the GUID text box is left
blank you can have a GUID automatically assigned based upon the current date/time or have the
current value of the Link field copied using the radio buttons.
(Optional)

Item Additional XML

This text will be added to the XML that makes up the <item>. It is an advanced feature that
should only be used by people who understand RSS and how to write XML. It is used to add
standard RSS elements (such as <category>) and namespace-specific elements (such as Apple
iTunes' <itunes:keywords>) that are not currently supported by this program. (You may want to
indent the tags with three spaces to line up this XML with the other Item elements in the final XML
output.)

Add Item | Add & Publish | Cancel

Note: To make adding new Items less tedious, default values for each of the fields may be set
using the Options Template settings. For example, you can make it so that when you add a new
item the PubDate "Set to current time" checkbox will start out being checked or the Title field will
have a particular prefix already entered.

Figure 8.8   Add a New Item screen (top)

Figure 8.9   Add a New Item screen—completed (bottom)

Now that there is an item in the feed, the Items screen has the following additional buttons:

- *Delete.* Clicking this button presents you with a list of your feed's items and gives you the option to delete them. Clicking the Delete button next to a particular item will remove that item from your feed (Figure 8.11).

- *Reorder.* Clicking this button presents you with a list of your feed's items along with Up and Down buttons next to each item (Figure 8.12). By clicking these buttons, you can modify the order in which your items are delivered within the feed. (Since we only have one item at this point, reordering won't make a difference.)

- *Add.* Clicking this button takes you to the Add Item screen, allowing you to add a new item to your feed.

- *Edit.* Clicking this button takes you to the same screen as the Add button, but instead of blank fields, they will be prepopulated with the information relating to the item, which you can edit as necessary.

It is important to note that when you add items and make changes using these buttons they only affect the version of your feed that's stored within the ListGarden program. You need to publish the feed before anyone can subscribe to it or see any changes you've made to a previously published feed.

To publish your first feed, click on the Publish tab at the top of ListGarden. You'll be presented with the Publish RSS Feed interface (Figure 8.13). Since you have not previously published this feed, you must first provide the program with some information. To do so, click on the Edit button, which will take you to the Edit Publish Information screen (Figure 8.14). There you'll need to provide the following information:

- *FTP URL.* The domain name of your FTP server. Do not include ftp://.

- *FTP Filename.* The filename of your RSS feed.

- *FTP Directory.* The path to the directory in which you want to place the RSS file. You will typically need to supply the full path from root.

- *FTP User.* Your username for the FTP server.

- *FTP Password.* Your password for the FTP server.

- *Local Filename.* If you want to save a copy of the RSS file on your local computer, enter the path and filename here. If you leave this blank, a local copy will not be created.

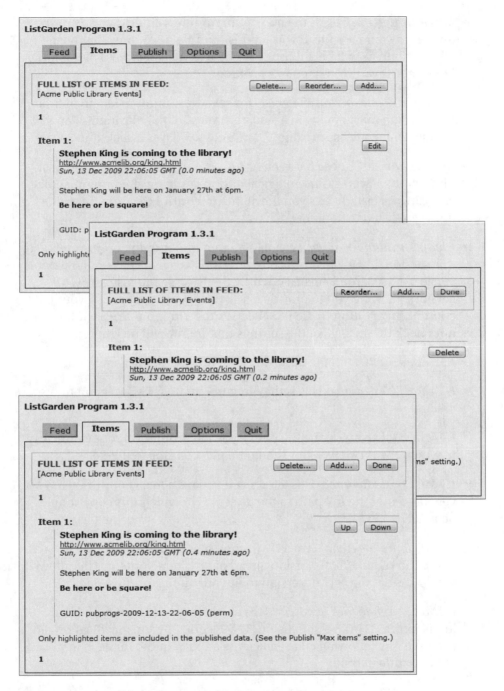

Figure 8.10   Full list of items in feed (top)

Figure 8.11   Delete button (middle)

Figure 8.12   Reordering buttons (bottom)

- *Maximum Items.* This is the maximum number of items you want to appear in your feed file. If you set this number at 25, only the most recent 25 items will be published in the RSS file, regardless of the number of items you've created in ListGarden.

- *Minimum Time to Publish Items.* This sets the minimum length of time that an item must appear in a feed, regardless of the maximum items setting. Your choices are None, 1 day, 2 days, 3 days, 1 week, and 2 weeks.

- *Item Sequence.* Choose between As Listed and Reverse Chronological. Though the Reverse Chronological option is the most common choice, choosing As Listed gives you the ability to control the order in which items are listed in your feed.

- *Create "human readable" version.* The remainder of the options relate to this section. If you check this box, choosing to create a human readable version, LinkGarden creates not only the RSS file but also an HTML version, allowing you to provide a link to a webpage showing your feed content (in addition to the RSS file for subscription purposes). If you do not check this box, all of the settings that follow will be ignored.

- *RSS File URL.* This is the full URL of the RSS file being generated.

- *HTML FTP Filename.* This is the filename of the HTML version to be created.

- *HTML FTP Directory.* The full path (typically from root) to the directory in which the HTML version should be placed is located here.

- *HTML Local Filename.* This allows you to save a local copy of the HTML version. Enter the full path to the directory in which this copy should be placed.

- *HTML Template Above.* Any HTML code placed in this field will appear at the top of the HTML version ahead of any item content. This allows you to format the HTML version to fit your site's current style.

- *HTML Template for Each Item.* This allows you to format individual items in the HTML version using HTML code of your specification. For example, the following code will create a block quote for each item, with the title in bold.

```
<blockquote><b>{{itemtitle}}</b><br />
{{itemlink}}<br />
{{itemdesc}}<br />
{{itempubdate}}</blockquote>
```

- *HTML Template Below.* Any HTML code placed in this field will appear at the bottom of the HTML version after any item content. This allows you to format the HTML version to match your site's current style.

- *HTML List All Items.* If checked, this option causes all items to appear in the HTML version regardless of any settings limiting the items in the RSS version.

When you've filled in all the appropriate information, click on the Save button in the upper right to save your changes and return to the Publish screen. On that screen, click Publish FTP, Publish Local File, or Publish Both, as your situation requires. You should receive a message letting you know that publishing was successful (Figure 8.15). If any errors occurred during publishing, you will be notified so you can re-edit your publishing settings to correct the error. To exit ListGarden, click on the Quit button at the top of any screen.

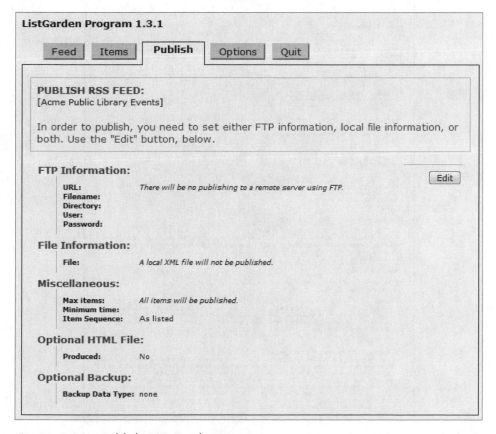

Figure 8.13   Publish RSS Feed screen

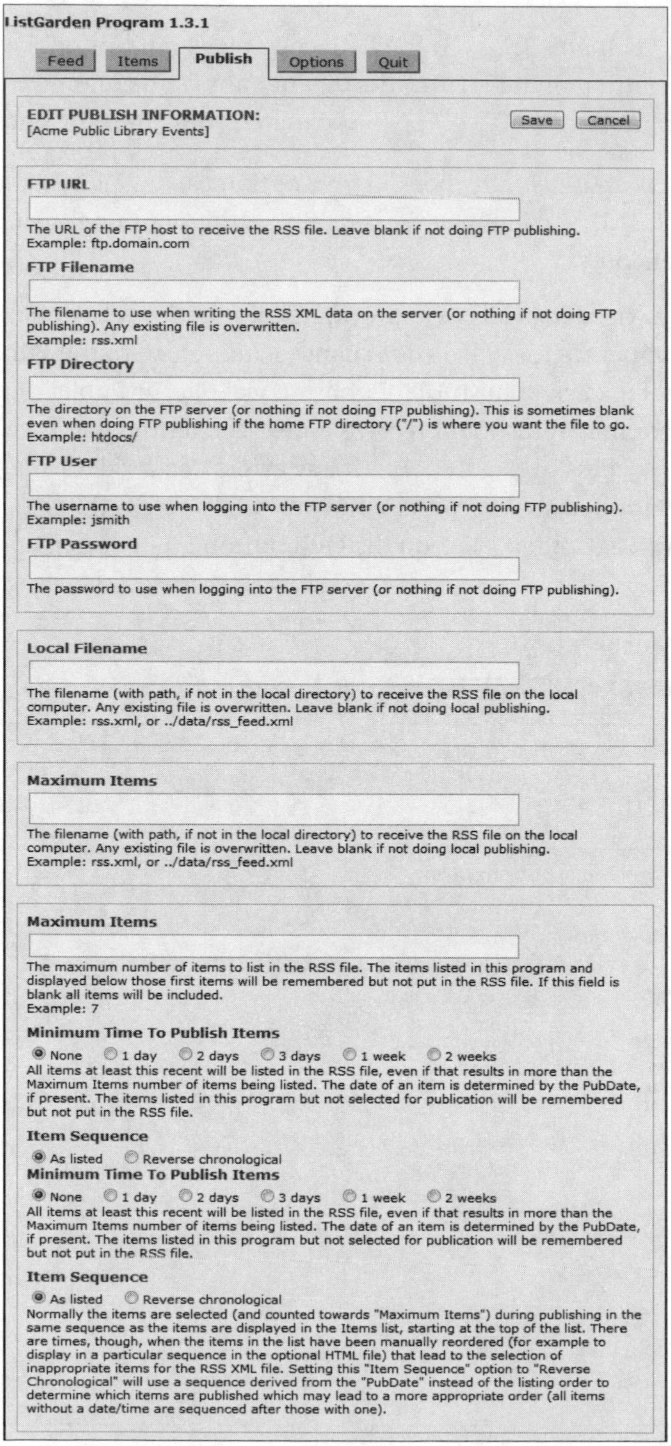

ListGarden Program 1.3.1

| Feed | Items | **Publish** | Options | Quit |

EDIT PUBLISH INFORMATION: Save   Cancel
[Acme Public Library Events]

FTP URL

The URL of the FTP host to receive the RSS file. Leave blank if not doing FTP publishing.
Example: ftp.domain.com

FTP Filename

The filename to use when writing the RSS XML data on the server (or nothing if not doing FTP
publishing). Any existing file is overwritten.
Example: rss.xml

FTP Directory

The directory on the FTP server (or nothing if not doing FTP publishing). This is sometimes blank
even when doing FTP publishing if the home FTP directory ("/") is where you want the file to go.
Example: htdocs/

FTP User

The username to use when logging into the FTP server (or nothing if not doing FTP publishing).
Example: jsmith

FTP Password

The password to use when logging into the FTP server (or nothing if not doing FTP publishing).

Local Filename

The filename (with path, if not in the local directory) to receive the RSS file on the local
computer. Any existing file is overwritten. Leave blank if not doing local publishing.
Example: rss.xml, or ../data/rss_feed.xml

Maximum Items

The filename (with path, if not in the local directory) to receive the RSS file on the local
computer. Any existing file is overwritten. Leave blank if not doing local publishing.
Example: rss.xml, or ../data/rss_feed.xml

Maximum Items

The maximum number of items to list in the RSS file. The items listed in this program and
displayed below those first items will be remembered but not put in the RSS file. If this field is
blank all items will be included.
Example: 7

Minimum Time To Publish Items

⦿ None   ○ 1 day   ○ 2 days   ○ 3 days   ○ 1 week   ○ 2 weeks

All items at least this recent will be listed in the RSS file, even if that results in more than the
Maximum Items number of items being listed. The date of an item is determined by the PubDate,
if present. The items listed in this program but not selected for publication will be remembered
but not put in the RSS file.

Item Sequence

⦿ As listed   ○ Reverse chronological

Minimum Time To Publish Items

⦿ None   ○ 1 day   ○ 2 days   ○ 3 days   ○ 1 week   ○ 2 weeks

All items at least this recent will be listed in the RSS file, even if that results in more than the
Maximum Items number of items being listed. The date of an item is determined by the PubDate,
if present. The items listed in this program but not selected for publication will be remembered
but not put in the RSS file.

Item Sequence

⦿ As listed   ○ Reverse chronological

Normally the items are selected (and counted towards "Maximum Items") during publishing in the
same sequence as the items are displayed in the Items list, starting at the top of the list. There
are times, though, when the items in the list have been manually reordered (for example to
display in a particular sequence in the optional HTML file) that lead to the selection of
inappropriate items for the RSS XML file. Setting this "Item Sequence" option to "Reverse
Chronological" will use a sequence derived from the "PubDate" instead of the listing order to
determine which items are published which may lead to a more appropriate order (all items
without a date/time are sequenced after those with one).

Figure 8.14   Edit Publish Information screen

Fill In The Following Fields Only If You Want The Optional HTML File

☐

If this box is checked a "human readable" version of the feed will be produced in HTML for reading with a browswer.

RSS File URL

[   ]

The URL of the published XML file containing the RSS information. This URL may be shown in the HTML file so that readers can give it to an RSS aggregator to "subscribe" to this feed. The file is created on the web server using the settings above either by FTP or by saving as a local file. In either case, a URL is used to access it from outside the web server. This program cannot derive the URL just from the FTP/file information and needs to be told the actual URL, hence the need for this field.
Example: http://www.aardvarkproject.com/rss.xml

HTML FTP Filename

[   ]

The filename to use when writing the feed HTML file on the server (may be blank if not doing FTP publishing or not producing the optional HTML file). Any existing file is overwritten.
Example: rss.html

HTML FTP Directory

[   ]

The directory on the FTP server for the HTML file (or nothing if not doing FTP publishing). This is sometimes blank even when doing FTP publishing if the home FTP directory is where you want the file to go. This must be set if doing FTP publishing of the HTML file even if it is the same as the XML FTP directory.
Example: htdocs/

HTML Local Filename

[   ]

The filename (with path, if not in the local directory) to receive the HTML file on the local computer. Any existing file is overwritten. Leave blank if not doing local publishing or not producing the optional HTML file.
Example: rss.html, or ../status/rss_feed.html

HTML Template Above

[   ]

☐ Set to default
The HTML code to be put in the HTML file before the section with the items. If blank, a default is used. If you want to see the default: Check the box, click "Save", and then edit again. The following "variables" expressed in the form "{(name)}" may be used: rsstitle, rsslink, rssdesc, rsspubdate, rssfileurl, rssfileurlraw (special characters not escaped).

HTML Template For Each Item

[   ]

☐ Set to default
The HTML code to be put in the HTML file for each item. If blank, a default is used. If you want to see the default: Check the box, click "Save", and then edit again. The following "variables" expressed in the form "{(name)}" may be used (in addition to those for Above and Below): itemtitle, itemlink, itemdesc, itemenclosureurl, itemenclosureurlraw, itemenclosurelength, itemenclosuretype, itempubdate, itemguid, itemnum (in this listing: 1, 2, ...).

HTML Template Below

[   ]

☐ Set to default
The HTML code to be put in the HTML file after the section with the items. If blank, a default is used. If you want to see the default: Check the box, click "Save", and then edit again. The following "variables" expressed in the form "{(name)}" may be used: rsstitle, rsslink, rssdesc, rsspubdate, rssfileurl, rssfileurlraw (special characters not escaped).

HTML List All Items

☐

If this box is checked all items in the feed will be included in the HTML file, not just those listed in the XML file. In addition, the order they are listed in the HTML file will be the same order as they are listed in the Items list (even if the Item Sequence option is set to "Reverse Chronological"). This has no effect on the XML RSS file (which is controlled by the Maximum Items, Minimum Time To Publish Items, and Item Sequence settings above).

Backup Type

⦿ No backup   ○ Single backup file   ○ Multiple -- a new one each time
☐ Include passwords
This determines whether or not to save backup copies of the current feed data at the same time as publishing. A single backup will repeatedly save to the same file. A multiple backup will save to a new file each time, with a filename that includes the date and time. Normally the FTP password values are NOT backed up and will need to be reentered if you use a backup file. If you want to save the passwords, too, then check the box.

To restore from a backup file, copy it into the directory where you keep the feed data file(s), give it a legal feed filename, and then run this program.

Backup Data FTP Filename

[   ]

The filename on the server to receive the Backup Data file by FTP. Leave blank if not doing FTP backup. The text "backup", the optional date/time (GMT), the feed name, and an extension will be appended to this name.
For example, if the filename given here is "rss", then the backup file will be "rss.backup.pubprogs.txt" or "rss.2005-07-26-14-43.backup.pubprogs.txt".

Backup Data FTP Directory

[   ]

The directory on the FTP server for the Backup Data file (or nothing if not doing FTP backup). This is sometimes blank even when doing FTP backup if the home FTP directory is where you want the file to go. This must be set if doing FTP backup even if it is the same as the XML or HTML FTP directories. The FTP URL, User, and Password are the same as used for FTP Publish.
Example: htdocs/

Backup Data Local Filename

[   ]

The filename (with path, if not in the local directory) to receive the Backup Data file on the local computer. Leave blank if not doing local backup. The text "backup", the optional date/time (GMT), the feed name, and an extension will be appended to this name.
For example, if the filename given here is "rss", then the backup file will be "rss.backup.pubprogs.txt" or "rss.2005-07-26-14-43.backup.pubprogs.txt". Another example value would be "../status/rss_feed".

[Save] [Cancel]

Figure 8.14   *(cont.)*

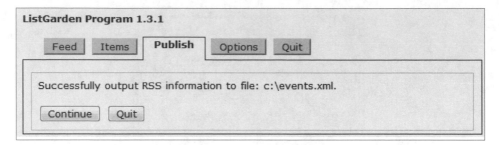

Figure 8.15　Successfully output RSS information

Fully Automated

If you have set up a blog using any of the standard blogging software, chances are this software can create a feed for you automatically. As an example, let's take Blogger.com (described in Chapter 4) and demonstrate how to have it create a feed automatically. (Blogger uses the Atom feed format as opposed to RSS, but as all of today's aggregators handle both formats, this is not a concern.)

To set up a feed for your blog in Blogger, log into your blog and select the Settings tab. Click on the Site Feed tab. By default, you'll be placed in the Basic Mode. Here you have three options:

- *Allow Blog Feeds.* Here you have three options: None, Short, and Full (the default.) Choosing None will turn off all feeds. Choosing Short will create a feed version showing only the beginning of your posts, specifically "the first paragraph, or approximately 255 characters, whichever is shorter." Leave the option on Full to distribute your complete posts. My suggestion is to leave it on Full.

- *Post Feed Redirect URL.* This field applies only for users of FeedBurner, a service that can automatically add content and features to your feeds. I won't be covering FeedBurner in this book so you can just leave this field blank. If you wish to investigate FeedBurner's services further, head over to www.feedburner.com.

- *Post Feed Footer.* Fill in this field if you wish to have additional content added to the end of an item in your feed. This content will not appear on your blog posts. For example, some feeds include advertising. This is where the code for the ads would be placed.

If you would like a little more control over your feeds, click on the Advanced Mode link on the Site Feed page to get three additional options: Blog Posts Feed, Blog Comment Feed, and Per-Post Comments Feed (Figure 8.16).

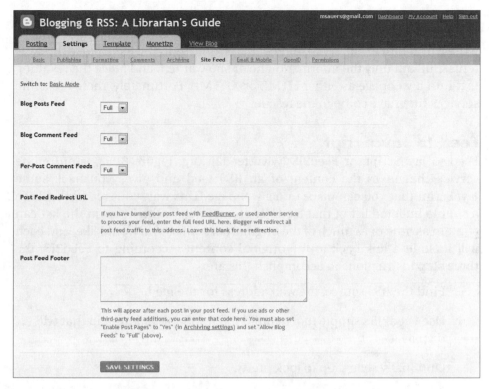

Figure 8.16   Blogger Settings: Site Feed

By default, Blogger automatically publishes three feeds: one for your blog posts, one for your blog's comments, and one for the comments on each individual blog post. Here you can control which of these feeds are published and how much content each includes. As on the previous screen, your choices are None, Short, and Full (the default.)

If you've made any changes on this screen, be sure to click the Save Settings button before moving on or Blogger will abandon your changes. If you're publishing to your own server, you'll also need to republish your blog to make the changes live.

Placing Outside RSS Content on Your Site

Whether you have a blog or just a traditional website, you might at times want to display the content of a feed from another site on your site. For example, you may want to have the headlines from the Washington Post business feed display on your library's business resources page. In the past, doing this required an extensive amount of programming knowledge. An author would need to have a clear understanding of XML and RSS formats and be able to write a program in either ASP or PHP that would grab the feed, parse the contents, pull out only the information he or she wanted, and place the resulting text into a webpage as either HTML or XHTML. Fortunately, there are some services that have come to the rescue.

Feed to JavaScript

Feed to JavaScript, or Feed2JS (www.feed2js.org; Figure 8.17), is an online service that takes the content of an RSS feed and gives you back some JavaScript that you can place into a webpage. This way, your readers will see a simple bulleted list of that feed's content. Each of the items in the list can contain as little or as much of the original content as you would like, and each will include a link back to the original content. According to Feed2JS, the three step instructions to accomplish this are:

1. Find the RSS source, the web address for the feed.

2. Use Feed2JS's simple tool to build the JavaScript command that will display it.

3. Optionally style it up to look pretty.

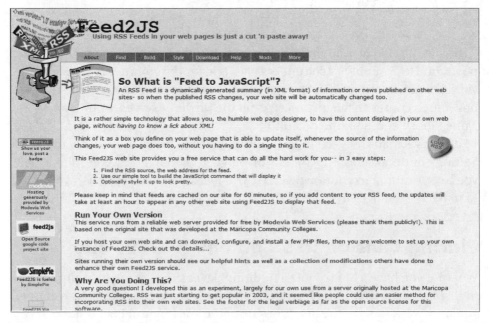

Figure 8.17   Feed to JavaScript

First, you need to find an RSS feed that you would like to republish on your site. As an example, let's say you'd like to display news headlines from Lincoln, Nebraska. Do a Google News search for *lincoln, ne* and find the URL for the results of that search (news.google.com/news?pz=1&cf=all&ned= us&hl=en&q=lincoln%2Cne&cf=all&output=rss).

Next go to Feed2JS and click on the Build tab, which takes you to the page shown in Figure 8.18. Here it's a question of filling in the form and choosing your options:

- *URL.* Paste the URL of your feed here.

- *Show channel?* Decide if you would like to display information about the source of the content. Being a good librarian, you know that you should always cite your sources, so select *Yes* to show the title and the description. You can also choose to display only the title or no information at all. (Eventually you may opt to display just the title or no information since choosing to show the title and the description on some feeds will cause this content to display twice.)

- *Number of items to display.* Leave this at zero if you would like to display every item in the feed. Chances are however, that you will not want that much. Five is generally a good number to start with.

- *Show/Hide item descriptions? How much?* Leaving this at one will display the entire content of each item. Change this to zero if you just want headlines; enter any other number to display the first *n* number of characters of the content.

- *Use HTML in item display?* If you only want to display headlines, leave this at *No*. However, if you are including item content in the display, choose *Yes* to include any HTML coding that may appear in that content such as formatting and hyperlinks. Set this to Preserve Paragraphs Only to just preserve paragraph formatting and remove all other HTML coding.

- *Show item posting date?* Your choice here will depend on the type of content in your feed. Since in this example we're displaying news headlines, the date and time of those headlines is important information, so change this to *Yes*.

- *Time Zone Offset.* Leave this as is unless you find that date and time stamps are not translating correctly between the source and your local time zone.

- *Target links in the new window?* Leaving this as *n* will cause links to be opened in the same window. Changing this to *y* will open links in a new window. There are additional options listed for those familiar with HTML window targeting. I recommend that you not change this option.

- *UTF-8 Character Encoding.* Only check this option if you are attempting to display content in non-Western character sets (Arabic, Cyrillic, Hebrew, etc.) and those characters are not displaying properly.

- *Podcast enclosures.* Choose this one if the content you are repurposing contains audio or video content (such as a podcast).

- *Custom CSS Class.* Here you can apply a CSS class to the Feed2JS output. I won't assume that you have any CSS knowledge, but for those who do, I'll point out the Feed2JS Guidelines link in this field, which provides more information on how CSS can be applied to make the output fit with your site's existing design.

Figure 8.19 shows the results of the form completed per my example.

Before adding the feed to your webpage, you will want to test it. Scroll back up the page and click the Preview Feed button on the right. A new window will appear showing you a preview of your content (Figure 8.20). If you're not happy with the results, close this window, try adjusting your settings, and preview again. Repeat these steps until you're happy with the results. (Any applied CSS styles will not appear in the preview version.)

Once you are satisfied, click the Generate JavaScript button. Your page will reload with a new box at the top of the page labeled Get Your Code Here. Copy all of the code in this box and paste it into the appropriate location in your webpage. Save your webpage and open it up in a browser. Your new RSS content should now appear and will update automatically whenever that page is loaded.

Figure 8.21 shows the sidebar of my blog containing a list of the five most recent bookmarks I've added to my Delicious account, which I accomplished using Feed2JS just as I've described here (with the addition of some CSS to get it to blend into the design of my site, which will take some trial-and-error, even for those with extensive CSS experience).

There's one more important thing I'd like to point out about Feed2JS: Back on the site's home page, there's a section labeled Run Your Own Version. If you plan on using Feed2JS long term, I highly recommend that you check out this section. Basically, the PHP code behind this service is freely available for you to download, so you can install it on your own web server (assuming you have one.) If you do, you should have your server administrator download and install it for you, as running it on your own server prevents one significant

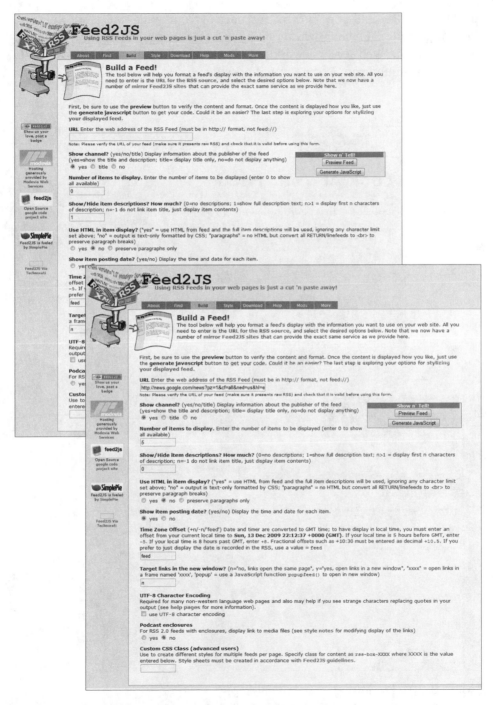

Figure 8.18   Build a Feed interface at Feed2JS (top)
Figure 8.19   Build a Feed interface—completed (bottom)

problem: If Feed2JS goes down, this part of your page will stop working. Running Feed2JS on your own server guarantees that it will continue to work as long as your web server is working. This is what I've done on my own site, and I recommend you do the same if possible.

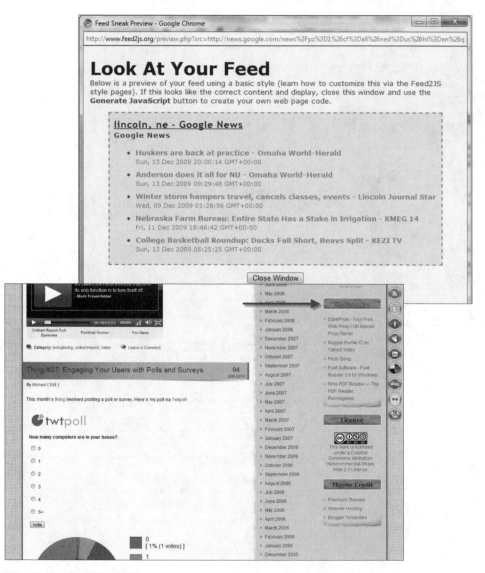

Figure 8.20   Previewing your content (top)

Figure 8.21   Recent Delicious bookmarks listed in my blog via Feed2JS (bottom)

Feed Informer

As good as Feed to JavaScript is, it doesn't do everything. What if you'd like to take the content from several RSS sources and output a single list of that content on your site? Taking that idea one step further, what if you would like to grab content from several sources, perform a keyword search on the combined content, and display only the results on your site? Either of these tasks would be beyond the capabilities of Feed to JavaScript. Fortunately, Feed Informer (feed.informer.com) can do both, just as I've described.

To get started go to the Feed Informer home page (feed.informer.com; Figure 8.22) and create a new account. Once you've created your account, you'll be taken to the Manage Digests page (Figure 8.23). Click Create New Digest on the left.

There are four basic steps to the Feed Informer process: Digest Sources, Digest Settings, Digest Design, and Publish Digest.

Digest Sources

Enter the URLs of the feed you wish to include here. With a free Feed Informer account, you are allowed to include up to five source feeds in a single digest. Paid accounts allow for more sources to be added into a digest (Figure 8.24).

Digest Settings

In Feed Informer, there are several options for controlling the output of your digest, based on your sources (Figure 8.25):

- *Digest Name.* Name your digest here. This is displayed only to you as the account holder and will not impact the output results.

- *Order Items By.* You can sort your output (either ascending or descending) based on item date, original order, item title, source feed, or randomly. Test each of these settings, especially when creating a digest with multiple feed sources.

- *Timezone.* Set the time zone for the date and time display on each item in a +/-*n* from GMT.

- *Max Items to Show.* Set the total number of items you wish to have displayed in your output.

- *Output Encoding.* Leave this set on UTF-8 (Default/International) unless you are having problems displaying characters from other non-Latin character sets.

- *Language.* Change to the language appropriate for your output. This setting affects only the day and month names in the item date stamps.

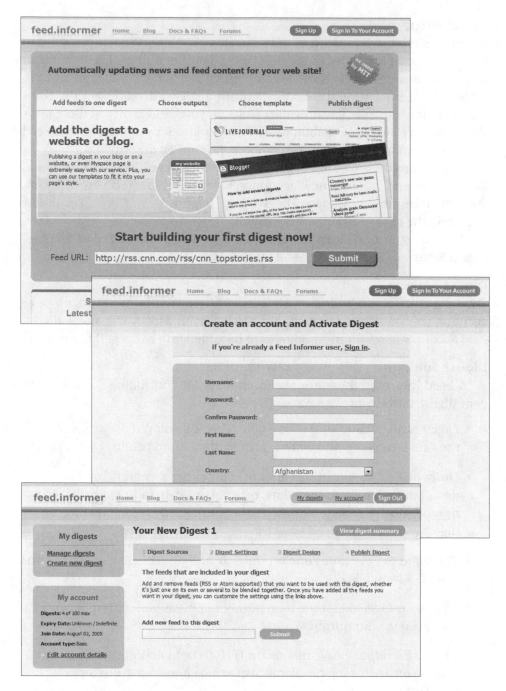

Figure 8.22   Feed Informer (top)

Figure 8.23   Create an Account and Activate Digest screen (middle)

Figure 8.24   Feed Informer: Digest Sources (bottom)

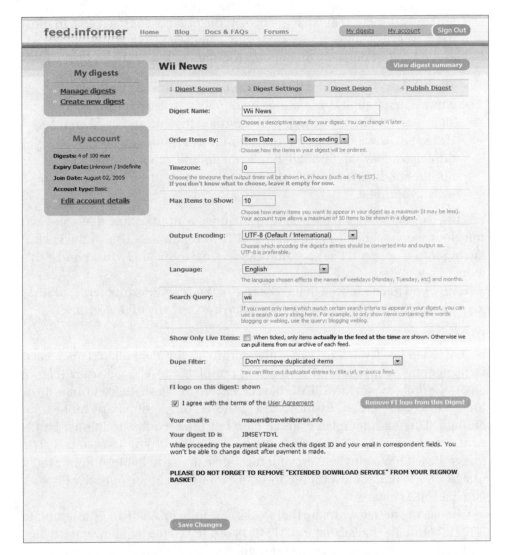

Figure 8.25   Feed Informer: Digest Settings

- *Search Query.* This is where the real power lies! Enter one or more keywords here, and your output will be limited to only those items that contain at least one of the keywords you've entered. (The field is based on a Boolean OR.) For example, if I had listed the feeds from several Nebraska newspapers but only wanted content that dealt with Lincoln, I'd enter *lincoln* into this field.

- *Show Only Live Items.* By default, Feed Informer caches the content of all feeds used in its digests. Checking this item will ignore the cache and only display items that are live on the original source feeds. In most cases, this will not be an issue for you. I suggest leaving this unchecked and only checking it if you notice a problem in the future.

- *Dupe Filter.* If your digest contains multiple source feeds, there is a chance that output content may be duplicated. Here you can choose to allow Feed Informer to attempt to de-dupe the output based on titles, URLs, or URLs ignoring anchors. This system is not perfect and some duplicates may slip through, but if you do find you're getting a large number of duplicate items, playing around with these options will be worth your time.

This Digest Settings page will also includes a notification that the Feed Informer logo will be displayed along with your content. This is the cost of having a free account. Paid account holders have the ability to remove this icon.

Lastly, you need to check that you agree to the Feed Informer terms of service. Be sure to click Save Changes if you have edited any of the settings.

Digest Design

Where Feed to JavaScript can only output a simple bulleted list, Feed Informer has many built-in formatting templates to choose from (Figure 8.26). Templates can be HTML-based, Flash- or Flash (legacy)-based, or image (pictures) based. In most cases, the HTML options are more than enough. The Flash templates are fancier, but they require additional bandwidth, and the viewer's browser must have the Flash plug-in installed. The image-based templates convert your text into a nonsearchable, nonindexable image and should be used only in cases where no other option will work (such as on MySpace).

Choose the design template that works best for you. A link to Edit Template HTML Manually is available for HTML-based templates to allow you to better fit the template into your site's design.

Publish Digest

At this point, you are ready to get the code for your website that will allow the output to appear on your page. Here again, Feed Informer excels in comparison with Feed to JavaScript. You can get the code needed as JavaScript, Flash, Flash (legacy), Picture, PDF, PHP (CURL with timeout), PHP (regular include), or ASP VBScript. Choose whichever one works best for your website; speak with your server administrator if you're not sure (Figure 8.27).

There are only two potential downsides to using Feed Informer rather than Feed to JavaScript. The first is that, although the free account will do the job for most, there may come a point when you need to consider paying for the service to get what you need out of it. The other is that there is no locally installable version available as there is with Feed2JS. When using Feed Informer, you are relying on a third-party service that could disappear in the future.

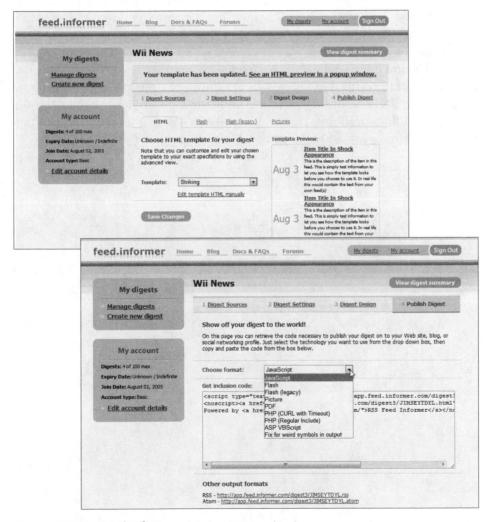

Figure 8.26   Feed Informer: Digest Design (top)
Figure 8.27   Feed Informer: Public Digest (bottom)

Further Thoughts About Republishing Content

If you are planning to add outside feed content using Feed to JavaScript, Feed Informer, or any other similar services, keep in mind that there is a potential fair-use issue because you are placing someone else's content on your site. Whenever you include content from other sites, be sure to clarify to readers that you (or your library) are not the creator of the content. In other words, cite your sources.

Another issue to consider is that when you rely on a third party to supply content, you run the risk of having that content suddenly disappear. Although this is unlikely with either Feed Informer or a major news source, it could happen.

There is one more way to create a feed, which combines both the power of blogging and the output of RSS with a minimum of time and effort. This new concept is called microblogging and is done through services such as Tumblr and the headline-grabbing Twitter. In this book's final chapter, I'll introduce you to microblogging and take you on a tour of Twitter.

Chapter 9

Microblogging With Twitter

Blogging, as I've presented it up to this point, has had a decade-long history of generally long-form content. Yes, there are exceptions such as photoblogging and those bloggers who tend to write shorter posts in general. But it was not until 2007 that a new form of blogging, which had been percolating in the background, finally made its primetime debut: microblogging.

Wikipedia defines microblogging as "a passive broadcast medium in the form of blogging. A microblog differs from a traditional blog in that its content is typically much smaller, in both actual size and aggregate file size. A microblog entry could consist of nothing but a short sentence fragment or an image or embedded video."[1] (According to this definition, you could say that the previously mentioned photoblogging is a type of microblogging.) There is one online service that, above all others, truly defines microblogging today. That service is Twitter.

Started in 2007 by Evan Williams, one of the original creators of Blogger, Twitter (twitter.com) asks a simple question, "What's happening?" The idea is to answer that question through short posts of 140 characters or less. As simple as this sounds, it's not as easy to do—or to understand—as it may seem.[2]

Before I get into how Twitter works, I want to point out a few things. First, there are many other popular (and not-so-popular) microblogging services available today, including FriendFeed (www.friendfeed.com), Jaiku (www.jaiku.com), and Tumblr (www.tumblr.com). However, at this writing, Twitter is the most popular, especially among librarians. Second, I could easily write an entire book dedicated to using Twitter, both personally and in a library environment. (And maybe I will someday.) However, this chapter is just meant to be an introduction to the service—enough to get you started.

Why Use Twitter?

If by this point I haven't convinced you of the benefits of blogging, either for yourself or for your library, there is absolutely no way that I'll be able to convince you that Twitter could have any value, ever. (It's a good sign that you've read this far!) And even for those convinced of the value of long-form blogging, Twitter can be a hard sell. Here are just a few questions and comments that I've heard after giving a basic intro to Twitter:

- "Why would I care what someone is doing every minute of the day?"

- "Why would someone else care what I'm doing every minute of the day?"

- "What could someone possibly say of any importance in 140 characters?"

- "It sounds like just shouting into the ether."

- "I tried it, but all anyone ever talked about was what they had for breakfast/lunch/dinner."

- "Great, one more thing I've got to keep track of!"

Does any of this sound familiar? In most cases, these comments are pretty much the same as what I heard when I started teaching people about blogging 10 years ago (with the exception of the 140-character limit).

One of the best responses I've ever heard to these sorts of comments is: What you get out of Twitter is completely dependent on what you put into it. Personally, the vast majority of my *tweets* (the term for an individual post to your Twitter account) are links to articles and resources that I've found online. In one day, I've posted links to Firefox security updates, the latest news on ebook hardware, free ebooks for download, and updates on copyright legislation.

People choose to follow me on Twitter because they find that the information I post is worthy of their time. Not all of it, granted, but enough to cause them to want to spend a bit of time reading my tweets. In return, I have more than 1,400 followers who I can turn to when I have a question that I can't answer. They are willing to assist me because they know that I am willing to assist them: directly, by answering their questions; or indirectly, by posting information they are interested in.

So, what might be some of the reasons for you to use a service like Twitter?

- It can be an additional method for disseminating existing content.

- Sometimes you have something to say that doesn't amount to enough to fill a longer blog post.

- Some of your followers may actually care about what you had for breakfast/lunch/dinner. (I think that having tried lambs brains once was an event worthy of immediate announcement.)

- Some people would rather receive short content and then decide whether to read linked longer content rather than receive the longer content in the first place.

- Tweets are easily read on small screens such as smartphones.

- Posting to Twitter can be automated, so it won't necessarily take up any more time than you're already spending on social media.

Twitter Basics

First, I'll cover how you can use Twitter to *provide* information. At the end of the chapter, I'll look at how you can use Twitter to *find* information, even if you don't have an account.

Creating an Account

In order to post information to Twitter, you must first create an account. At Twitter.com, click on Sign Up Now (Figure 9.1). On the signup screen, you will see the following fields (Figure 9.2):

- *Full name.* This name will be associated with your account and may be shown to other users depending on the software or service they are using to read your tweets.

- *Username.* This is the name you will use to log into Twitter and the name that will be shown on your account to all users. This will also be part of the URL for your Twitter page. My username is *msauers* and my Twitter URL is www.twitter.com/msauers.

- *Password.* Type this in carefully and make a note of it; you are asked to type it twice to confirm that you typed it correctly the first time.

- *Email.* This address will allow Twitter to send you notifications based on the preferences you will set up later and if necessary can be used to recover you password.

- *I want the inside scoop.* Leave this box checked if you want to receive emails from Twitter about the service. These are generally not sent out more than once a month.

- *CAPTCHA.* Type in the words you see in the box. This is used to prevent nonhumans from setting up accounts in an automated fashion.

When you're done, click Create My Account. Once your account has been created, you'll see your Twitter page. You may also be tempted to start tweeting immediately, but I highly recommend that you take a moment and do a little more work before you start posting (I'll cover this shortly).

I'd also like to mention that from this point forward when you need to log into your account, you'll do so through the screen shown in Figure 9.3. You can get to this screen by going to twitter.com and clicking on the Sign In link, or it may be presented to you via one of the other posting methods I'll discuss later. The important thing is that you can do nothing with your account, including posting, without first logging in.

Before You Tweet

It is very tempting to start tweeting away the moment you've set up your account. It may also be tempting to immediately start following other people's tweets. And although there's nothing stopping you from doing so, I highly recommend you don't do either just yet, as there are a few other things you should do first. Let me explain why, using my own behavior on Twitter as an example.

If you decide to follow me on Twitter, I will receive an email informing me of the fact. At that point, I'm likely to look at your account and decide if I want to follow you back. Because I currently follow more than 500 other accounts on Twitter, when it comes to deciding whom I wish to follow, there are several factors I take into consideration. First, I consider whether I actually know the person. (Short of finding me and introducing yourself, which I do encourage, there's not much you can do about that one.) Second, I consider whether I find what you have to say interesting. (I am sure you will try to be interesting, but there's not much you can do if your definition of "interesting" is different than mine.)

Next, I look at certain things in your Twitter account that you *can* control such as your avatar, biography, and link. If I don't know you but I think you might have something interesting to say, these are the things that are going sway my final decision on whether to follow you. So address these matters at the outset, before you do anything else. If this information is missing or poorly crafted, I'll likely assume that you're not serious about your account and decide not to follow you.

With that in mind, go ahead and click on the Settings link in the upper-right corner of your Twitter page to get to your Account Settings page.

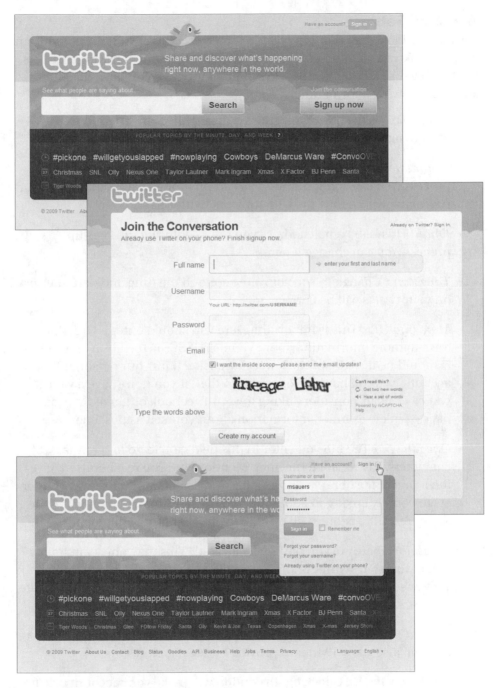

Figure 9.1   Twitter (top)

Figure 9.2   Twitter signup screen (middle)

Figure 9.3   Twitter login screen (bottom)

Account Settings

Let's take a look at all that is available under Account Settings. I'll point out what I think you should address immediately and what can wait until later. On the Account screen (mine is shown in Figure 9.4), you have the ability to add the following information:

- *Name.* This is the name you entered during the sign-up process. You can change it here.

- *Username.* This is the username you entered during the sign-up process. You can change it here. Be careful though, since changing your username will change the URL for your Twitter page.

- *Email.* This is the email address you entered during the sign-up process. You can change it here.

- *Time Zone.* Change this to your time zone so the time and date stamps on your tweets will be correct.

- *More Info URL.* This is important. Here you should enter a URL that links to more information about yourself. If this is the library's account, it should be the URL of the library's website. If it's your personal Twitter account and you have a blog, point to that. If you don't have a website you can link to, consider linking to your Facebook or LinkedIn profile pages. Link to as much information about yourself as possible.

- *One Line Bio.* The bio you enter in this field can be no longer than 160 characters. You must be succinct: Mention that you're a librarian, give the name of the library you work for, and list a few other things of interest to you. By linking to additional biographical information using the More Info URL, people will be able to discover more about you.

- *Location.* Where are you physically located? This may not seem important at first, but Twitter is location aware, and it is possible to limit a Twitter search based on the location of tweets. Enter your city and state here or, better yet, enter your ZIP code for more accurate results.

- *Language.* Choose the language in which you will be tweeting. This setting will also allow Twitter to provide better search results.

- *Protect my tweets.* Checking this option will make your account private, meaning that anyone wishing to follow you must be approved by you. Additionally, your tweets will only be viewable by those you approve, and your tweets will not be searchable by others. This is a decision I can't make for you, but I do have an opinion: While you may be tempted to protect your tweets, it defeats the purpose of the "social" part of "social web," so I don't recommend it.

When you've finished setting these options, be sure to click the Save button at the bottom of the page to make the changes permanent. (This is true for all of the other settings pages.)

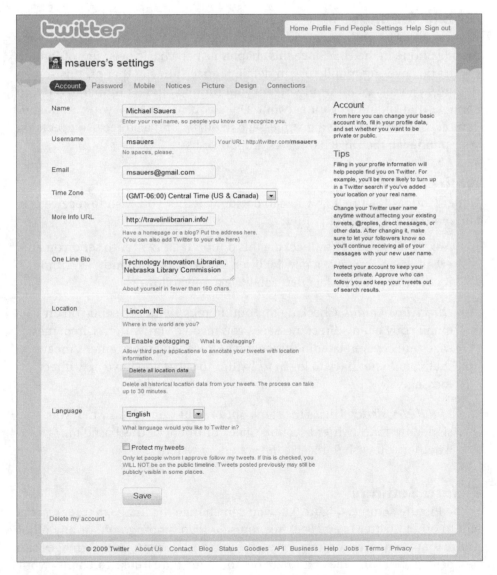

Figure 9.4   Account settings

There is also a Delete My Account link at the bottom of this page should you ever wish to end your relationship with the "twitterverse."

Password Settings

On the Password page (Figure 9.5), you can change your account password. Just enter your current password and then the new password you wish to use (you'll need to enter it twice). Click the Change button to commit the change.

Mobile Settings

It is possible to both post and receive tweets via SMS messages on your mobile phone in the U.S. Since this chapter is just a basic overview of Twitter, I won't be covering mobile use in detail. Suffice it to say that on this screen (Figure 9.6), you can inform Twitter of your mobile phone number in order to connect that phone to your account. Once you've done so, you can post to your account by sending a text message to 40404 and also receive tweets on your phone via the Device Updates dropdown list.

Notices Settings

Under Notices (Figure 9.7), you can decide whether you wish to receive certain types of emails from Twitter:

- *New Follower Emails.* Checking this option tells Twitter to send you an email when you have a new follower. I find this very handy, as without it you may miss the fact that you have a new follower.

- *Direct Text Emails.* Checking this option tells Twitter to send you an email copy of any direct messages you receive via Twitter. (Direct messages are covered later in this chapter.) Receiving these emails means that you do not have to log in to Twitter to see if you have new direct messages.

- *Email Newsletter.* This is the same option you were given when you signed up for a Twitter account. Check or uncheck this based on whether you wish to receive the system newsletter.

Picture Settings

In the Picture settings (Figure 9.8), you can change the image that represents you to other Twitter users. Feel free to use a logo, photograph, or any other image that you feel accurately represents you and/or your library. Images can be .jpeg, .gif, or .png files and may be no larger than 700k. To change your image, click the Choose File button, browse your computer for the image, choose the image, and click the Save button. You can also click Delete Current to reset the image to the default Twitter icon.

Design Settings

Under the Design tab (Figure 9.9), you can choose from a variety of built-in backgrounds for your Twitter account by clicking on one of the images on this screen. If you have a different image you wish to use, click on Change Background Image to browse for that image on your computer. You can also change the colors used via the Change Design Colors link. There are also many websites such as Themeleon (www.colourlovers.com/themeleon/twitter) and TwitBacks (www.twitbacks.com) from which you can download and even customize a background.

Connections Settings

There are many third-party services on the web today that interact with Twitter. I'll be introducing a few of them to you at the end of this chapter. When you use any of these third-party services, you are giving that service access to your Twitter account. On the Connections screen (Figure 9.10), you will see a list of all the third-party services to which you have granted access to your Twitter account. You can revoke that permission for any particular service by clicking the appropriate Revoke Access link.

Once you have your settings completed to your satisfaction (most specifically, your URL, bio, time zone, and background), it is time to start tweeting.

Tweeting 101

Many new users of Twitter start by following others for a while before posting any content themselves. While this may sound logical, there is a problem with that logic—and also a way around it. The problem is one I've already mentioned: If you follow me, I'll receive a notification and then take a look at your account to decide whether to follow you back. If you have no content, my decision will pretty much be an instant "no," since without content, I can't tell whether what you have to say is going to interest me. So, I suggest you add some content before you start following other users.

But what if you want to read the postings of others before posting yourself? Simple: Just bring up their Twitter pages by going to www.twitter.com/*username* (assuming their account isn't private). There you can easily read their content at your leisure. You can also use the RSS feed link on a person's Twitter page to subscribe to their tweets via Google Reader or another aggregator of your

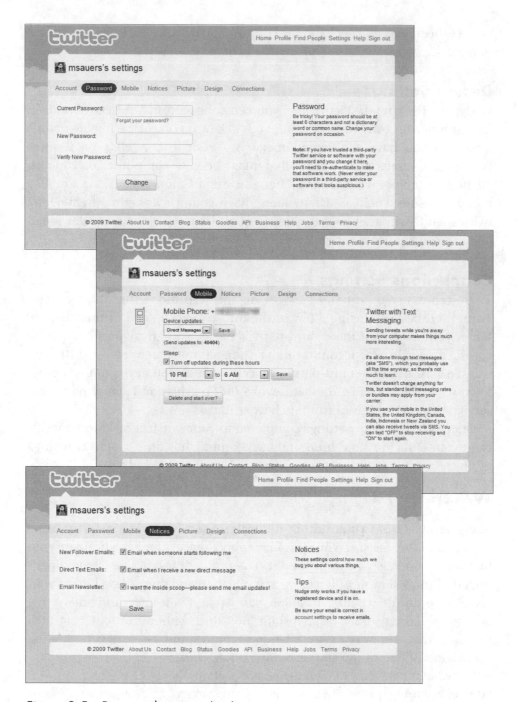

Figure 9.5   Password settings (top)

Figure 9.6   Mobile settings (middle)

Figure 9.7   Notices settings (bottom)

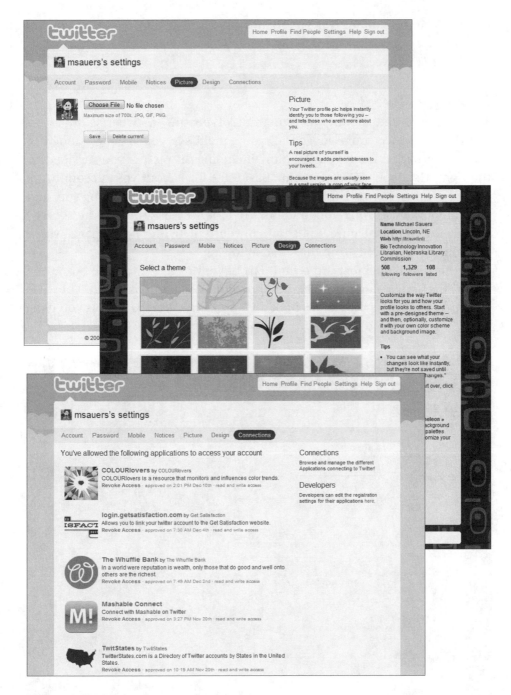

Figure 9.8   Picture settings (top)

Figure 9.9   Design settings (middle)

Figure 9.10 Connections settings (bottom)

choice. This is another way to follow someone without first having an account.

So, let's start tweeting!

Posting a Tweet

The simplest and most direct method of posting a tweet is to go to Twitter.com. Once you're logged in, you should see your background with other information about your account, including the picture you supplied, to the right. Here you'll also see some basic statistics about your account (the number of people you're following, the number of people following you, and the number of lists you're on) and links to other screens that will be covered later in the chapter. Figure 9.11 shows my current Twitter home page, which contains recent tweets from those I'm following.

At this point, the most important part of your page is the large box at the top of the screen labeled "What's happening?" This box is where you type your tweet. Above and to the right of this box is the number *140*. As you type,

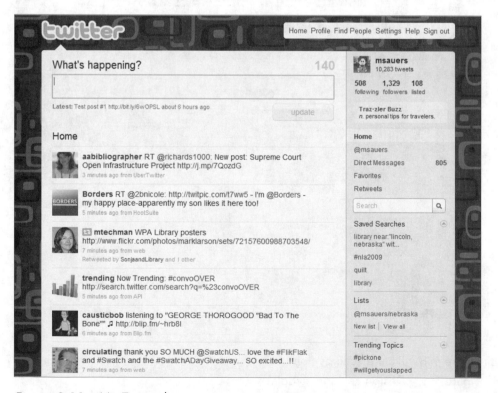

Figure 9.11 My Twitter home page

this number will decrease, letting you know how many characters you have left. If you reach zero and keep going, the number will become negative and turn red. If this happens, you will be unable to post your tweet.

Go ahead and type in your first tweet. What you say is completely up to you. When you're finished, click the Update button, and you'll see your tweet appear on the screen. As you post additional tweets, they will appear on this page in reverse-chronological order.

Each tweet posted includes the account holder's picture and username, the content of the tweet including clickable links, if there are any, a date and time stamp, and the name of the software or service used to post the tweet. (Tweets posted via the Twitter website will be labeled "from web.")

Once you start following other users, their tweets will be displayed along with yours on your home page in the same reverse-chronological order. The 20 most recent tweets will be shown on this page. Once that limit has been reached, older tweets will "fall off" but will still be accessible via a More link at the bottom of the page.

When posting tweets, there are two special characters that have very specific meanings in the Twitterverse: @ and #. I will explain how these characters work and also discuss *retweets* and *direct messages*, in the following sections.

@mentions and @replies

Let's say you want to tweet that you're currently learning how to use Twitter by reading this book. You could say "Learning how to use Twitter by reading Michael Sauers's book" and, while I would greatly appreciate you doing so, I might not notice. Instead, since you know that my Twitter username is *msauers*, you could instead say "Learning how to use Twitter by reading the book by @msauers." In this case, *@msauers* will create a link back to my account and appear on the page in my account located at www.twitter. com/#replies. (You can also click on the *@username* link in the right sidebar of your account to get to this page.)

Since you included an *@username* in your post but not at the beginning of your post, this is known as an "at mention." In other words, you've mentioned another Twitter user, and he or she will be able to see it.

What if you wanted to post a tweet specifically to me but wouldn't mind if the tweet was read by all of your followers? For example, say you want to let me know what you think of this book and are OK with others reading it. In this case, you could start your tweet with *@username* to get my attention, such as "@msauers I really love your book, *Blogging and RSS*!" Even though you're not replying to something I said, since you started your tweet with *@username*, this is known as an "at reply."

Let's take a look at a better example of an "at reply." Let's say you read a tweet of mine that said, "Having dinner at Fuji, a new sushi place in town," and you want to directly respond to me regarding this particular tweet. If you were to read this as part of your Twitter home page (assuming you're following me) and you hover your pointer over my tweet, you should see two additional links in the lower-right corner of the tweet: Reply and Retweet (Figure 9.12). Clicking the Reply link will automatically place *@msauers* in the box at the top of the page, allowing you to send a reply asking what I thought of dinner since you have been thinking of checking out this restaurant yourself.

Because you used the Reply link, when your tweet is posted, it will include (in addition to the date/time stamp and the posting method) a note that says "in reply to msauers." That last bit will also be a hyperlink back to my original tweet. This is how conversations happen on Twitter.

The Retweet link allows you to automatically repost someone else's tweet to your account. I'll be covering this in more detail later in the chapter.

Hash Tags

Hash tags, indicated by #, are a convention that has developed over the life of Twitter as a way to indicate the topic for a tweet even if the topical word or phrase doesn't appear in the core content of the tweet. For example, many of

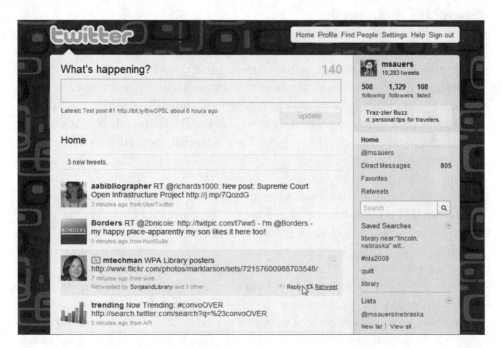

Figure 9.12   Twitter Reply and Retweet links

the tweets that I post have to deal with ebooks; therefore, these tweets include *#ebooks*.

Here's an actual tweet of mine: "HarperCollins joins S&S, Hatchette plan to encourage piracy—MobileRead Forums http://ow.ly/KIue #ebooks." In this example, the general topic of the tweet is ebooks but it is specifically about recent announcements from a few publishers concerning ebook release schedules. Had I not included *#ebooks*, people searching Twitter for ebooks may never have found this particular tweet. Additionally, other Twitter users can click on the hash tag to automatically perform a search for content on that topic. In other words, hash tags are tagging for tweets (Figure 9.13).

Another instance in which hash tags are commonly used is at conferences. In the past few years, both the Computers in Libraries and Internet Librarian conferences have used the *#cil2010* and *#il2010* hash tags respectively (the year changes to whatever is appropriate). This way, all tweets relevant to these conferences can be easily collected, indexed, and searched without each tweeter having to spell out the name of the conference in each and every tweet.

Retweets

When someone posts an interesting tweet that you think others should know about, you can "retweet" their tweet to your account. The syntax for this is to repeat the content with *RT* (short for retweet) and the *@username* of the original

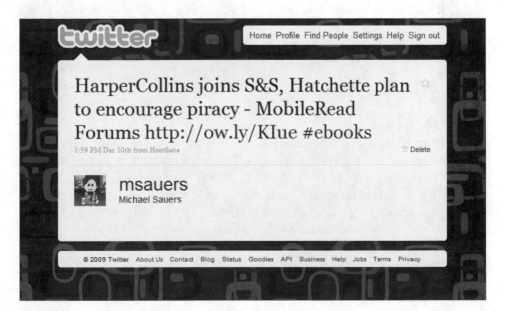

Figure 9.13   Hash tag example

tweeter at the beginning of the tweet. Editing of the original content is generally frowned upon but is acceptable if you're shortening to get the retweet to
fit within the 140-character limit.

Retweets posted via Twitter's retweet link (next to the @reply link) will
appear with a small circular arrow icon at the beginning of the tweet. (Figure
9.14 shows examples of both.)

Figure 9.14   Retweet example

Direct Messages

There is another kind of tweet known as a direct message. This is a way for
Twitter users to share private messages. To send a direct message to another
Twitter user, start your tweet with *D username,* with *username* being that of
the recipient. Direct messages can only be sent between users who are following one other. So if I am following you, but you aren't following me, I cannot send you a direct message via Twitter.

Direct messages you have sent and received can be found by clicking on
the Direct Messages link in the sidebar. On this screen, you can also create a
direct message to another user by selecting their username from the Send a
Direct Message dropdown list (Figure 9.15). If the user you are looking for is
not in this list, you are not reciprocal followers.

Figure 9.15   Sending a direct message

Following Others

Once you've tweeted a bit and have a handle on the different types of tweets that you can create, you are ready to start following some other Twitter users. To follow someone, just go to their Twitter page (www.twitter. com/*username*) and click the Follow button (Figure 9.16). His or her icon will now show up in your sidebar as someone you follow (Figure 9.17), and this icon will also link back to his or her Twitter page. Beneath these icons is a View All link where you can see a list of all the people you follow and additional details about each of them, along with options such as mentioning them and sending them direct messages (Figure 9.18). To unfollow someone, go to their Twitter page and click the Unfollow button.

You might be wondering how to find Twitter users to follow. There are many ways to do this. Here are just a few suggestions to get you started:

- Follow me. By now you know that my Twitter username is *msauers*. So head on over to www.twitter.com/msauers and click the Follow button. (Send me a message that you've read the book, and I'll be sure to follow you back.)

- Once you've followed me, look at the list of people I follow. Chances are, if you find what I say interesting, you might also find some of the

Figure 9.16   Follow button (top)

Figure 9.17   List of your followers (middle)

Figure 9.18   View of everyone you follow (bottom)

folks I follow interesting. Click on their icons, read their tweets, and choose a few to follow.

- Click on one of the trending topics in the sidebar. These are keywords that are getting mentioned a lot right now. If one interests you, it could be a great way to find others with similar interests to follow.

- Do a Twitter search on a topic that interests you. (We'll be covering searching next.) As with trending topics, this is another way to find folks with similar interests.

- If you are looking for someone specific but you can't remember or don't know their username, click on the Find People link at the top right of any Twitter page. Here you can search for people by their real names or email addresses, invite your friends to join directly, or get suggestions from Twitter itself.

- If all else fails, just do a Google search for a topic you're interested in, adding the keyword *twitter* to your search terms. Chances are you'll find someone to follow.

Searching Twitter

Although the central focus of *Blogging and RSS* is not on how to search the internet, I would be remiss if I didn't take a few minutes of your time to talk about how to search Twitter just as I did with searching in Google Reader. While the debate continues as to whether content on Twitter has no value, some value, or much value, there are undoubtedly certain instances in which the ability to search Twitter can have value. Here are just a few examples:

- *During conferences.* As I've mentioned previously, many conferences today establish a hash tag in advance of the conference. While this can be of use to conference attendees to help them in connecting with each other, a conference hash tag can be of even more use to those unable to attend. By searching for the conference's hash tag, those not physically present can follow along and even participate in the conversation that's happening at the conference.

- *Finding out what's happening locally.* Remember how you set your physical location in your account earlier in this chapter? That's because Twitter is location aware. You can search Twitter and limit results to tweets within a certain radius of your location or another location. This can be a great way to see what others are up to in your town. Maybe someone's tweeting about a local event that you missed reading about in the local paper.

- *Immediate reactions to current events.* The death of Michael Jackson is just one example of an event that got a lot of people talking via Twitter. In some such instances, information is released by someone on Twitter before the major news outlets receive it. In a more practical example, not long ago there was an accident involving a train and a car three miles from my house; I was able to find postings by others in my area about what had happened and so didn't get caught in the resulting traffic jam. That's not something I could have found on Google.

So, let's go through the basics of searching Twitter. First, you can search Twitter either on the Twitter home page (if you're not logged in), via the search box in the sidebar (if you are logged in) or by going to search.twitter.com (Figure 9.19).

The basics of a Twitter search are conventions that you're probably already used to. Enter a keyword or two (Boolean AND is the default) and use quotation marks to indicate phrases. In addition, on Twitter you can specify that you're searching for a particular hash tag by preceding your keyword with # or specify a particular user by including his or her username as a keyword. (To search for mentions of a user, search for *@username*.)

Figure 9.20 shows a search result for *public library*. From here, you can view a particular tweet or reply to a tweet. You can also get an RSS feed for this search and tweet the results. This search will continue to update itself. If you wait long enough (and if you have performed a search that will precipitate many new results quickly), you will eventually see a message stating "X more results since you started searching. Refresh to see them" (Figure 9.21). To see the newest results, click on the Refresh link.

There is also an advanced Twitter search interface, available through the Advanced Search link on any Twitter search screen. Here you will find a form-based version of Twitter's advanced search features (Figure 9.22). All of these options may also be typed manually into any search box. To learn the syntax, click on the Search Operators link on this screen.

As with the advanced search screens in other search engines, Twitter's advanced search allows you to create a more specific, Boolean-based search query. Additionally, you can limit your results to tweets from or to a specific user; within a specific distance of a location; before or after a certain date, or within a certain date range; with a certain attitude (based on the inclusion of certain emoticons); and that contain links to non-Twitter resources. The options you use will depend on the results you're looking for. For example, in the Twitter search syntax, searching for *library near:"lincoln, nebraska"*

Figure 9.19   Search on Twitter (top)

Figure 9.20   Search results for *public library* (middle)

Figure 9.21   More results since you started searching (bottom)

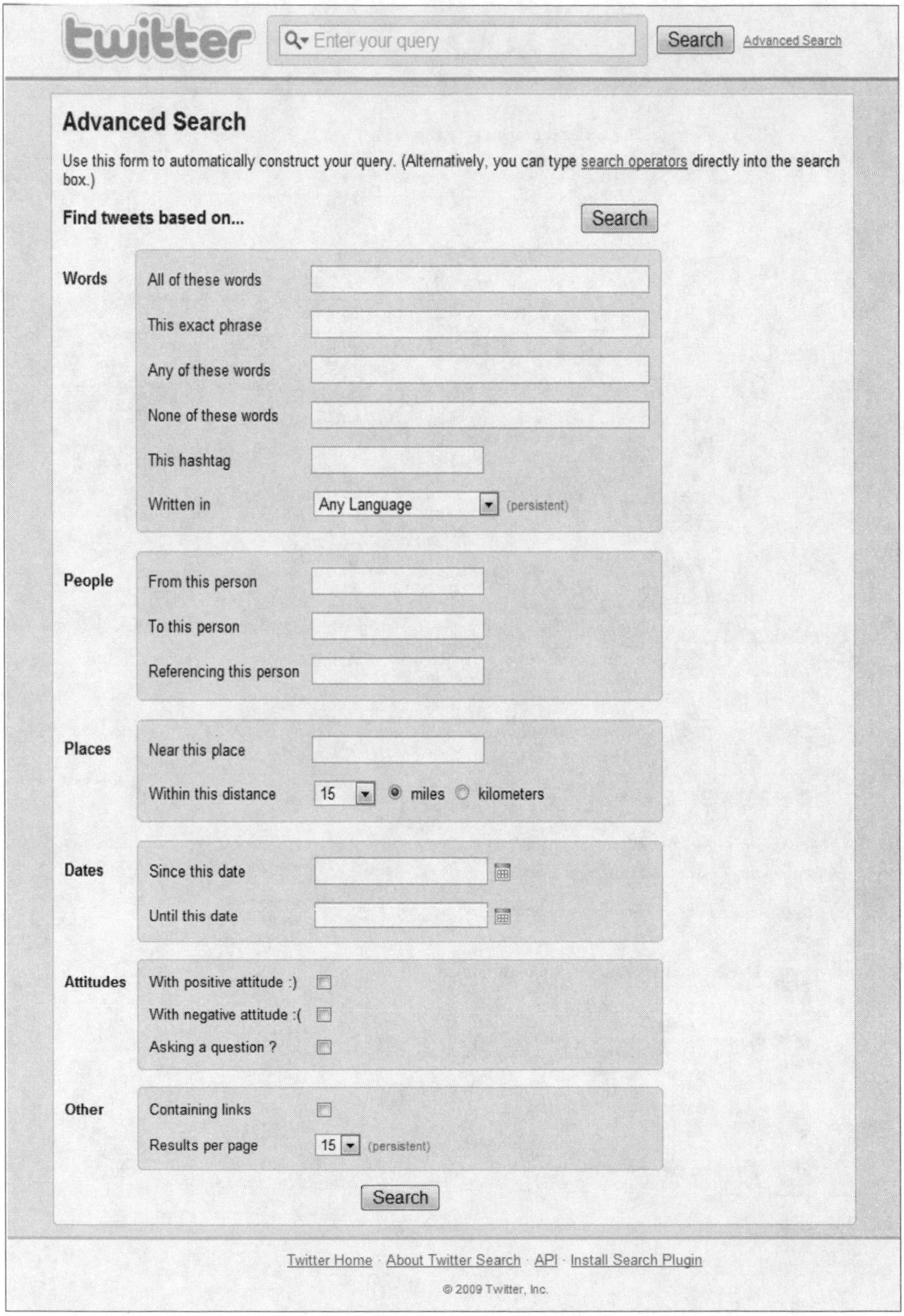

Figure 9.22 Twitter's advanced search interface

within:25mi provides me with tweets that contain the word *library* by individuals who are within a 25-mile radius of Lincoln, Nebraska. This allows me to periodically get the pulse of the town when it comes to the local libraries.

Lastly regarding searching, I'd like to point out one more feature that is available only if you search via the sidebar of your Twitter page: the ability to save searches. For example, if you look at my Twitter page in Figure 9.23, you'll see that I have some saved searches in the sidebar. To do this, enter a term into this search box and then view the results that are displayed on your page. To the right of where it says "Real time results for ..." you'll see a Save This Search link. Click that and your search will be listed in your sidebar for use again in the future.

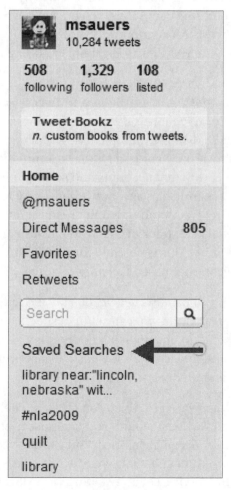

Figure 9.23   Saved searches

Next Steps

Before I leave you to all your blogging, RSS reading, and tweeting, I'd like to point out a few of the additional tools and services that have grown up around Twitter. This list is by no means exhaustive. For a much longer list (pushing 300 at the time of this writing), check out my Delicious bookmarks tagged *Twitter* (delicious.com/travelinlibrarian/twitter). In the meantime, here are some particularly interesting ones you might want to check out:

- *TweetDeck (www.tweetdeck.com)*. This desktop Twitter client offers many additional features beyond what is available via the Twitter website, including retweeting, built-in searching, and organizing the accounts you follow into columns. You can also sync your TweetDeck settings across multiple computers, so you can have the same settings at home and at work. Most importantly for some, TweetDeck provides access to your Twitter, MySpace, Facebook, and LinkedIn accounts in a single interface (Figure 9.24).

- *HootSuite (www.hootsuite.com)*. Similar to TweetDeck, HootSuite is an online Twitter client. It allows one person to view and post to multiple Twitter accounts and allows multiple users to post to a single account. We use HootSuite at the Nebraska Library Commission so I can keep an eye on our several different accounts and so multiple staff members can post to our accounts. It has many other useful features, including the ability to write tweets and schedule them for later posting. Importantly, it will keep track of click-though statistics on links you post using HootSuite. This is possibly the best Twitter client available today for organizational-based tweeting (Figure 9.25).

- *Twitter Your Flickr (blog.flickr.net/en/2009/06/30/Twitter-your-flickr)*. If you have a Flickr account, you can set up a special email address so that when you send an image to that address it will appear in your Flickr account, and a tweet pointing back to that photo will be automatically generated (Figure 9.26).

- *FuelFrog (www.fuelfrog.com)*. Once you create a FuelFrog account and connect it to your Twitter account, you can post tweets to @fuelfrog that include your mileage, field price, and gallons used. FuelFrog will collect this information and chart your fuel expenses. To get the most benefit out of this service, set up tweeting via SMS so you can send this information from your cell phone after you fill up (Figure 9.27).

Figure 9.24   TweetDeck (top)

Figure 9.25   HootSuite (middle)

Figure 9.26   Twitter Your Flickr (bottom)

- *Twistori (twistori.com).* This is a data visualization project that finds and displays live tweets containing the phrases "I love," "I hate," "I think," "I believe," "I feel," and "I wish." It's an interesting way to gauge the pulse of the Twitterverse (Figure 9.28).

- *Is Twitter Down? (www.istwitterdown.com).* Sometimes Twitter isn't working, but how can you be sure it's not just you? Head on over to this website to find out if Twitter is down (Figure 9.29).

- *BackupMyTweets (backupmytweets.com).* If you're worried that Twitter might someday lose everything you've posted, or you're just interested in reading everything you've ever tweeted as a Word document, give this service a try. Once you've set it up, you can download your backed-up content in several different formats (Figure 9.30).

- *Twitterfeed (twitterfeed.com).* This service allows you to take RSS-based content and automatically tweet whenever a new item is added to that feed. A common use is to set the feed for your blog and have this service tweet for you whenever you post to your blog. Tweets will automatically contain the title of your blog post and a link to that blog post, subject to the 140-character limit, of course (Figure 9.31).

- *Twitter Analyzer (www.twitteranalyzer.com).* After you've been tweeting for a while, you might start to wonder things like: What time of the day do you tweet the most? What hash tags do you use most frequently? Who do you converse with the most often? Just put your name into the Twitter Analyzer and get answers to these questions and more all with colorful charts and graphs (Figure 9.32).

Endnotes

1. "Microblogging," Wikipedia, The Free Encyclopedia, en.wikipedia.org/wiki/Microblogging (accessed May 5, 2010).
2. In the fall of 2009, Twitter redesigned its interface and on individual account pages, the question is now "What are you doing?" or "What's happening?"

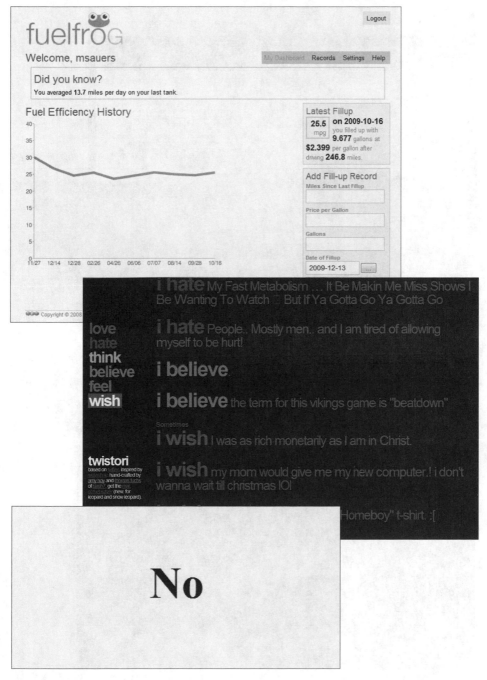

Figure 9.27   FuelFrog (top)
Figure 9.28   Twistori (middle)
Figure 9.29   Is Twitter Down? (bottom)

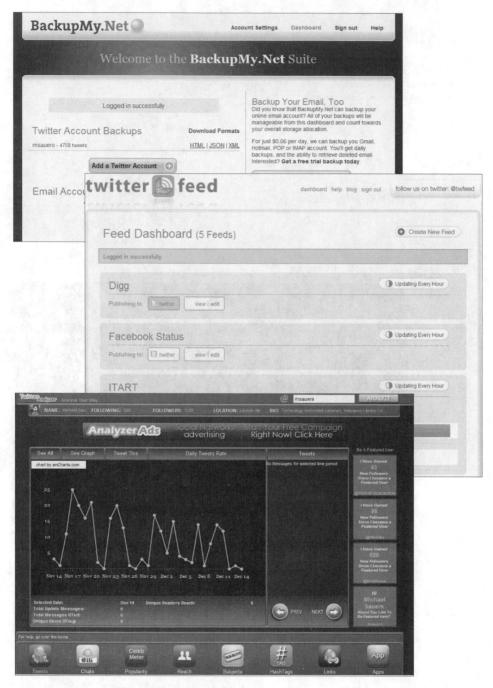

Figure 9.30   BackupMyTweets (top)
Figure 9.31   Twitterfeed (middle)
Figure 9.32   Twitter Analyzer (bottom)

Afterword

What if the real attraction of the internet is not its cutting-edge bells and whistles, its jazzy interface or any of the advanced technology that underlies its pipes and wires? What if, instead, the attraction is an atavistic throwback to the prehistoric human fascination with telling tales? Five thousand years ago, the marketplace was the hub of civilization, a place to which traders returned from remote lands with exotic spices, silks, monkeys, parrots, jewels—and fabulous stories.

—From *The Cluetrain Manifesto* by Rick Levine,
Christopher Locke, Doc Searls, and David Weinberger (2000)

Will You Tell Me a Story?

In writing this book, I've focused mostly on the mechanics of creating blogs and RSS feeds, and my hope is that I've shown you how to use those mechanics easily. Now comes the hard part—putting those mechanics into action.

The next step is to take your blog or your library's blog and use it to its full advantage. The best way to go about that is to use it to tell a story—your story, the library's story, the conference's story. The story itself isn't as important as the fact that you tell it.

Libraries are notoriously bad at promotion. Every other time I've printed those words, the editor with whom I'm working has responded by telling me, "You can't say that. Be less direct. You'll upset people." The trouble is, every time I make that statement to a librarian, he or she instantly agrees with me. Sorry, folks, we librarians, even after the intervening years since the first edition of this book, are *still* bad at publicity.

Yes, we make fliers, post announcements on our websites, and use word of mouth to let people know what's going to happen at the library. Then we cross our fingers and hope that enough people show up at the event to make it worth the time and effort. We need a better way to promote both the library's events and the library itself.

One way is to promote the event not only before it happens but also after it happens. Tell the story of the planning, what happened at the event, and the results after the fact. Include pictures and comments from the participants. Tell a story and people will want to come back for more. In this age of recessions, ever-shrinking budgets, furloughs, and even threats of closing not only branches but whole library systems, storytelling is now more important than ever.

A blog can accomplish this. Blogs are inherently story-based. A blog tells the story of its author or authors. Let your blog be the place where your patrons come to hear that story.

Why does a blog work for storytelling? Because it takes the complexity out of web publishing: No XHTML, CSS, or messing around with servers required. Blogs are conversational. If you let your blog have its own voice, people will respond as if they're talking to you—not reading a press release drafted by a PR department.

So, go forth and blog. Tell your story.

Recommended Reading

The following is a list of books and online resources that contain further information on blogs, blogging, bloggers, and RSS. This list is by no means complete and does not contain any of the blogs or feeds covered in previous chapters. Those interested in more resources should look at BlogBib (blog-bib.blogspot.com) and my Information Superhighway bibliography (travelin librarian.info/home/bibliography.html).

Books

Banks, Michael A. *Blogging Heroes*. Indianapolis, IN: John Wiley and Sons, 2008.

Beal, Andy and Strauss, Judy. *Radically Transparent: Monitoring and Managing Reputations Online*. Indianapolis, IN: Sybex, 2008.

Blood, Rebecca (ed.). *We've Got Blog: How Weblogs are Changing Our Culture*. Cambridge, MA: Perseus Publishing, 2002.

Casey, Michael E. and Savastinuk, Laura C. *Library 2.0: A Guide to Participatory Library Service*. Medford, NJ: Information Today, Inc., 2007.

Coombs, Karen and Griffey, Jason. *Library Blogging*. Santa Barbara, CA: Linworth Publishing Company, 2007.

Clyde, Laurel A. *Weblogs and Libraries*. Oxford: Chandos House, 2004.

Farkas, Meredith G. *Social Software in Libraries*. Medford, NJ: Information Today, Inc., 2007.

Gant, Scott. *We're All Journalists Now*. New York: Free Press, 2007.

Gillmor, Dan. *We the Media: Grassroots Journalism by the People, For the People*. Cambridge, MA: O'Reilly, 2004.

Graham, Alan and Burton, Bonnie (eds.). *Never Threaten to Eat Your Co-Workers: Best of Blogs*. Berkeley, CA: Apress, 2004.

Hastings, Robin. *Microblogging in Libraries*. New York, Neal-Schuman, Inc., 2010.

Hewitt, Hugh. *Blog: Understanding the Information Reformation That's Changing Your World*. Nashville, TN: Nelson Books, 2005.

Hunt, Tara. *The Whuffie Factor*. New York: Crown, 2009.

King, David Lee. *Designing the Digital Experience*. Medford, NJ: CyberAge Books, 2008.

Kline, David and Burstein, Dan. *Blog!* New York: CDS Books, 2005.

Rosenberg, Scott. *Say Everything: How Blogging Began, What It's Becoming, and Why It Matters*. New York: Crown, 2009.

Scoble, Robert and Israel, Shel. *Naked Conversations: How Blogs Are Changing the Way Businesses Talk With Customers*. Hoboken, NJ: John Wiley & Sons, 2006.

Stone, Biz. *Who Let the Blogs Out? A Hyperconnected Peek at the World of Weblogs*. New York: St. Martin's Griffin, 2004.

Trippi, Joe. *The Revolution Will Not Be Televised: Democracy, the Internet, and the Overthrow of Everything*. New York: Regan Books, 2004.

Wojtowicz, Peter. *I Blog, Therefore I Am*. Bloomington, IN: AuthorHouse, 2005.

Wright, Jeremy. *Blog Marketing: The Revolutionary New Way to Increase Sales, Build Your Brand, and Get Exceptional Results*. New York: McGraw-Hill, 2005.

Online or Print Articles

Albanese, Andrew. "UM Library Offers Free Blogs." *Library Journal* 129, no. 9 (May 15, 2004): 18.

Angeles, Michael. "K-Logging: Supporting KM With Web Logs." *Library Journal* 128, no. 7 (April 15, 2003). Retrieved from www.libraryjournal.com/index.asp?layout=article&articleid=CA286642 (accessed May 6, 2010).

Ayre, Lori Bowen. "Want To Go Blogging? Infopeople Webcast." March 2004. Retrieved from infopeople.org/training/webcasts/webcast_data/102/index.html (accessed May 6, 2010).

Baker, Marcia Dority and Pearlman, Stefanie S. "Tweet Treats: How One Law Library Uses Twitter to Educate and Connect With Patrons." *AALL Spectrum* 14, no. 3 (December 2009). Retrieved from www.aallnet.org/products/pub_sp0912/pub_sp0912_Tweet.pdf (accessed July 7, 2010).

Balas, Janet L. "Here a Blog, There a Blog, Even the Library Has a Web Log." *Computers in Libraries* 23, no. 10 (November–December 2003): 41–43.

Bannan, Karen J. "RSS: Lo-fi Content Syndication." *EContent* 25, no. 1 (January 2002).

Barron, Daniel D. "Blogs, Wikis, Alt Com, and the New Information Landscape: A Library Media Specialist's Guide." *School Library Media Activities Monthly* 20, no. 2 (October 2003): 48–51.

Bates, Mary Ellen. "Would You Trust Joe Isuzu's Blog?" *EContent* 27, no. 12 (December 2004).

Berger, Pam. "Are You Blogging Yet?" *Information Searcher* 14, no. 2: 1–4. Retrieved from infosearcher.typepad.com/infosearcher/articles/ISblogs 2.pdf (accessed May 6, 2010).

Bradley, Phil. "Weblogs: What, Why, Where & When." Retrieved from www.philb.com/weblogsppt/Weblogs_files/frame.htm (accessed May 6, 2010).

Broun, Kevin. "New Dog, Old Trick: Alerts for RSS Feeds." *Library Journal* (July 15, 2004). Retrieved from www.libraryjournal.com/article/CA428129.html (accessed May 6, 2010).

Carver, Blake. "Is It Time To Get Blogging?" *Library Journal* 128, no. 1 (January 15, 2003). Retrieved from www.libraryjournal.com/article/CA266428.html (accessed May 6, 2010).

Clyde, L. Anne. "Library Weblogs." *Library Management* 25, no. 4/5 (2004): 183–189.

___. "Shall We Blog?" *Teacher Librarian* 30, no. 1 (October 1, 2002): 44–46.

___. "Weblogs and Blogging, Part 1." *Free Pint* 111 (May 2, 2002). Retrieved from www.freepint.com/issues/020502.htm#feature (accessed May 6, 2010).

___. "Weblogs and Blogging, Part 2." *Free Pint* 112 (May 16, 2002). Retrieved from www.freepint.com/issues/160502.htm (accessed May 6, 2010).

Cohen, Steven M. "RSS for Non-Techie Librarians." LLRX (June 3, 2002). Retrieved from www.llrx.com/features/rssforlibrarians.htm (accessed May 6, 2010).

Crawford, Walt. "Starting a Bicycle Club: Weblogs Revisited." *American Libraries* 35, no. 1 (January 2004): 90–91. Retrieved from www.ala.org/ala/alonline/thecrawfordfiles/crawford2004/january2004starting.cfm (accessed May 6, 2010).

___. "'You Must Read This': Library Weblogs." *American Libraries* 32, no. 9 (October 2001): 74–79.

Creese, Jennifer. "Talking With Pods: A Look Inside UQ Library's Podcasting Project." Retrieved from espace.library.uq.edu.au/eserv/UQ:200813/Talking_with_PodsVALA2010.pdf (accessed July 7, 2010).

Curling, Cindy. "A Closer Look at Weblogs." LLRX (October 15, 2001). Retrieved from www.llrx.com/columns/notes46.htm (accessed May 6, 2010).

Efimova, Lilia and Hendrick, Stephanie. "In Search for a Virtual Settlement: An Exploration of Weblog Community Boundaries." Retrieved from doc.novay.nl/dsweb/Get/Document-46041 (accessed May 6, 2010).

Estep, Erik S. and Gelfand, Julia. "Weblogs." *Library Hi Tech News* 20, no. 5: 11–12.

Faisal, S. L. "Blogs and Online Social Networks as User Centric Service Tools in Academic Libraries: An Indian Library Experience." International Conference on Academic Libraries (ICAL-2009), October 5–8, 2009, Delhi, India. Retrieved from crl.du.ac.in/ical09/papers/index_files/ical-83_162_349_1_RV.pdf (accessed July 7, 2010).

Fichter, Darlene. "Blogging Software for Intranet Applications: You Can Put Your Own Creative Juices to Work Thinking Up Ways to Use Weblog Software." *ONLINE* 27, no. 1 (January–February, 2003): 61–64.

___. "Blogging Your Life Away." *ONLINE* 25, no. 3 (May 2001): 68–71.

___. "Using RSS to Create New Services." *ONLINE* 28, no. 4 (July–August 2004).

___. "Why and How to Use Blogs to Promote Your Library's Services." *Marketing Library Services* 17, no. 6 (November–December 2003): 1–4. Retrieved from www.infotoday.com/mls/nov03/fichter.shtml (accessed May 6, 2010).

Garrod, Penny. "Weblogs: Do They Belong In Libraries?" *Ariadne* 40 (July 30, 2004). Retrieved from www.ariadne.ac.uk/issue40/public-libraries (accessed May 6, 2010).

Goans, Doug and Vogel, Teri M. "Building a Home for Library News with a Blog." *Computers in Libraries* 23, no. 10 (November–December 2003): 20–26. Retrieved from www.infotoday.com/cilmag/nov03/goans_vogel.shtml (accessed May 6, 2010).

Grady, Jenifer. "Who's Blogging?" *Library Worklife* 1, no. 5. Retrieved from www.ala-apa.org/newsletter/vol1no5/worklife.html (accessed May 6, 2010).

Hammond, Tony, Hannay, Timo, and Lund, Ben. "The Role of RSS in Science Publishing: Syndication and Annotation on the Web." *D-Lib Magazine* 10, no. 12 (December 2004).

Hane, Paula. "Blogs Are a Natural for Librarians." *NewsLink* no. 24 (October 2001). Retrieved from www.infotoday.com/newslink/newslink0110.htm (accessed May 6, 2010).

Henning, Jeffrey. "The Blogging Iceberg: Of 4.12 Million Hosted Weblogs, Most Little Seen, Quickly Abandoned." Retrieved from findarticles.com/p/articles/mi_m0EIN/is_2003_Oct_6/ai_108559565 (accessed May 6, 2010).

Herring, Susan, Scheidt, Lois Ann, Bonus, Sabrina, and Wright, Elijah. "Bridging the Gap: A Genre Analysis of Weblogs." *Proceedings of the 37th Annual Hawaii International Conference on System Sciences* (HICSS'04)—Track 4 (January 5–8, 2004): 40101b. Retrieved from csdl.computer.org/comp/proceedings/hicss/2004/2056/04/205640101b.pdf (accessed May 6, 2010).

Hinton, Melissa J. "Reading the Academic Library Blog Through the Lens of Genre Theory: A Preliminary Discussion." *Internet Reference Services Quarterly* 13, no. 4 (October 2008): 347–361.

Humphries, Lee. "Historicizing Microblogging." CHI 2010, April 10–15, 2010, Atlanta, Georgia. Retrieved from www.cs.unc.edu/~julia/accepted-papers/Humphreys_HistoricizingTwitter.pdf (accessed July 7, 2010).

Huwe, Terence K. "Born to Blog." *Computers in Libraries* 23, no. 10 (November–December 2003): 44–45.

International Association of School Librarianship (IASL). "Weblogs and Blogging: Resources For School Libraries. School Libraries Online." Retrieved from www.iasl-slo.org/weblogs.html (accessed July 7, 2010).

Jacobs, James R. "Blogosphere: Exploring the New Killer App for Librarians." *Documents to the People* (DttP) 31, no. 2 (Summer 2003): 6–7.

___. "RSS: It's Only XML But I Like It." *Documents to the People* (DttP) 32, no. 2 (Summer 2004).

Johnson, Sarah L. and Gordon, Rachel Singer. "Library Job Gurus Create Career Blog Site." *Computers in Libraries* 24, no. 2 (February 2004): 48.

Kroski, Ellyssa. "Should Your Library Have a Social Media Policy?" *School Library Journal* (October, 1, 2009). Retrieved from www.schoollibraryjournal.com/article/CA6699104.html (accessed July 7, 2010).

LaGuardia, Cheryl and Tallent, Ed. "Interviewing: Beware Blogging Blunders." *Library Journal* 127, no. 15 (September 15, 2002).

Lenhart, Amanda, Purcell, Kristen, Smith, Aaron, and Zickuhr, Kathryn. "Social Media and Young Adults. Pew Internet and American Life Project." February 3, 2010. Retrieved from www.pewinternet.org/Reports/2010/Social-Media-and-Young-Adults.aspx (accessed July 7, 2010).

Mattern, Jennifer. "Why Blog Controversy Is a Good Thing (Even When It's About You)." DIRJournal Web Directory, March 1, 2010. Retrieved from www.dirjournal.com/articles/why-blog-controversy-is-a-good-thing-even-when-its-about-you (accessed July 7, 2010).

Mattison, David. "So You Want to Start a Syndicated Revolution." *Searcher* 11, no. 2 (February 2003): 38–48.

Nardi, Bonnie, Schiano, Diane, and Gumbrecht, Michelle. "Blogging as Social Activity, or, Would You Let 900 Million People Read Your Diary?" *Proceedings of Computer Supported Cooperative Work* 2004, November 6–10, 2004. Chicago: ACM. Retrieved from home.comcast.net/~diane.schiano/CSCW04.Blog.pdf (accessed May 6, 2010).

Newman, Bobbi. "Sneaking the Social Web into Your Library." Retrieved from www.slideshare.net/librarianbyday/sneaking-the-social-web-into-your-library (accessed July 7, 2010).

Notess, Greg. "The Blog Realm: News Sources, Searching with Daypop, and Content Management." *ONLINE* 26, no. 5 (September–October 2002). Retrieved from www.onlinemag.net/sep02/OnTheNet.htm (accessed May 6, 2010).

___. "Harvesting Blogs for Emergent Information." Internet Librarian 2003, November 4, 2003. Retrieved from notess.com/speak/talks/il03harvesting blogs.pps (accessed May 6, 2010).

___. "RSS, Aggregators, and Reading the Blog Fantastic." *ONLINE* 26, no. 6 (November–December 2002).

Paquet, Sébastien. "Personal Knowledge Publishing and Its Uses in Research (1/2)." KnowledgeBoard. January 10, 2003. Retrieved from www.knowledge board.com/item/253/2010/5/2008 (accessed July 7, 2010).

Quint, Barbara. "Blogs and Currency." *Information Today* 21, no. 5 (May 2004): 7.

Rainie, Lee. "How Libraries Can Survive in the New Media Ecosystem." *El profesional de la información* 19, no. 3 (May–June 2010): 308–314. Retrieved from www.elprofesionaldelainformacion.com/contenidos/2010/mayo/rainie.pdf (accessed July 7, 2010).

___. "The State of Blogging." Pew Internet & American Life Project (January 2005). Retrieved from www.pewinternet.org/PPF/r/144/report_display.asp (accessed May 6, 2010).

Sauers, Michael. "Integrating RSS Into Your Web Site." Retrieved from www.slideshare.net/travelinlibrarian/integrating-rss-into-your-web-site-long-presentation (accessed July 7, 2010).

___. "An Introduction to RSS." Business Information Alert (August 2003). Retrieved from www.travelinlibrarian.info/writing/introtorss.html (accessed May 6, 2010).

Sauers, Michael and Burns, Christa. "What Are You Doing Now? The Twitterification of the Web." Retrieved from www.slideshare.net/travelin librarian/what-are-you-doing-now-the-twitterfication-of-the-web-presentation (accessed July 7, 2010).

Schwartz, Greg. "Blogs for Libraries." WebJunction (August 3, 2003). Retrieved from webjunction.org/do/DisplayContent?id=767 (accessed May 6, 2010).

Skinner, Geoffrey. "Filters and Rogue Librarians: Weblogs in the Library World." November 8, 2002. Retrieved from www.redgravenstein.com/people/gs/mlis/289/weblog (accessed May 6, 2010).

Stone, Steven A. "The Library Blog: A New Communication Tool." *Kentucky Libraries* 67, no. 4 (Fall 2003).

Tay, Aaron. "Using RSS Feeds to Distribute Library News—6 Ways." Musings About Librarianship. March 22, 2010. Retrieved from musingsaboutlibrarianship. blogspot.com/2010/03/using-rss-feeds-to-distribute-library.html (accessed July 7, 2010).

Tennant, Roy. "Feed Your Head: Keeping Up by Using RSS." *Library Journal* 128, no. 9 (May 15, 2003).

Thomsen, Elizabeth B. "RSS: Really Simple Syndication." *Collection Building* 23, no. 4 (2004).

Viégas, Fernanda. "Blog Survey: Expectations of Privacy and Accountability (2004)." Retrieved from web.media.mit.edu/~fviegas/survey/blog/results. htm (accessed May 6, 2010).

Wakeman, Denise. "Why Blog When You've Got Facebook?" Build a Better Blog. July 6, 2009. Retrieved from www.buildabetterblog.com/2009/07/why-blog-when-youve-got-facebook.html (accessed July 7, 2010).

Feed Code Examples

RSS 0.90

This version has been superseded by RSS 0.91 and is rarely used any more. The following sample was created for this book.

```
<?xml version 1.0"?>
<rdf:RDF xmlns:rdf=http://www.w3.org/1999/02/22-rdf-syntax-ns#
xmlns="http://my.netscape.com/rdf/simple/0.9">
   <channel>
      <title>Sample RSS 0.90 Feed</title>
      <link>http://www.foo.bar/</link>
      <description>A sample RSS feed for Blogs & RSS: A librarian's
      handbook</description>
   </channel>
   <image>
      <title>Michael rendered in Lego</title>
      <url>http://travelinlibrarian.info/blog/lego.jpg</url>
      <link>http://travelinlibrarian.info/</link>
   </image>
   <item>
      <title>The Misadventures of Hello Cthulhu</title>
      <link>http://www.hello-cthulhu.com</link>
   </item>
   <item>
      <title>Browse Happy</title>
      <link>http://browsehappy.com</link>
   </item>
</rdf:RDF>
```

RSS 0.91

This version has been superseded by RSS 0.92. The following sample is from Librarian's Rant, Louise Alcorn (lblog. jalcorn.net/rss.php?version=0.91).

```xml
<?xml version="1.0" encoding="utf-8" ?>
<rss version="0.91">
  <channel>
    <title>Librarian's Rant</title>
    <link>http://lblog.jalcorn.net/</link>
    <description>Planning the Revolution....</description>
    <language>en</language>
    <image>
    <url>http://lblog.jalcorn.net/templates/default/img/s9y_banner_small.png</url>
    <title>RSS: Librarian's Rant - Planning the Revolution....</title>
    <link>http://lblog.jalcorn.net/</link>
    <width>100</width>
    <height>21</height>
    </image>
    <item>
    <title>Our New Foreign Policy</title>
    <link>http://lblog.jalcorn.net/archives/615-Our-New-Foreign-Policy.html</link>
    <description>&lt;br /&gt;Talk tough, shoot first, ...&lt;a
    href=&quot;http://lblog.jalcorn.net/exit.php?url_id=1264&amp;amp;entry_id=615&quot;
    title=&quot;http://story.news.yahoo.com/news?tmpl=story&amp;u=/nm/20050128/pl_nm/
    holocaust_cheney_dress_dc&quot;
    onmouseover=&quot;window.status='http://story.news.yahoo.com/news?tmpl=story&amp;u=
    /nm/20050128/pl_nm/holocaust_cheney_dress_dc';return true;&quot;
    onmouseout=&quot;window.status='';return true;&quot;&gt;dress casual&lt;/a&gt;.
    &lt;blockquote&gt;&lt;b&gt;Cheney Criticized for Attire at Auschwitz
    Ceremony&lt;/b&gt;&lt;br /&gt; &lt;br /&gt; Vice President Dick Cheney raised
    eyebrows on Friday for wearing an olive-drab parka, hiking boots and knit ski cap
    to represent the United States at a solemn ceremony remembering the liberation of
    Auschwitz. &lt;br /&gt; &lt;br /&gt; ...&quot;The vice president...was dressed in
    the kind of attire one typically wears to operate a snow blower,&quot; Robin
    Givhan, The Washington Post's fashion writer, wrote in the newspaper's Friday
    editions. &lt;br /&gt; &lt;br /&gt; Between the somber, dark-coated leaders at the
    outdoor ceremony sat Cheney, resplendent in a green parka embroidered with his name
    and featuring a fur-trimmed hood, the laced brown boots and a knit ski cap reading
    &quot;Staff 2001.&quot; &lt;br /&gt; &lt;br /&gt; &quot;And, indeed, the vice
    president looked like an awkward boy amid the well-dressed adults,&quot; Givhan
    wrote. &lt;/blockquote&gt; &lt;i&gt; Thanks to Todd G.&lt;/i&gt;&lt;br /&gt; &lt;br
    /&gt;</description>
    </item>
    <item>
    <title>Education secretary condemns public show with gay characters</title>
    <link>http://lblog.jalcorn.net/archives/614-Education-secretary-condemns-public-
    show-with-gay-characters.html</link>
    <description>&lt;br /&gt;Cuz heaven forbid this administration shouldn't follow the
    oh-so-progressive viewpoint of James Dobson and Focus on the Family, a la &lt;a
    href=&quot;http://lblog.jalcorn.net/exit.php?url_id=1262&amp;amp;entry_id=614&quot;
    title=&quot;http://lblog.jalcorn.net/archives/609-UCC-Welcomes-
    Spongebob!.html&quot;
```

```
onmouseover=&quot;window.status='http://lblog.jalcorn.net/archives/609-UCC-
Welcomes-Spongebob!.html';return true;&quot;
onmouseout=&quot;window.status='';return true;&quot;&gt;the Spongebob
controversy&lt;/a&gt;.  Article about the Ed. Secy is at &lt;a
href=&quot;http://lblog.jalcorn.net/exit.php?url_id=1263&amp;amp;entry_id=614&quot;
title=&quot;http://www.cnn.com/2005/EDUCATION/01/26/education.secretary.pbs.ap/
index.html&quot;
onmouseover=&quot;window.status='http://www.cnn.com/2005/EDUCATION/01/26/education.
secretary.pbs.ap/index.html';return true;&quot;
onmouseout=&quot;window.status='';return true;&quot;&gt;CNN.com&lt;/a&gt;:
&lt;blockquote&gt;The not-yet-aired episode of &quot;Postcards From Buster&quot;
shows the title character, an animated bunny named Buster, on a trip to Vermont --
a state known for recognizing same-sex civil unions. &lt;b&gt;The episode features
two lesbian couples, although the focus is on farm life and maple
sugaring&lt;/b&gt;.&lt;br /&gt; &lt;br /&gt; A PBS spokesman said late Tuesday that
the nonprofit network has decided not to distribute the episode, called
&quot;Sugartime!,&quot; to its 349 stations. She said the Education Department's
objections were not a factor in that decision.&lt;/blockquote&gt;  I'm so
disappointed with PBS...&lt;br /&gt; &lt;br /&gt; &lt;i&gt;Thanks to Amy M. on
Library Underground.&lt;/i&gt;&lt;br /&gt; &lt;br /&gt;</description>
    </item>
  </channel>
</rss>
```

RSS 0.92

This version has been superseded by RSS 2.0. The following sample is from Thoughts From Eric, Eric Meyer (meyerweb. com/feed/rss).

```
<?xml version="1.0" encoding="UTF-8"?>
<rss version="0.92">
  <channel>
    <title>Thoughts From Eric</title>
    <link>http://meyerweb.com</link>
    <description>Things that Eric A. Meyer, CSS expert, writes
    about on his personal Web site; it's largely Web standards
    and Web technology, but also various bits of culture,
    politics, personal observations, and other miscellaneous
    stuff</description>
    <lastBuildDate>Thu, 03 Feb 2005 19:16:34
    +0000</lastBuildDate>
    <docs>http://backend.userland.com/rss092</docs>
    <language>en</language>
    <item>
      <title>S5 1.1b5</title>
      <description>The last beta before 1.1 final is released.
      The only change is the addition of Home and End handling,
      but we're still looking for a fix to alpha handling of
```

```
      background PNGs in IE/Win. (431 words | Tools S5 |
      comments and pings allowed)</description>
      <link>http://meyerweb.com/eric/thoughts/2005/02/03/
      s5-11b5/</link>
    </item>
    <item>
      <title>Be A Parent</title>
      <description>An old favorite returns, and in so doing
      inadvertantly touches off a rant about parenthood and baby
      blogs. (962 words | Personal | pings
      allowed)</description>
    </item>
  </channel>
</rss>
```

RSS 2.0

The following example is from Library Web Chic, Karen Coombs (www.librarywebchic.net/rss.xml).

```
<?xml version="1.0"?>
<!-- RSS generated by Radio UserLand v8.0.8 on Sun, 30 Jan 2005 20:55:47 GMT -- >
<rss version="2.0">
  <channel>
    <title>Library Web Chic</title>
    <link>http://www.librarywebchic.net/</link>
    <description></description>
    <language>en-us</language>
    <copyright>Copyright 2005 Karen Coombs</copyright>
    <lastBuildDate>Sun, 30 Jan 2005 20:55:47 GMT</lastBuildDate>
    <docs>http://backend.userland.com/rss</docs>
    <generator>Radio UserLand v8.0.8</generator>
    <managingEditor>kac@mailcity.com</managingEditor>
    <webMaster>kac@mailcity.com</webMaster>
    <skipHours>
      <hour>0</hour>
      <hour>2</hour>
      <hour>3</hour>
      <hour>4</hour>
      <hour>5</hour>
      <hour>1</hour>
      <hour>8</hour>
      <hour>23</hour>
      <hour>15</hour>
      <hour>16</hour>
```

```
      <hour>10</hour>
      <hour>6</hour>
      <hour>11</hour>
      <hour>7</hour>
      </skipHours>
<ttl>60</ttl>
<item>
      <title>Free E-books</title>
      <link>http://www.librarywebchic.net/2005/01/30.html#a196</link>
      <description>&lt;h4&gt;Free E-books&lt;/h4&gt; &lt;p&gt;This week I spent
      some time adding free e-books collections to our OpenURL resolver. The
      most important set I got added as the Escholarship editions from the
      University of California Press. Information about how to link to these
      titles and a list of them is available on the web at &lt;a
      href=&quot;http://texts.cdlib.org/escholarship/help.html&quot;&gt;&lt;a
      href=&quot;http://texts.cdlib.org/escholarship/help.html&quot;&gt;http:
      //texts.cdlib.org/escholarship/help.html&lt;/a&gt;&lt;/a&gt; This
      collection contains almost 500 publically available titles. The best
      part is if you have SFX (which we do) there is a target already set up
      for you. You don&apos;t have to create one on your own. This basically
      means all you have to do is turn things on. Since our monography budget
      has taken a serious hit this year, access to these e-books is very
      helpful. Does anyone have other collections of freely available e-books
      that they have added to their OPAC or OpenURL resolver? If so, drop me
      a note using the email link and let me know. I&apos;m very interested
      in trying to make as many free resources available to my users as
      possible.&lt;br&gt; &lt;/p&gt;&lt;br&gt;</description>
      <guid>http://www.librarywebchic.net/2005/01/30.html#a196</guid>
      <pubDate>Sun, 30 Jan 2005 20:55:47 GMT</pubDate>
      <category>Ongoing Projects</category>
      <category>OpenURL</category>
</item>
<item>
      <title>Integrateable Standards compliant WYSIWYG Editor</title>
      <link>http://www.librarywebchic.net/2005/01/27.html#a195</link>
      <description>&lt;h4&gt;Integrateable Standards compliant WYSIWYG
      Editor&lt;/h4&gt; &lt;p&gt;&lt;a
      href=&quot;http://www.themaninblue.com&quot;&gt;The Man in
      Blue&lt;/a&gt; has created a JavaScript-driven &lt;a
      href=&quot;http://www.themaninblue.com/experiment/widgEditor/&quot;&gt;
      web-based WYSIWYG editor&lt;/a&gt; that can be added to any web page.
      This is similar to tools such as &lt;a
      href=&quot;http://www.kevinroth.com/rte/demo.php&quot;&gt;RichText
      Editor&lt;/a&gt; and &lt;a
      href=&quot;http://www.dynarch.com/demos/htmlarea/examples/core.html&quo
      t;&gt;HTMLArea&lt;/a&gt;, but highly streamlined, standards-compliant,
      and much easier to integrate. It is very cool. If you have a home-grown
      content management system in which you have people contribute content
      by adding html into a textarea field, this tool will eliminate the need
      for content creators to know HTML. I&apos;m integrating it into our
      XML-base blogging tool (which was using RichTextEditor before) and a
```

```
        small content management system I&apos;ve built. Thanks Man in Blue for
        such a cool and very useful tool!&lt;br&gt;
        &lt;/p&gt; &lt;br&gt;</description>
        <guid>http://www.librarywebchic.net/2005/01/27.html#a195</guid>
        <pubDate>Fri, 28 Jan 2005 01:28:02 GMT</pubDate>
        <category>General Thoughts</category>
      </item>
    </channel>
</rss>
```

RSS 1.0

This version is not preceded or superseded by any other RSS version. The following sample is from Free Range Librarian, Karen G. Schneider (freerange librarian.com/index.rdf).

```
<?xml version="1.0" encoding="utf-8"?>
<rdf:RDF
 xmlns:rdf="http://www.w3.org/1999/02/22-rdf-syntax-ns#"
 xmlns:dc="http://purl.org/dc/elements/1.1/"
 xmlns:sy="http://purl.org/rss/1.0/modules/syndication/"
 xmlns:admin="http://webns.net/mvcb/"
 xmlns:cc="http://web.resource.org/cc/"
xmlns="http://purl.org/rss/1.0/">
  <channel rdf:about="http://freerangelibrarian.com/">
    <title>Free Range Librarian</title>
    <link>http://freerangelibrarian.com/</link>
    <description></description>
    <dc:language>en-us</dc:language>
    <dc:creator></dc:creator>
    <dc:date>2005-02-01T08:11:58-08:00</dc:date>
    <admin:generatorAgent
    rdf:resource="http://www.movabletype.org/?v=3.14" />
    <items>
      <rdf:Seq>
        <rdf:li rdf:resource="http://freerangelibrarian.com/
        archives/020105/podcasting_test.php" />
        <rdf:li rdf:resource="http://freerangelibrarian.com/
        archives/013105/the_last_mile_a_cha.php" />
        <rdf:li rdf:resource="http://freerangelibrarian.com/
        archives/013105/mustread_blogs_lib.php" />
        <rdf:li rdf:resource="http://freerangelibrarian.com/
        archives/013005/frl_rss_1_or_rss_2.php" />
        <rdf:li rdf:resource="http://freerangelibrarian.com/
        archives/012905/lists_versus_blogs_.php" />
```

```
            <rdf:li rdf:resource="http://freerangelibrarian.com/
            archives/012905/newspaper_archives_.php" />
            <rdf:li rdf:resource="http://freerangelibrarian.com/
            archives/012805/frl_spotlight_review.php" />
            <rdf:li rdf:resource="http://freerangelibrarian.com/
            archives/012805/bookqueuetoo_previe.php" />
            <rdf:li rdf:resource="http://freerangelibrarian.com/
            archives/012805/proposals_and_dispos.php" />
            <rdf:li rdf:resource="http://freerangelibrarian.com/
            archives/012605/still_kicking_myself.php" />
            <rdf:li rdf:resource="http://freerangelibrarian.com/
            archives/012605/united_church_of_chr.php" />
            <rdf:li rdf:resource="http://freerangelibrarian.com/
            archives/012505/factcheck_asks_you_t.php" />
            <rdf:li rdf:resource="http://freerangelibrarian.com/
            archives/012405/pensees_du_webcred.php" />
            <rdf:li rdf:resource="http://freerangelibrarian.com/
            archives/012405/public_library_inter.php" />
            <rdf:li rdf:resource="http://freerangelibrarian.com/
            archives/012405/webcred_and_libraria.php" />
        </rdf:Seq>
    </items>
</channel>
    <item rdf:about="http://freerangelibrarian.com/
    archives/020105/podcasting_test.php">
        <title>Podcasting Test</title>
        <link>http://freerangelibrarian.com/archives/020105/
        podcasting_test.php</link>
        <description>This is a test of podcasting (a special type
        of audio webcasting you can think of as &quot;radio on
        demand&quot;; the &apos;casters produce audio files which
        you can download to your MP3 player or--now you will
        understand the name--iPod). I...</description>
        <dc:subject>Podcasting</dc:subject>
        <dc:creator>kgs</dc:creator>
        <dc:date>2005-02-01T08:11:58-08:00</dc:date>
    </item>
    <item rdf:about="http://freerangelibrarian.com/
    archives/013105/the_last_mile_a_cha.php">
        <title>The Last Mile: A Chance to Get Started</title>
        <link>http://freerangelibrarian.com/archives/013105/
        the_last_mile_a_cha.php</link>
        <description>This Friday I&apos;m giving a talk at the
        Ontario Library Association Superconference , and months
        ago, I wrote a wide-open program description. I said I
        would &quot;describe the outer limits of digital
```

```
        libraries,&quot; share &quot;radical and contrarian
        views,&quot; and offer...</description>
        <dc:subject>The Last Mile (Digital Divide
        Issues)</dc:subject>
        <dc:creator>kgs</dc:creator>
        <dc:date>2005-01-31T10:31:41-08:00</dc:date>
    </item>
</rdf:RDF>
```

Atom

The following sample is from The Travelin' Librarian, Michael Sauers (www.travelinlibrarian.info/atom.xml).

```
<?xml version="1.0" encoding="UTF-8" standalone="yes"?>
<?xml-stylesheet href="http://www.blogger.com/styles/atom.css"
type="text/css"?>
<feed version="0.3" xml:lang="en-GB"
xmlns="http://purl.org/atom/ns#">
   <link href="http://www.blogger.com/atom/5543214"
   rel="service.post" title="Travelin' Librarian"
   type="application/atom+xml"/>
   <link href="http://www.blogger.com/atom/5543214"
   rel="service.feed" title="Travelin' Librarian"
   type="application/atom+xml"/>
   <title mode="escaped" type="text/html">Travelin' Librarian</title>
   <tagline mode="escaped" type="text/html"/>
   <link href="http://www.travelinlibrarian.info/" rel="alternate"
   title="Travelin' Librarian" type="text/html"/>
   <id>tag:blogger.com,1999:blog-5543214</id>
   <modified>2005-01-31T20:47:36Z</modified>
   <generator url="http://www.blogger.com/"
   version="5.15">Blogger</generator>
   <info mode="xml" type="text/html">
      <div xmlns="http://www.w3.org/1999/xhtml">This is an Atom
      formatted XML site feed. It is intended to be viewed in a
      Newsreader or syndicated to another site. Please visit the <a
      href="http://help.blogger.com/bin/answer.py?answer=697">Blogger
      Help</a> for more info.</div>
   </info>
   <entry xmlns="http://purl.org/atom/ns#">
      <link
      href="http://www.blogger.com/atom/5543214/110720445691459308"
      rel="service.edit" title="LC, ISBN &amp;amp; XML"
      type="application/atom+xml"/>
      <author>
```

```
      <name>Michael</name>
   </author>
   <issued>2005-01-31T13:45:36-07:00</issued>
   <modified>2005-01-31T20:47:36Z</modified>
   <created>2005-01-31T20:47:36Z</created>
   <link href="http://www.travelinlibrarian.info/2005/01/lc-isbn-
   xml.html" rel="alternate" title="LC, ISBN &amp;amp; XML"
   type="text/html"/>
   <id>tag:blogger.com,1999:blog-5543214.post-
   110720445691459308</id>
   <title mode="escaped" type="text/html">LC, ISBN &amp;amp;
   XML</title>
   <content type="application/xhtml+xml"
   xml:base="http://www.travelinlibrarian.info/"
   xml:space="preserve">
      <div xmlns="http://www.w3.org/1999/xhtml">This article, <i>
      <a href="http://www.xml.com/pub/a/2004/06/02/dijalog.html">
      Putting ISBNs to Work</a></i>, is going to take me a while to
      digest but it looks very interesting. What the author's done
      is "a command line tool that let me input an ISBN... which
      outputs a Library of Congress Call Number, which I could then
      affix to a book."</div>
   </content>
</entry>
<entry xmlns="http://purl.org/atom/ns#">
   <link
   href="http://www.blogger.com/atom/5543214/110720428926175088"
   rel="service.edit" title="Firefox 1.1 delayed"
   type="application/atom+xml"/>
   <author>
      <name>Michael</name>
   </author>
   <issued>2005-01-31T13:42:49-07:00</issued>
   <modified>2005-01-31T20:44:49Z</modified>
   <created>2005-01-31T20:44:49Z</created>
   <link href="http://www.travelinlibrarian.info/2005/01/firefox-
   11-delayed.html" rel="alternate" title="Firefox 1.1 delayed"
   type="text/html"/>
   <id>tag:blogger.com,1999:blog-5543214.post-
   110720428926175088</id>
   <title mode="escaped" type="text/html">Firefox 1.1
   delayed</title>
   <content type="application/xhtml+xml"
   xml:base="http://www.travelinlibrarian.info/"
   xml:space="preserve">
      <div xmlns="http://www.w3.org/1999/xhtml">According to <a
```

```
            href="http://weblogs.mozillazine.org/ben/archives/007434.html
            ">Ben Godger's blog</a>, Firefox 1.1 will not be making an
            appearance in March as originally scheduled. (He's the lead
            engineer on the project, he should know.) </div>
         </content>
      </entry>
   </feed>
```

Glossary

Aggregator. A program or web service that tracks and receives RSS feed content and presents that content to the user in a readable format.

Archive. To transfer old posts from a blog's home page to pages that display posts only from a certain time period. Typically an archive page contains posts from a single month or week.

ASP. Active Server Pages. A Microsoft scripting language.

Atom. An XML-based structured language for syndicating content. Similar to RSS.

BitTorrent. A peer-to-peer internet file-sharing system that uses a distributed model for sharing content.

Blog/blogging/blogger. A blog is a website in the form of an online journal that presents information in reverse chronological order. Blogging is the act of posting to a blog, and a blogger is a person who is doing the posting.

Blogosphere. The totality of all blogs on the web.

Blogroll. A list of blogs and/or feeds read or recommended by a user.

Client software. Software installed on a user's personal computer (typically a desktop or laptop) as opposed to software installed on a server.

CSS. Cascading Style Sheets. A language for controlling the design elements of webpages.

Enclosures. Nontext files that are attached to feed items. Similar to email attachments.

Encoding scheme. The method used to control and identify which character set is being used in a file. For example, English and Russian use different encoding schemes.

Feed. Short for RSS feed or Atom feed. A file used to syndicate content.

FTP. File Transfer Protocol. An internet protocol for transferring files from one computer to another.

FTP server. The computer that the user is either receiving from or sending to.

Google bomb. A prank in which millions of webpages are directed to create links of the same type, in an attempt to influence the ranking of Google search results.

GUID. Globally Unique Identifier. A string of characters that identifies a feed item.

Hand rolling. Creating a feed without using any software. In this method, all feed code and content is entered by hand.

HTML. Hypertext Markup Language. A markup language used for creating webpages.

HTTP authentication. A method of verifying the identity of a user attempting to access a webpage using a username/password combination.

LAN. Local Area Network.

Lifestreaming. The practice of collecting all online postings and events associated with a single individual into one online location.

Metadata. Information associated with an item (typically a document) that describes the content of that item.

Microblogging. A form of blogging in which posts are very short or contain single images as with Twitter and Tumblr, respectively.

Moblogging. Mobile blogging. Typically refers to the creation of a photo-based blog using a cell-phone camera.

MP3. MPEG Level 3. An open-source standard for the creation of digital audio files.

PHP. An open-source scripting language. Typically used to automate the content of webpages.

Podcast. Syndicated audio content using RSS.

Posts. Individual entries in a blog.

RDF. Resource Description Framework. An XML-based metadata format.

RFID. Radio Frequency Identification. A small chip containing data that can be read via radio frequency from a short distance.

RSS. Really Simple Syndication, Rich Site Summary, or RDF Site Summary. An XML-based language for syndicating content online.

Semi-Automated. A method for creating a feed in which a user types the content but software creates the required code.

Server root. The directory on the web server that contains the home page of the website.

Server software. Software installed on a server as opposed to software installed on a user's computer.

Server-based aggregator. An aggregator installed on a server.

SFTP. Secure File Transfer Protocol. A method of FTP that encrypts the content of the files being transferred.

SGML. Standard Generalized Markup Language. A set of rules for creating markup languages. Predates XML.

SMS. Short Messaging Service. The protocol used for sending text messages of up to 160 characters between cell phones.

SSL/HTTPS. Secure Sockets Layer/Hypertext Transport Protocol. Methods for encrypting and securing connections between a web server and client computer.

Stand-alone clients. Software installed on a client computer that does not integrate into any other software on that computer.

Style sheet. File containing the code controlling the style of a document. Typically refers to files containing CSS code.

Sync. Synchronize. A procedure for comparing the data in two systems to make sure that both systems contain the same data.

Twitter. A microblogging platform on which users create individual posts (called tweets) of up to 140 characters. Posts can be delivered to the service via a variety of methods including text message, web interfaces, and mobile applications.

Tweet. An individual post on Twitter.

Tweeting. The act of posting to Twitter.

Web server. Computer that houses website files.

Web-based aggregators. An aggregator housed on a web server that can be accessed from any web-accessible device.

Web-based service. A program installed on a web server and accessible from any web-accessible device.

Weblog. Pronounced "We blog." The longer version of the more commonly used "blog."

WYSIWYG. What You See Is What You Get. Any interface that displays what you are typing exactly as you will see it once the information has been processed.

XHTML. eXtensible Hypertext Markup Language. A markup language used for creating webpages. Similar to HTML but follows the rules of XML.

XML. A set of rules for creating markup languages. A follow-up to SGML.

About the Author

Michael P. Sauers is currently the Technology Innovation Librarian for the Nebraska Library Commission in Lincoln, Nebraska, and has been training librarians in technology for more than 15 years. He has also been a public library trustee, a bookstore manager for a library Friends group, a reference librarian, serials cataloger, technology consultant, and bookseller. He earned his MLS in 1995 from the University at Albany's School of Information Science and Policy. He has written nine previous books and dozens of articles for various journals and magazines. In his spare time, he blogs at travelin librarian.info, runs websites for authors and historical societies, is chair of the Nebraska Library Association's Information Technology and Access Round Table, takes many, many photos, and reads about 120 books per year.

Index

+ Google (Add to Google) link, 169, 171, 172

\# (hash tags), 272–273, 278

@mentions, 271

@replies, 271–272

A

Absolute RSS Editor, 232

access to blog, granting, 123, 125

Add Enclosure Link option, Blogger, 114

addresses
    blog, 84, 86, 87, 110
    post, 114

Add Star option (Google Reader), 180–181, 182

Add to Google, 169, 171, 172

administrators, blog, 88, 125

adult post content, 107, 108, 110

aggregators, 151, 155–162, 207, 220. *See also* Google Reader

Amazon.com RSS web feed, 210, 211

Ann Arbor District Library blog, 3, 43, 48

archive index date format, 111, 113, 115

archiving posts, 119, 121–122

"at mention," 271

Atom feeds, 138, 139, 142–144. *See also* RSS

"at reply," 271–272

audio posts, 98

authors, adding, 123, 125

Awful Library Books blog, 11, 15, 73, 74

B

backgrounds
    blog, 129–130, 131
    Twitter, 267, 269

backlinks, 118

BackupMyTweets, 284, 286

baseball blogs, 4

BBC news feeds, 213, 217

behind-the-scenes feeds, 147–148

Beyond the Job blog, 12, 15

Bigwood, David, 13, 67–70

Bisson, Casey, 30

Blogger
    Add Enclosure Link option, 114
    Compose tab, 92, 93
    creating accounts, 83–84, 85
    creating feeds, 246–247
    creating posts, 90, 92–95
    Dashboard, 87–90
    described, 2
    directories, 104, 107, 108
    Edit HTML page, 133, 134
    Email and Mobile screen, 123
    Enclosures link, 116
    features, 82
    float alignment setting, 114
    following other blogs with, 194
    Formatting screen, 110–111, 113, 114
    help tools, 83, 135
    link fields, 114, 116
    monetize feature, 135
    Navbar, 126–127
    notifications, 84, 90, 91
    Permissions screen, 123, 125
    posting tab, 99

Blogger (*cont.*)
    profiles, 89–90, 91
    Publishing settings, 112
    Reading List, 88
    security, 123
    Settings tab, 104
    site feed settings, 122
    tags, 130, 133
    template, choosing, 86–87
    time zone setting, 111, 113, 116
    View Blog link, 95
    WYSIWYG interface, 92, 96–97, 108
Blogger Buzz, 88
Blogger Help, 83, 135
bloggers, 1. *See also* librarians who blog
blogging, 1, 81–82
Blogging Fifth Nail, 4
Bloglines, 160–161
blogosphere, 1
blogrolls, 148, 195, 197
blogs
    address, 84, 86, 87, 110
    archives, 122
    backgrounds, 129–130, 131
    characteristics, 7
    comments in, 2
    creating, 82, 83–87, 88
    deleting, 104
    described, 1–2
    design, XHTML in, 124–125, 130
    editing, 107, 108, 109
    email settings, 124
    importing, 87
    making + Google available, 171, 172
    media and, 3, 4
    name, selecting, 84, 86
    numbers, 7
    previewing changes, 129
    search engines, effect on, 3, 5
    search engines, making available to, 107
    templates, 123–124
    titles, 104, 107
    types, 2–3
    viewing live, 95
BlogSend Address, 123
blog services, 82–83
blogspot.com publishing screen, 108, 110

BlogThis! 96–97
blog tools, 104
Blue Skunk Blog, 72
BoingBoing blog, 76
bookmarklets, 169, 170, 197–198, 199, 200
Boule, Michelle, 40
Bromberg, Peter, 23
browsers, integrating with Google Reader, 168
bundles, feed set, 177
Bush, George W., "miserable failure" Google bomb, 5, 6
business/shopping feeds, 223, 225, 226, 227, 228

C

C|Net feed, 216, 217
Carver, Blake, 29
Casady, Tom, 65
Catalogablog, 13, 16, 67, 68, 70
catalog search feeds, 209, 211
Catalogs of Babes blog, 69
Channel 9 blog, 3, 52–53, 56
The Chief's Corner blog, 65–66
Christina's LIS Rant blog, 72
Chrome browser, Google, 150, 152, 169, 198
classic template, 133, 134
clips, adding to website (Google Reader), 192, 193, 195, 197
colors, blog, 130, 131, 132
comment form, 118
comments, 2, 104, 114, 118–120, 121
comment spam, 114, 118, 136
complete feeds, 144
compose mode, 108
Compose tab, Blogger, 92, 93
conferences, Twitter tools for, 273, 277
confirm when marking all as read setting (Google Reader), 194
convert line breaks option, 113
Coombs, Karen, 3, 25
Copyfight blog, 13–14, 16
copyright on blog content, 136

Coverville podcast, 203–204, 205
craigslist feed, 222, 226
Crawford, Walt, 39, 69, 70–72
creating
    Blogger accounts, 83–84, 85
    blogs, 82, 83–87, 88
    feeds, 231–232, 246–247
    Google accounts, 83–84, 85
    Google Reader accounts, 162
    pages, 102–103
    posts, 2, 90, 92–95, 99–100, 123, 125
Custom Domain publishing screen, 108,
    110

D

Dashboard feature, Blogger, 87–90
dates, formatting, 111, 113, 115
Dawdlr blog, 79
Deeplinks blog, 53, 56
deleting
    blogs, 104
    posts, 2, 100, 101, 105
Delicious, 228, 229
demotions due to blog content, 4
Dempsey, Lorcan, 30
Dewey Blog, 9–11, 15
digests, information, 253–257, 258
Digitization 101 blog, 14, 17, 21
direct messages, 274–275
directory, Blogger, 104, 107, 108
domain, custom, 108, 110
Dornfest, Rael, 139
Duncan, Joseph, 4

E

eBay feed, 225, 227
Edit HTML page, Blogger, 133, 134
editing
    blogs, 107, 108, 109
    pages, 102, 103–104, 105–106
    posts, 99–101, 107, 108
    templates, 125–126, 127
Electronic Frontier Foundation, 53

email
    Blogger settings, 123, 124
    Google Reader settings, 182, 195, 196
    posting via, 97–98, 123, 181
    post links, 107, 108
    reading via aggregator, 220
embedded client aggregators, 156, 158
Emily Chang's eHub blog, 78
Enclosures link, Blogger, 116
Encyclopædia Britannica Online feed,
    213, 215
Engadget blog, 73
Everything Is Miscellaneous blog, 53–54,
    56
exporting
    feeds, 179–180
    posts, 104

F

Farkas, Meredith, 18
Fark blog, 76
Fark feeds, 216, 219
Fat Man Walking blog, 4
favicon settings (Google Reader), 194
Feed2JS, 248–252
feed aggregators, 151, 155–162, 207, 220.
    See also Google Reader
FeedBurner, 246
FeedDemon, 156
feed files, contents, 139–142, 155
Feed Informer, 253–257, 258
Feedity, 232
Feed on Feeds, 158, 160
Feedreader, 156
feed readers, 151, 155–162, 207, 220. *See
    also* Google Reader
feeds. *See also* aggregators; Google
    Reader
    adding content to website, 247–248,
        253–257, 258
    adding items, 234, 236–239
    Atom, 138, 139, 142–144
    behind-the-scenes, 147–148
    bundling, 177
    catalog search, 209, 211

feeds (*cont.*)
  complete, 144
  creating, 69, 231–232, 233, 234,
      246–247
  defined, 138
  deleting, 234, 236
  development, 138
  editing, 234, 235
  exporting, 179–180
  filtering, 179
  finding, 148–149
  Google News link, 146
  hidden, 147–148
  icons, 144–148
  identifying, 144–148, 162
  images, 144–148
  importing, 179–180
  links, 144–148
  managing subscriptions, 178–179
  organizing, 164–165, 179
  publishing, 240, 242–246
  reading, 155
  renaming, 164, 174, 179
  republishing, 247–248, 253–257, 258
  on-screen, 144–147
  selecting, 233
  sharing, 177
  site settings, 122
  sorting, 164
  subscribing to, 150, 162–164, 168–173
  summary, 144
  types, 142
  unsubscribing from, 164, 178, 179
  uses, 138
  using, 149–152
  viewing in Google Reader, 166
feeds, available
  business/shopping, 223, 225, 226,
      227, 228
  library/library-related, 209–213,
      214–215
  news, 213, 216–218, 228, 229
  photo, 225, 226
  research, 225, 227
  RSS-based services, 220–223
  social bookmarking, 228, 229
  traffic, 228–229, 230

Feed to JavaScript (Feed2JS), 248–252
filtering
  feeds, 179
  posts, 92, 94, 100
finding feeds, 148–149
Firefox browser, Mozilla, 144–145, 148,
      150–151, 158–159, 168
firing due to blog content, 4, 82
*First Have Something to Say: Writing for
      the Library Profession* (Crawford),
      69
Flickr feed, 225, 226
float alignment setting, Blogger, 114
folders, Google Reader, 178, 179, 195,
      196
following others
  blogs, 148, 184–185, 188–189,
      190–191, 194
  Twitter, 275–277
fonts, blog, 130, 132
Formatting screen, Blogger, 110–111,
      113, 114
Freedom to Tinker blog, 79
FreeGovInfo blog, 79
Free Range Librarian blog, 17–18, 21
FriendFeed microblogging service, 259
FuelFrog, 282, 285
fully automated feed setup, 246–247

G

gadgets, 98–99, 102–103, 104, 127, 128
Gavin, Jennifer, 44
Gizmodo blog, 3, 54, 57
Gmail RSS service, 220, 222
goodies (Google Reader), 195, 197–198,
      199
Google
  creating accounts, 83–84, 85
  manipulating search results, 5–6, 8
  ranking results, 5
  Toolbar, installing, 97
Google AdSense system, 135
Google Blog, 54–55, 57, 148–149, 150
Google bombing, 5–6, 8
Google Gears for offline reading, 198

Google News, 146, 220, 221
Google Profile page, 188
Google Reader. *See also* aggregators
   accounts, creating, 162
   Add Star option, 180–181, 182
   blogroll settings, 195, 197
   clip settings, 192, 193, 195, 197
   confirm when marking all as read set-
      ting, 194
   custom URLs, 192
   described, 160–162
   email settings, 182, 195
   favicon settings, 194
   feeds, managing, 162–166, 167,
      168–174, 178–179, 198–199
   folders, 195, 196
   following others, 148, 184–185,
      188–189, 190–191, 194
   goodies, 195, 197–198, 199
   integrating into browser, 168
   interface, 171–173
   items, liking, 184, 185, 186, 194
   items, sharing/unsharing, 184–185,
      187–190, 191–193, 195, 196
   items, tagging, 184, 186
   items in, 173–174, 175, 176, 180–183
   Keep Unread option, 181, 182
   language settings, 193
   logging in, 162, 163
   navigation pane settings, 193–194
   offline reading in, 199
   on phones, 198, 199
   podcasts, 204, 207
   preferences, 193
   public page settings, 195
   scroll tracking settings, 193
   searching for content, 201–202
   send to feature, 181, 182, 183, 198,
      200–201
   Settings options, 165, 177–180, 193,
      195, 196
   sort options, 164, 173
   start page settings, 193
   subscriptions, managing, 174,
      177–179
Gordon, Rachel Singer, 12
GovTrack.us feeds, 216, 218

Griffey, Jason, 31, 72–73
groups of followers (Google Reader), 188,
   190

H

hand rolling feeds, 231–232
hash tags, in tweets, 272–273, 278
help, Blogger, 83, 135
Hennepin County Library feed, 209, 211
Herzog, Brian, 36
Hibner, Holly, 11, 73–76
hidden feeds, 147–148
Hide Compose Mode option, 108
Hirtle, Peter, 24
HootSuite, 282, 283
Houghton-Jan, Sarah, 23, 76–78, 81
HTML, post creation using, 90, 92,
   96–97, 108
The Huffington Post blog, 3
Hurst-Wahl, Jill, 14
hyper-linking posts to a webpage, 114

I

icons, feed, 144–148
IEBlog, 55, 58–59
iGoogle, 168, 197, 199
images
   blog background, 129–130
   on comments, 119
   feed, 144–148
   in posts, 102
   profile, 90
   template background, 129
   Twitter, 266–267, 269
importing
   blogs, 87
   feeds, 179–180
   posts, 104
individual blogs, 2–3
information digests, 253–257, 258
Information Wants to Be Free blog,
   18–19, 22, 72, 73
Internet Explorer browser, Microsoft,
   144–145, 148, 150–151, 158–159,
   169

ipl2 feed, 210, 212, 214
isbn.nu RSS service, 220–221, 222
Is Twitter Down? tool, 284, 285
ITART blog, 19–20, 22, 145
iTunes, 204, 205, 206, 225, 227

J

Jaiku microblogging service, 259
"Jew" Google bomb, 5, 6, 8
Johnson, Joel, 54
Johnson, Sarah, 12
Journal Tables of Contents feed service,
    213, 214

K

Keep Unread option (Google Reader),
    181, 182
Kelly, Mary, 11, 73–76
Kerry, John, running mate selection, 4
keyword search of posts, 100

L

labels, post, 92, 94, 100
language, post, 111, 113, 116. *See also*
    transliteration, post
language settings (Google Reader), 193
Lawson, Steve, 32
layout, blog, 130, 132
Libby, Dan, 138
librarian blogs, 9. *See also individual
    blogs*
Librarian in Black blog, 23, 27, 76
librarian.net blog, 20, 22, 70, 78, 79
librarians who blog, 67. *See also individ-
    ual librarians*
libraries, blogs as tools for, 7–8
library blogs, 43, 82. *See also individual
    blogs*
LibraryElf RSS service, 221, 223, 224
library feeds, 214–215
Library Garden blog, 23–24, 28
LibraryLaw blog, 24–25, 28

Library of Congress blog, 44–45, 48
library-related feeds, 209–213
Library Suggestion blog, 45–46, 48
Library Web Chic blog, 3, 25–26, 28
A Library Writer's Blog, 26–27, 29
Lifehacker blog, 73, 76, 78
liking items, Google Reader, 184, 185,
    186, 194
line breaks, converting, 113
link fields, Blogger, 114, 116
Link List gadget, 127
links, feed, 144–148
LISNews blog, 3, 29, 34
ListGarden
    accessing, 232–233
    described, 232
    feeds, managing, 233, 234, 235,
        236–240, 242–246
    items, managing, 240, 241
    version, choosing, 232
listings, including blog in, 108
Listverse blog, 76
A look at what's new page, 172–173
Lorcan Dempsey's Weblog (OCLC), 30,
    34, 70

M

MacManus, Richard, 59
"magic elements," 130. *See also* Blogger,
    tags
MaisonBisson.com blog, 30–31, 34
MakeUseOf.com blog, 76
Marin County Free Library blog, 46, 49
Mars Rover Blog, 4
media and blogs, 3, 4
"Memogate," blog exposure of error by, 4
@mentions, 271
microblogging, 258, 259. *See also* Twitter
Microsoft Developer Network blog, 3,
    52–53, 56
Microsoft Internet Explorer browser,
    144–145, 148, 150–151, 158–159,
    169
Microsoft Outlook, 158, 159
Microsoft Word, posting via, 95–96

Minnow, Mary, 24
"miserable failure" Google bomb, 5–6, 8
Mitchell, Joan, 9
MLBlogs, 4
mobile devices
    blog access, 123, 124
    Google Reader on, 198, 199
    posting via, 98, 123
    Twitter access, 266, 268
Modcult blog, 79
moderation, comment, 104, 118–119, 121
monetize feature, Blogger, 135
Movable Type, 2, 83
The Mozilla Blog, 59, 63
MP3 files, sharing, 202–207, 210
MP3 format posts, 98–99
multi-author blogs, email notifications, 123

N

name of blog, selecting, 84, 86
name of feed, changing, 164, 174, 179
Navbar, Blogger, 126–127
navigation pane settings (Google Reader), 193–194
NCompass blog, 46–47, 49
Neatorama blog, 76
Nebraska Library Commission, 46, 204, 205, 210, 212
Netscape and RSS development, 138
news feeds, 213, 216–218, 228, 229
news readers, 151, 155–162, 207, 220. See also Google Reader
New York Times feeds, 216, 217
NewzCrawler, 156
nGenera Insight, 62
notifications
    Blogger, 84, 90, 91
    of comments, 119
    of posts, 123
    Twitter, 261, 263, 266, 268

O

Obama, Barack, election and social media, 4
OCLC, 210, 212
Oddee blog, 76
offline reading of feeds, 198, 199
Old Bridge Library Weblog, 47, 50, 51
Old Editor, 108
on-screen feeds, 144–147
OpenID, 123
OPML (Outline Processing Markup Language), for subscription import/export, 179–180
organizational blogs, 3
Outlook RSS reader, Microsoft, 158, 159

P

Packagetrackr feed, 225, 228, 229
Page Elements, 126–129
pages, blog, 102–106
Pattern Recognition blog, 31–32, 35, 72
Pegasus Librarian blog, 72
Permissions screen, Blogger, 123, 125
phones, 98, 198, 199. See also mobile devices
photo feeds, 225, 226
photos. See images
Podcast Alley feed link, 147
podcasting, 202–207, 210
Poll gadget, 127
polls, 126, 128
posting
    by multiple posters, 88
    via BlogThis! 96–97
    via email, 97–98, 123, 181
    via mobile devices, 123
    via phone, 98
    via SMS, 98
    via Word add-in, 95–96
posting tab, Blogger, 99
post links, email, 107, 108
post pages, 118, 121–122
posts
    address, 114

posts (*cont.*)
    archiving, 119, 121–122
    audio, 98
    changing, 2
    comments to, 114, 118–119, 120
    controlling ability to create, 123, 125
    creating, 2, 90, 92–95, 99, 100
    defined, 2
    deleting, 2, 100, 101, 105
    drafts, saving, 93–94
    editing, 99–101, 107, 108
    exporting, 104
    filtering, 100
    hyper-linking to a webpage, 114
    images in, 102
    importing, 104
    MP3 format, 98–99
    notifications of, 123
    previewing, 94, 101–102
    publishing, 94–95, 100, 108, 110
    republishing, 94–95
    searching, 100
    shown, limit on, 111
    tags, 92, 94, 100
    templates, 113, 114, 117
    titles, 111, 113
    transliteration, 107, 108
    via email, 97–98, 123, 181
    via phone, 98
    viewing in Blogger, 94, 101–102
    XHTML code in, 90
previews
    of blog changes, 129
    of posts, 94, 101–102
    of templates, 133
privacy, blog owner, 90
profiles, Blogger, 89–90, 91
public page settings (Google Reader), 195
publishing posts, 94–95, 100, 108, 110
Publishing settings, Blogger, 112
Pueblo RSS feeds, 219

Q

quick editing of blog, 107, 108

R

Raymond, Matt, 44
RDF (Resource Description Framework), 139, 153
Reader. *See* Google Reader
Reading List, Blogger, 88
ReadWriteWeb blog, 59–60, 64, 78
renaming feeds (Google Reader), 164, 174, 179
@replies, 271–272
reply link, Twitter, 271–272
reporting, blogger preemption of, 3, 4
republishing
    blogs, 133
    feed content, 247–248, 253–257, 258
    posts, 94–95
    tools for, 248–252
research feeds, 225, 227
Resig, John, 228
Resource Description Framework (RDF), 139, 153
ResourceShelf blog, 78
retweet link, Twitter, 272
retweets, 272, 273–274
reverting templates, 133–134
RSS, 137–138, 142–144, 202–207
RSS-based services feeds, 220–223
RSS feed icons, 144–145, 148
RSS feeds. *See* feeds
RSS Feeds Generator, 232
RSS files in Chrome (Google browser), 152
RSS reader in browsers, 158, 159
RSS services, 220–223
RT (retweets), 272, 273–274

S

Sauers, Michael P., 3, 38
saving drafts of posts, 93–94
saving templates, 133
Schneider, Karen G., 17
Schneier on Security blog, 61–62, 64
scriptingNews, 138
scroll tracking settings (Google Reader), 193

Search Box gadget, 127

search engines and blogs, 3, 5, 107

searching for content, 100, 201–202

security, Blogger, 123

See Also . . . blog, 32–33, 35, 72

Seeman, Corey, 26

semi-automated feed creation, 232. *See also* ListGarden

send to feature (Google Reader), 181, 182, 183, 198, 200–201

server-based aggregators, 158, 160

server-based packages, 82–83

services, blog, 2

Settings options (Google Reader), 165, 177–180, 193, 195, 196

Settings tab, Blogger, 104

sharing feeds, 177

sharing items (Google Reader), 184–185, 187–190, 191–193, 195, 196

shopping feeds, 223, 225, 226, 227, 228

showing post options, 111

site feed settings, Blogger, 122

60 Minutes, blog exposure of error by, 4

Smarterware blog, 73

SMS, posting via, 98

social bookmarking feeds, 228, 229

sort options (Google Reader), 164, 173

stand-alone client aggregators, 156, 157

start page settings (Google Reader), 193

Stephens, Michael, 3, 36, 82

Sturgeon's Law, 73

subject blogs, 3

subject portals, 69

subscribe as you surf feature (Google Reader), 169, 170, 198, 199

subscriptions
   to feeds, 150, 162–164, 169, 178–179
   importing/exporting, 179–180
   managing in Google Reader, 174, 177–179
   as you surf feature (Google Reader), 169, 170, 198, 199

summary feeds, 144

Sun Microsystems blog, 3

Swiss Army Librarian blog, 36, 40, 79

Syndic8 blog, 148–149, 150

syndicated feeds. *See* feeds

T

tags
   Blogger, 130, 133
   on items (Google Reader), 184, 186
   post, 92, 94, 100
   Twitter, 272–273, 278

Tame the Web blog, 3, 36–37, 41, 82

Tapscott, Don, 62

Template Designer, 126, 129–134

templates, Blogger, 86–87, 123–127, 129, 131, 133–135

templates, post, 113, 114, 117

"Ten Guidelines for Developing Your Internal Blog" (Stephens), 82

Tennant, Roy, 37

Tennant: Digital Libraries blog, 37–38, 41

"Ten Things a Blogging Librarian Must Do (an exercise in common sense)" (Stephens), 82

Text gadget, 127

Themelion website, 267

Thingology Blog, 69

timestamp formatting, Blogger, 111, 113, 115, 118

time zone setting, Blogger, 111, 113, 116

titles
   blog, 104, 107
   post, 111, 113

TOCs Journal Tables of Contents feed service, 213, 214

Topeka and Shawnee County Public Library blog, 50, 51, 52

Topix.net feed, 228, 229

traffic conditions feeds, 228–229, 230

translate feeds (Google Reader), 164

translation, automatic, 107, 108

transliteration, post, 107, 108

The Travelin' Librarian blog, 3, 38–39, 42, 146

Tumblr microblogging service, 259

TweetDeck, 282, 283

Twistori, 284, 285

TwitBacks website, 267

Twitter
   account management, 261–266, 284
   background, 267, 269

Twitter (*cont.*)
    described, 259
    following others, 275–277
    history, 259
    home page, 270
    images, 266–267, 269
    logging in, 262, 263
    mobile access, 266, 268
    notifications, 261, 263, 266, 268
    passwords, 261, 263, 266, 268
    posting to, 270–275
    reading another's postings, 267, 270
    searching, 277–281
    services, 267, 269, 282–284
    tags, 272–273, 278
    value, 259–261
Twitter Analyzer, 284, 286
Twitterfeed, 284, 286
Twitter Your Flickr, 282, 283
TypePad web service, 83
Typo of the Day for Librarians blog, 70

U

University of Saskatchewan Library feed,
    213, 215
unsharing items (Google Reader),
    184–185, 187–190, 191–193, 195,
    196
Unshelved feed, 210, 214
unsubscribing from feeds (Google
    Reader), 164, 178, 179
Updated Editor, 108
URLs
    blog, 84, 86, 87, 110
    blog archive, 122
    custom (Google Reader), 192
USA.gov RSS feeds, 219

V

Vaught, Steve, 4
View Blog link, Blogger, 95
Virginia Commonwealth University
    Libraries, 45

W

Walking Paper blog, 73, 78
Walt at Random blog, 39–40, 42, 70, 71
A Wandering Eyre blog, 40–41, 42
Washington Post RSS feeds, 216, 218
web-based aggregators, 160–162
web-based services, 82
web feeds. *See* feeds
weblog (term), 1, 8
websites, adding feed content to,
    247–248, 253–257, 258
Weinberger, David, 53
West, Jessamyn, 20, 78–80
What You See Is What You Get (WYSI-
    WYG) interface, Blogger, 92, 96–97,
    108
Wikinomics blog, 62–63, 64
Wikipedia feed, 225, 227
Williams, Evan, 259
Winer, Dave, 138, 139
Word, posting via Microsoft, 95–96
WordPress web service, 83
word verification for comments, 119, 136
WorldCat feeds, 213, 215
WYSIWYG (What You See Is What You
    Get) interface, Blogger, 92, 96–97,
    108

X

XHTML, 90, 124–125, 130